Praise for
Planting the Seeds of Algebra, 3–5

"The classroom demonstration lessons are so detailed that after perusing the lesson, creating a few charts, and gathering materials, teachers will be able to implement the lesson immediately."

—Stacey Bennett Ferguson, Fourth-Grade Teacher
North Bay Elementary School, Bay Saint Louis, MS

"This book will make classroom instruction more effective while transitioning to Common Core State Standards requirements. Elementary students will benefit greatly after making meaningful connections to foundational algebraic concepts in later grades."

—Nancy J. Larsen, Sixth-Grade Teacher
Coeur d'Alene, ID

"This book is terrific! Well-written and FULL of information. The writer is *so* knowledge-able and presents the information *so* well. Background information and sample lessons are provided that will make the teacher the expert and the students active learners who carry a positive attitude and better understanding of math with them to middle and high school."

—Joyce Sager, Inclusion Math Teacher
Gadsden City High School, Gadsden, AL

"Discover how math is about more than just learning the algorithm to get the right answer. If given stimulating problems to explore, children can discover how to solve problems using algebraic thinking! Teachers who engage in the strategies presented in this book will be able to support students as they learn. Whether you love math or find it intimidating, this book will lead you to enjoy thinking mathematically."

—Amy Krumich, Third-Grade Teacher
Middleburg, VA

"Dr. Neagoy artfully combines theory, research, and practice to transform the way elementary teachers think about and teach algebraic concepts. Teachers who read this book will enter the classroom with enhanced knowledge, confidence, passion, and a deep understanding about how teaching algebraic concepts will delight and inspire students while setting them up for future mathematical success. If you want your teachers to understand foundational algebraic principles, read detailed math explorations that they can replicate in their classrooms, learn how upper elementary mathematics leads to higher level algebraic thinking, and inspire their students to love math, then give them a copy of *Planting the Seeds of Algebra, 3–5*."

—Bob Weiman, Lower School Director/Assistant Head of School
St. Stephen's & St. Agnes School, Alexandria, VA

"This is an invaluable resource for any teacher hoping to offer their students a deeper understanding of mathematical concepts. Filled with engaging and interactive activities and lessons based on extensive research, it will help teachers learn the math in depth, allowing for greater differentiation in their teaching."

—**Ann Bremner, Math Resource Teacher**
FCPS, Fairfax, VA

"Monica Neagoy's extensive knowledge of mathematics is surpassed only by her exceptional ability to impart that knowledge to others. She thrives on helping educators and their students arrive independently at solutions in order to construct their own understanding of concepts. In this text, Dr. Neagoy directly addresses the teaching of many of the most challenging topics in elementary mathematics, explaining them in clear and precise terms. This enriching text belongs on the bookshelf of every mathematics teacher."

—**Kerianne Gritt, Fifth-Grade Teacher**
St. Stephen's & St. Agnes School, Alexandria, VA

"This book demonstrates Dr. Neagoy's deep commitment to helping our students think critically and develop a deep understanding of mathematical concepts. Dr. Neagoy describes where we can incorporate algebra concepts into our classrooms so our students are better prepared."

—**Jay Tucker, Fourth-Grade Math Teacher**
Georgetown Day School, Washington, DC

"Dr. Monica Neagoy's passion for mathematics is contagious: it comes through her writings and even more when she presents her ideas in person. Working with Dr. Monica Neagoy over two years, and getting her book ideas firsthand, has given me a deeper appreciation for mathematics and has made me a stronger math teacher. Her energy inspires teachers, students, and parents to want to learn more about the magic of algebra."

—**Jennifer Gibbs, Firth-Grade Teacher**
Benjamin Franklin International School, Barcelona, Spain

"Dr. Neagoy's lessons and ideas dramatically changed my approach to teaching mathematics and my students' approach to thinking mathematically. Math time became about solving complex problems, debating over solutions, and articulating processes in ways that demonstrate deep understanding. My students became collaborators and co-constructors in their own learning. Through Dr. Neagoy's work, I realized that I no longer need to be the content expert and impart that content to my students through tired lessons. Rather, I am the facilitator of guided discovery and rich discussions."

—**Mollie Cura, International Educational Consultant**
Cura Literacy Consulting, Dublin, Ireland

3-5

Planting the Seeds of
ALGEBRA

Explorations for the Upper Elementary Grades

Monica Neagoy

Forewords by Francis (Skip) Fennell and Keith Devlin

A Resource for Meeting
CCSS

CORWIN
A SAGE Company

CORWIN
A SAGE Company

FOR INFORMATION:

Corwin

A SAGE Company

2455 Teller Road

Thousand Oaks, California 91320

(800) 233-9936

www.corwin.com

SAGE Publications Ltd.

1 Oliver's Yard

55 City Road

London EC1Y 1SP

United Kingdom

SAGE Publications India Pvt. Ltd.

B 1/I 1 Mohan Cooperative Industrial Area

Mathura Road, New Delhi 110 044

India

SAGE Publications Asia-Pacific Pte. Ltd.

3 Church Street

#10-04 Samsung Hub

Singapore 049483

Photos by Monica Neagoy unless otherwise credited.

Printed in the United States of America

A catalog record of this book is available from the Library of Congress.

ISBN: 978-1-4129-9661-7

Acquisitions Editor: Robin Najar

Associate Editor: Desirée A. Bartlett

Editorial Assistants: Ariel Price and
                                    Andrew Olson

Production Editor: Melanie Birdsall

Copy Editor: Cate Huisman

Typesetter: C&M Digitals (P) Ltd.

Proofreader: Caryne Brown

Indexer: Amy Murphy

Marketing Manager: Amanda Boudria

This book is printed on acid-free paper.

Certified Chain of Custody
Promoting Sustainable Forestry
www.sfiprogram.org
SFI-01268

SFI label applies to text stock

14 15 16 17 18 10 9 8 7 6 5 4 3 2 1

Contents

Foreword by a Mathematics Educator

She's done it again! Monica Neagoy has authored a second book that deftly presents important foundations of algebra while celebrating mathematics through carefully crafted explorations, all of which include student and teacher vignettes and comments about the mathematics they have learned and are teaching. Wow. When I read this book I felt like I was in a classroom!

Monica Neagoy's gift is in her ability to "tell a story" while she deeply and carefully explores really important, and challenging, mathematics. This "story" digs deep into mathematics topics in grades 3–5 (and beyond) that are foundational to algebra as it is developed at the elementary school level and extended through the middle and high school grades.

Classroom teachers, particularly those for whom this book is intended, need this book. They will deepen and extend their mathematical understandings from the discussions provided in each chapter and leave each discussion with a treasure trove of activities that they can use in their own classrooms. But this book is so much more than a professional contribution for mathematics content and pedagogy. It's a resource that will be used—regularly—as in daily. *Monica's Mottos* themselves could provide the topic for grade level or building learning community discussions. Consider discussing "Address the Whys, Not Just the Hows," "Instill a Sense of Wonder," or "Foster Friendliness With Numbers."

Finally, as most of the country addresses and moves forward in implementing the Common Core State Standards for Mathematics, a key issue will be the establishment of curricular opportunities that focus on important mathematics, are coherent across both developmental levels of students and mathematical topics and expectations, and, indeed, that challenge students to dig deeper! This book does that. Read it! Enjoy the story.

—Dr. Francis (Skip) Fennell

McDaniel College, Westminster, MD
Past President of the National Council
of Teachers of Mathematics (NCTM)
L. Stanley Bowlsbey Professor of Education
and Graduate and Professional Studies
Project Director, Elementary Mathematics Specialists
and Teacher Leaders Project (ems&tl)

Foreword by a Mathematician
Algebra: What's the Big Deal?

In a world where we all carry powerful computing devices around with us in our pockets, the need to be skilled in arithmetic has greatly diminished. Instead, today we have to be skillful users of those computing machines. That has greatly ramped up the importance of algebra. For algebra is, to all intents and purposes, the language computers use.

Unfortunately, the education system has not kept pace with the changes in our lives brought about by the computing revolution. Algebra teaching today is largely unchanged from the ninth century, when the Arabic-speaking mathematician al-Khwārizmī wrote the world's first algebra textbook. (The term *al-jabr* in the book's title, *al-Kitab al-mukhtasar fi hisab al-jabr wa'l-muqābala*, is where we get the name *algebra*.) Back then, and right up to the 1960s, one of the keys to a successful and hopefully prosperous life was mastery of arithmetical and algebraic tools for solving numerical problems. But today, cheap computers we carry around in our pockets do arithmetic computations for us, compute the values of algebraic formulas, and solve algebraic equations. What's more, they do so faster and more accurately than we can. People no longer need to acquire that mastery.

That does not mean that arithmetic and algebra are no longer important. Indeed, they are used much more today than at any other time in history. It's just that the grunt work is now done by machines. That shifts the focus people must bring to arithmetic and algebra. Today, we have to be accomplished users of those computers. This is why mathematicians and math teachers have started using the terms "arithmetical thinking" and "algebraic thinking" (and more generally, "mathematical thinking"). Those terms mean the kind of thinking required in order to solve problems—real problems that arise in today's world—with the aid of arithmetic and algebra, frequently using computers. Modern computer systems also eliminate the need to craft artificial problems that can be solved using paper-and-pencil methods. Today, it is possible for learners to work on real problems—though it still makes sense for beginners to start with simple ones.

Algebraic thinking, the focus of this book, requires far more conceptual understanding than the basic algebraic skills of times past. Today, we don't (at least, we shouldn't) teach algebra with the goal of fast, accurate (and generally mindless) manipulation of symbolic expressions. Our machines can do that, far faster and more reliably than we can. Rather, what today's world requires is people who can look at a real-world problem and understand it from an algebraic perspective, see what steps are required to solve it, and then set about finding a solution—using a computer where appropriate. Put simply, our computers can do almost everything that was the focus of most algebra teaching of the past. Give a computer a problem from an old algebra book, and it will give you a correct solution. But that's all the computer can do. It does not understand the world. It actually does not *understand* anything. It can just follow rules. To use a computer to solve a real-world problem, a person has to first turn that problem into an algebraic expression or equation that a computer can accept, and then take the computer's solution and interpret it in real-world terms. That requires not only knowing what the rules are that the computer will follow but also *understanding* them—the part the computer cannot do.

That is why the focus in this book is on *understanding* problems in an algebraic way, and *understanding* the methods of algebra. This is a very different way of teaching algebra than today's parents experienced (and today's teachers, for that matter). As a result, both parents and teachers may initially find some things unfamiliar. But if you use the book as your guide, you should do okay. People who learned algebra in the past would frequently be heard to say, "I can *do* algebra, but I never really understood it." Back in earlier times, you could often get by with that level of mastery. But those days are gone, never to return. In today's world, if your mastery of algebra is purely procedural (i.e., manipulation of symbolic expressions), you will lose out every time to a faster, cheaper, more accurate computer. In fact, once you get past that initial strangeness, you will make a surprising discovery. Once you approach algebra from an understanding perspective, it actually turns out to be a whole lot easier than trying to master all those rules for moving symbols around! So much so, that there is no reason why algebra (i.e., algebraic thinking) cannot be taught in the elementary grades. Indeed, that's when we should start teaching it!

Remember, in the 21st century, no one is going to be hired for being able to do something a computer can do. (Better, faster, and cheaper wins every time.) Instead, our students—indeed, everyone—need to master something the computer cannot: *understanding* algebra! This book will help you, your children, and your students do just that.

—Dr. Keith Devlin

Stanford University, CA
Co-Founder and Executive Director of
the Stanford University's H-STAR Institute
Co-Founder of the Stanford Media X Research Network
The Math Guy on NPR's Weekend Edition

Acknowledgments

Writing this second book has been yet another edifying journey. The process took me to private places of the mind, spirit, and heart as I dug deeply into my multiple teaching and learning experiences; it also took me to public places—different countries, schools, and classrooms—where I connected with teachers and teacher leaders who directly or indirectly inspired me, enriched me, and enlightened me. Collectively, they helped me shape the goals and content of *Planting the Seeds of Algebra, 3–5*.

I thank my parents who instilled a value for mathematics, my schoolteachers who nurtured my love for mathematics, my university professors who opened windows onto new learnings, and my favorite authors and researchers who shed new light on old ideas. I especially thank the myriad teachers and administrators of the elementary schools—public, private, independent, and international—I have worked with over the past 25 years. Their questions, comments, and insights always prompted me to go deeper and search further. Their desire to excite children about mathematics nurtured my own. I will not risk listing all their names for fear of leaving out an important one. For this reason, I hope they will understand—as they know well who *they* are—that my gratitude to them is endless.

That said, I would be remiss not to specifically acknowledge a few individuals who helped me bring this book to life: I thank Cathy Hernandez, who first contacted me to write for Corwin; associate editor Desirée Bartlett and her assistants Ariel Price and Andrew Olson, who supported my work with patience and consideration through the development stage; and Melanie Birdsall, who diligently and graciously guided the production stage of the book. In short, I thank the entire Corwin team. A special thanks also goes to my wonderful copy editor Cate Huisman.

On a more personal note, I have been blessed with a supportive and thoughtful husband, who has lived this book with me through its countless iterations. I am profoundly grateful to Didier, a writer and artist in his own right, my intellectual companion and loving mate, and the first editor of all my writings. *Merci infiniment!*

Last, I wish to express my gratitude to all teachers who believe that children are capable of sophisticated and creative mathematical thinking and who guide them to delve deeper into the wondrous world of mathematics. They will help change the face of school mathematics in our culture!

Publisher's Acknowledgments

Corwin gratefully acknowledges the contributions of the following reviewers:

Stacey Bennett Ferguson, Fourth-Grade Teacher
North Bay Elementary School
Bay Saint Louis, MS

Dr. Nancy J. Larsen, Sixth-Grade Teacher
Coeur d'Alene Charter Academy
Coeur d'Alene, ID

Dr. Joyce Sager, Inclusion Math Teacher
Gadsden City High School
Gadsden, AL

About the Author

Photo by Tim Coburn

Monica Neagoy, international consultant and popular keynote speaker, has a contagious passion for mathematics. In addition to authoring books, over the course of a 25-year mathematics career she has done national program directing, teacher professional development, math specialist training, national and international conference speeches, live television courses, video creation and hosting, math apps conception, live math shows, including her popular *MathMagic Show*, and last but not least has helped the game of SWISH become a reality for *Thinkfun*. Whether in the United States or abroad, whether presenting in English, French, or Spanish, whether working with teachers, students, or parents, Monica's life-long goal is to infuse people with a fascination for the beauty, power, and wonder of mathematics.

The seeds of Dr. Neagoy's love for mathematics took root on the beaches of Saipan, in the Northern Mariana Islands, where her father wrote problems in the sand for his daughters to solve. Pleasure, beauty, and mathematics were intertwined for her from the age of four. Her career in mathematics teaching began at Georgetown University. Later, she was invited to become a program director at the National Science Foundation, where she directed K–12 national math projects. As an independent consultant, she has served numerous school districts and systems across the country and notable organizations, including the Carnegie Institution of Washington, PBS TeacherLine, MATHCOUNTS, and the American Association for the Advancement of Science. Since 2004, her consulting has expanded to serve Europe, the Middle East, and Africa as well.

Dr. Neagoy has had a parallel career in theatre as actor, choreographer, and stage director, notably with the professional LE NEON Theatre, which she codirected, in the Washington, DC, area. Her exposure to many cultures, mastery of several languages, double career in the arts and the sciences, and mindfulness training through yoga practice and teaching provide her with a unique perspective on the learning and teaching of mathematics. Her passions for mathematics and the arts converge in her popular keynote presentation, *The Mathematics of Beauty and the Beauty of Mathematics*.

Dr. Neagoy combined her love for the arts and the sciences in the creation of a series of innovative mathematics videos for teachers and students—about 60 in all, including *Discovering Algebra With Graphing Calculators* for Discovery Education and *Mathematics: What's the Big Idea?* for the Annenberg Channel (now available on Annenberg Learner). Lately, she has been collaborating with two colleagues in the conception and creation of math apps for teachers and students.

Dr. Neagoy was educated in the French school system, grades 1–12, in Asia and the United States. She has a BS in mathematics and philosophy from Georgetown University, an MA in pure mathematics from Catholic University, and a PhD in mathematics education from the University of Maryland.

*To Didier, my partner on stage and in life who shares
my ineffable joy of creation, I dedicate this book.*

Introduction

Algebraic thinking is a major area of school mathematics that is crucial for students to learn but challenging for teachers to teach.

—Maria Blanton, Linda Levi,
Terry Crites, and Barbara Dougherty (2011, p. 1)

Everywhere we turn these days, we encounter another article, report, or book on the importance of algebra. In 2000, with the publication of *Principles and Standards for School Mathematics*, the National Council of Teachers of Mathematics (NCTM) made algebra one of five mathematics content standards for preK–12 mathematics, describing it as a way of thinking that cuts across all math content areas and unifies the curriculum. In 2008, the final report of the president's National Mathematics Advisory Panel identified algebra as a main concern "for Algebra[1] is a demonstrable gateway to later achievement" (p. xiii). In 2010, the National Governors Association Center for Best Practices and the Council of Chief State School Officers, building on the NCTM standards and heeding the Advisory Panel's recommendations, echoed the importance of algebraic thinking starting in kindergarden, embodied in the Common Core State Standards for Mathematics published that year. Yet major publications continue to acknowledge a serious national mathematics problem and regularly identify algebra as the main culprit. Why? Because the mathematics achievement curve begins a sharp decline as students reach late middle school, precisely when U.S. students begin their study of algebra. Classic comments such as "I liked math until I began algebra" or "math made sense until algebra" add anecdotal evidence to scientific results.

To help remedy this situation, policy makers and math educators are calling for a strong foundation for algebra in the early grades in order to help students get a deeper understanding of mathematics early on and prepare them for success in algebra later on. But questions arise about how best to answer this call. After all, elementary teachers were not educated to teach algebra, and, what's more, they may barely remember high school algebra. Some may even harbor unpleasant memories of their algebra experience.

Algebra in the early years, a relatively new focus area in mathematics education, has received much attention in the past decade or two. The movement, known as "early algebra," is *not* about teaching traditional school algebra *early*. Rather, it's about fostering ways of thinking, doing, and communicating about mathematics, and of teaching and learning mathematics with understanding. It's about making connections, analyzing relationships, noticing structure, studying change, and solving problems; it's about justifying, conjecturing, generalizing, symbolizing, and mathematizing, all of which are critical habits of mind for all of mathematics.

---

1. The word *Algebra* capitalized refers to a particular course or course sequence in middle or high school.

But this begs further questions: How can elementary teachers learn to cultivate these habits of mind? Where can they find the research on children's algebraic thinking in forms that are clear and useful to them? In what ways can they use their present curriculum to meet algebra expectations? In short, what does it *mean* to plant the seeds of algebra in the elementary grades, and what do these seeds *look like* in grades 3–5? One answer is in your hands. *Planting the Seeds of Algebra, 3–5: Explorations for the Intermediate Grades* (*Planting Seeds*) is a pioneer in its genre: It takes the reader into real classrooms, describes students engaged in important mathematics, models teaching strategies, connects the early mathematics with advanced algebra concepts, and makes suggestions for further explorations. Based on existing research, these different components converge to offer meaningful algebraic experiences for young students.

To be more specific, I have written this book for teachers in the elementary grades to help instill in them a very different view of algebra than the popular one captured in Glasbergen's cartoon below! It is my hope that readers will

- *Unlearn* any negative lessons about algebra they may be harboring and *release* any negative beliefs or attitudes that impede a full appreciation of the topic.
- *Experience* algebraic acculturation; that is, *cultivate* new thought and behavior patterns that naturally weave into algebra's cognitive fabric.
- *Conceptualize* algebra as a domain that makes sense and connects to the world we live in, rather than as a set of meaningless symbolic formulas and procedures.
- *Understand* the continuum—and visualize meaningful bridges—between the mathematics they teach and the mathematics taught in secondary school algebra.
- *Visualize* concrete embodiments of what algebra actually looks like in the early grades, giving it color, light, and texture.
- *Enjoy* the usefulness, power, and beauty of algebra as an integral part of mathematics.

"Algebra will be useful to you later in life because it teaches you to shut up and accept things that seem pointless and stupid."

Why Write This Book?

I wish to articulate the hoped-for outcomes that are the motivating force behind this work as well as the anticipated macro-level consequences of reading and implementing the teachings within. There are six broad-ranging results to be gained from mathematical instruction that routinely "plants the seeds" of algebraic thinking.

Student Achievement and Teacher Empowerment. As teachers learn to "algebrafy" elementary mathematics by weaving into it a web of algebraic ideas and actions, words and symbols, their students become better at doing mathematics, and together they enjoy the subject more. Teachers will be able to answer rather than dread *why* questions, such as, "Why invert and multiply when dividing fractions?" They will be motivated to pose deeper questions, and their students will gain deeper number sense, spatial sense, and symbol sense. When algebra becomes an organizing principle for elementary mathematics, the potential for increased math proficiency is huge. Mindful explanations engender profound understanding, which contributes to richer mathematical experiences now, which in turn lead to successful mathematics experiences later. After reading *Planting Seeds*, teachers will feel empowered, and students will feel *they can*.

> Mindful explanations → Profound understanding → Richer experiences → Joy and success

Respect for Elementary Teachers. Throughout my 25 years of professional development with preK–14 teachers, I've heard high school teachers too often blaming elementary teachers for their students' algebra ills. Granted, we have a national math problem, and algebra is clearly at center stage. But good will is not the missing ingredient: I've worked with many reflective, inquisitive, and assiduous elementary school teachers who are open minded and eager to learn.

The reasons for high school students' poor preparation for algebra are at least two-fold: (1) Elementary teacher preparation programs require little by way of mathematics, and (2) the elementary teachers who venture to take an algebra course are given traditional, advanced algebra material that doesn't serve them directly in their elementary classrooms. Therefore, this book meets an urgent need: It provides elementary teachers with the tools to create a new classroom culture of algebraic approaches to mathematics, the fruits of which will have an upward domino effect, forcing secondary math teachers, in turn, to rethink their own algebra teaching practices. As a result of this inevitable change, high school teachers will stop trivializing the mathematics learned and taught in elementary school and begin valuing elementary teachers.

Lower School Math

The indoctrination begins. Students learn that mathematics is not something you do.... Emphasis is placed on sitting still, filling out worksheets, and following directions. Children are expected to master a complex set of algorithms...unrelated to any real desire or curiosity on their part....Multiplication tables are stressed, as are parents, teachers, and the kids themselves.

—Paul Lockhart (2009, p. 134)

A Mathematics Revolution With Teachers as Agents of Change. There is a dire need to educate the public about algebra and mathematics in general; to reintroduce these noble intellectual achievements back into our culture as valuable assets; to change beliefs, attitudes, and behaviors. This can happen only through education. This education must start with the young. Elementary school teachers can be change agents in this burgeoning revolution: They educate the leaders and decision makers of tomorrow. Only they can model for our children a mathematics that is vibrant, useful, exciting, and rich. Hence, this book will plant the seeds of a new awareness of the nature of algebra (and mathematics as a whole) that will begin to change current attitudes. It will spread from teachers to students and outward to society. A new awareness about the role of algebra in our world will gradually deviate from Opinion 1, below, and align itself with Opinion 2.

> (1) Algebra isn't essential to much of anything. . . . It is useless torture. . . . It's for the few, not the many.
>
> —Coleman McCarthy (1991, p. A21)
>
> (2) Algebra represents one of mankind's great intellectual achievements—the use of symbols to capture abstractions and generalizations, and to provide analytic power over a wide range of situations, both pure and applied.
>
> —Alan Schoenfeld (2008, p. 506)

The Democratization of Algebra. High school Algebra has served as a gatekeeper in education: It lets some people in to enjoy STEM careers (in science, technology, engineering, and/or mathematics) but keeps many out. I have been passionate about the need to widen algebra's narrow gate since the inception of my mathematics career. Still today, too few students pass Algebra with understanding. Since proficiency in algebra continues to be considered a criterion for success in higher education, failure in high school Algebra disadvantages a slice of the population that includes many female, Black, and Hispanic students, depriving them of scientific careers. Recent reports have further correlated success in higher education with completion of Algebra II. Reconceptualizing the nature of algebra in the early grades will provide *all* students opportunities to engage with big ideas in meaningful ways, thereby increasing the chances for more students to thrive in high school Algebra. This book will contribute to the early algebra reform efforts to transform Algebra from "a gateway for some to a highway for all" (Neagoy, 2010).

> Solving the algebra problem serves four major goals . . . [including] to democratize access to powerful ideas by transforming algebra from an inadvertent engine of inequity to a deliberate engine of mathematical power.
>
> —James Kaput (2008, p. 6)

Narrowing of the Global Achievement Gap. Beyond college and graduate school, we must also consider the quality of work and life itself. A growing number of educational scholars and leaders are concerned about our students' disadvantages on a larger scale. Harvard education professor Tony Wagner warns of a global achievement gap (Wagner, 2008). He argues that the 2001 No Child Left Behind Act, instead of narrowing the achievement gap, has left us with ineffective schools that are unable to prepare our students for college, work, and life. With judicious reasoning, he makes the case that our students are unprepared to analyze arguments, weigh evidence, or detect biases. He draws a list of seven survival skills for today's teenagers, the core competencies deemed necessary for success in college and the workplace. Wagner's survival skills are strikingly similar to the habits of mind exhibited in classrooms where mathematics is taught and learned with meaning, as modeled in *Planting Seeds*. Four of them follow.

- Critical thinking and problem solving
- Agility and adaptability
- Effective oral and written communication
- Curiosity and imagination

Planting Seeds focuses on rethinking algebra as a network of ideas, actions, and symbols, and on fostering mathematical habits of mind that will serve students all the way through high school and beyond. These ways of thinking and doing will transfer to other areas of education and life and will be foundational to developing Wagner's survival skills.

> One's intellectual and aesthetic life cannot be complete unless it includes an appreciation of the power and the beauty of mathematics.
>
> —Jerry P. King (1992, p. 3)

A Love for Mathematics Akin to the Love for Language Arts. When it comes to mathematics, and especially algebra, we almost always justify its importance to students by portraying it as a prerequisite to (1) high school graduation, (2) college achievement, or (3) a lucrative career. A main ingredient is missing in this utilitarian portrayal of "one of humanity's most ancient and noble intellectual traditions" (RAND Mathematics Study Panel, 2003). The missing ingredient is a passion for mathematics, one akin to the delight in reading or the joy of writing. A deep appreciation is lacking for the intrinsic nature of mathematics: its art, elegance, and creativity. The many "wow moments" and "aha moments" teachers and students will experience when using explorations from *Planting Seeds* will begin to foster a profound enjoyment of mathematics that will lead to a contagious love for its awesome beauty.

I wish to emphasize the critical role schoolteachers play in kindling a child's love for mathematics. Their effect is critical not only on students' achievement but also on students' appreciation for the topic. It may be hard to prove, but those who were inspired by a teacher when they were young know the vital role the teacher played in their lives. Once students enter middle school, their minds are pretty much made up about mathematics. For the disheartened, there's a slim chance of any rekindling. We must therefore reach children while they are young and *turn their hearts and minds on* to mathematics. A child *turned off* to mathematics is a tragedy for the child and a tragedy for our country.

What Background Do I Bring to this Book?

First, *Planting Seeds* is the outgrowth of 25 years of working with teachers. I have worked specifically on algebra both in site-based contexts, where I taught professional development courses and workshops for teachers of all grade bands, in the United States and abroad; and at venues such as Georgetown University and the Carnegie Institution of Washington, where I designed, directed, and taught summer institutes for K–14 teachers.

Second, this book is based on the research knowledge acquired throughout my career, both through conducting and consuming research and especially through guiding large-scale, national algebra-related projects as a program director at the National Science Foundation under the umbrellas of the Teacher Professional Continuum (TPC) and the Centers for Learning and Teaching (CLT) programs.

Third, this book is also the fruit of my work over the past 18 years in creating, writing, and hosting television programs (e.g., on the Annenberg CPB Channel, www.learner.org) and video series (e.g., for Annenberg Media, Discovery Education, http://store.discovery education.com, and T3 Europe, www.t3europe.org) on the teaching and learning of algebra in grades K though–14.

Last, this book draws on webinars, keynote speeches, and Math Show performances I've given on the topic of algebra at national and international conferences, cultural events, and back-to-school or math nights for parents. I am grateful to the many people who insisted that I "write a book on algebra that would inspire more people."

Who Will Benefit From This Book?

On a pragmatic level, I've written *Planting Seeds* primarily for preservice and in-service elementary school teachers, elementary math specialists, coaches, and teacher educators who work with elementary school teachers. Since more and more parents today are homeschooling their children, this book will also serve parents, as well administrators trying to make sense of the rapidly shifting K–12 algebraic landscape. On a philosophical level, this book joins my lifelong professional efforts to inspire teachers, students, and all lovers of learning by *infusing*, *infecting*, and *injecting* them with a fascination for the power, the value, and the beauty of mathematics.

I envision this book being used as a resource for the following:

- Courses for preservice teacher preparation and workshops, courses, and institutes for in-service teachers
- Site-based lesson study or other teacher collaborations
- Sessions for elementary teachers run by math specialists and coaches
- Math workshops for parents of young children
- Individual learning by teachers, administrators, and other readers interested in children's mathematical development and education

How Is This Book Organized?

At the heart of this book are three in-depth Explorations—I, *Circling Circles*; II, *Fancy Fences*; and III, *Multiplication Musings*. Explorations I, II, and III address core material for grades 3–5 students and are in turn composed of three chapters each:

1. *The Lesson* chapter (Chapters 1, 4, and 7) builds on actual lessons recorded in elementary classrooms, in public or private schools. Only the names of the students and teachers are changed.

2. The *Algebra Connections* chapter (Chapters 2, 5, and 8) revisits each stage of the exploratory lesson, bringing to light the often hidden connections between elementary mathematics and secondary algebra.

3. The *More Problems to Explore* chapter (Chapters 3, 6, and 9) begins with a *Next Steps* section offering suggestions for follow-up lessons. It also provides suggestions for further explorations for the teacher's own learning and ten additional explorations for the students' learning.

Chapter 10 describes a fourth exploration—IV, *Fractions in Action,* which is the fruit of professional development meetings with teachers, math lessons with students, and math night or math academy sessions with parents on fundamental aspects of fractions and rational numbers.

Finally, Chapter 11, titled *Final Thoughts,* summarizes the big ideas of the book—what algebraic thinking, talking, and doing means in grades 3–5—and offers six new "Monica's Mottos," maxims for teachers often inspired by them.

Exploration Topics

In characterizing "early algebra," *Developing Essential Understanding of Algebraic Thinking for Teaching Mathematics in Grades 3–5* (NCTM, 2011) states, "Early algebra brings a more eclectic perspective to the kinds of activities that we might describe as algebra. . . . It offers multiple points of entry that draw on arithmetic, functional thinking, mathematical modeling, and quantitative reasoning" (p. 8). All four areas are addressed extensively throughout this book.

Exploration I looks at geometry, measurement, and data from an algebraic perspective. We learn that algebra stems from arithmetic and geometry and that, in fact, geometry and algebra are two complementary ways of thinking about mathematical ideas. Using modeling and quantitative reasoning, students discover a surprising property of a circle, the perfect Euclidean shape known since before the beginning of recorded history.

Exploration II focuses on geometric and numeric growing patterns and the not-so-obvious connections between patterns and functions and between functions and algebra. Again, through mathematical modeling and quantitative reasoning, the worlds of shapes, numbers, and algebra converge in meaningful ways. Students examine functions, or relationships between quantities that change, in two ways: recursively (looking at what changes) and rule-wise (looking at what remains the same or *invariant*).

Exploration III examines multiplication from multiple perspectives, beginning with images of multiplication children bring with them from their early experiences. Multiplicative thinking, a new big idea students encounter in grade 3, is the foundation for an entire network of interconnected concepts, including multiplication, division, fractions, ratios, rational numbers, proportional relationships, and linear functions—all of which are central to algebra. The connecting thread throughout Exploration III, and another big idea bridging basic computation to higher mathematics, is the distributive property of multiplication over addition. It is important for at least two reasons: It connects the two fundamental operations, and it helps students make sense of computational algorithms. Key aspects of division, such as partitive versus quotative, are also discussed.

Guided by eight challenging questions, such as, "Can $\frac{2}{5}+\frac{3}{4}$ ever equal $\frac{5}{9}$?" Exploration IV walks the reader through what is considered by many educators the most difficult topic for students to learn and teachers to teach: fractions and rational numbers. "Historically, the development of algebra grew from the arithmetic of fractions and rational numbers (Saul, 1998, p. 137)." Because they represent a big stumbling block for middle school students, solid groundwork must be laid in grades 3–5. Consequently, Exploration IV addresses five foundational aspects of fractions and rational numbers: meanings of $\frac{a}{b}$, representations of $\frac{a}{b}$, the whole or the unit, equivalence and comparison, and the meanings of division.

Grade Bands

Explorations I through IV are labeled Grade 3, Grades 4–5, Grades 3–4, and Grades 3–5 respectively. Nevertheless, with minor modifications, all explorations can be used in *any* of the three grade levels. Moreover, all elementary school teachers will find the wide range of algebraic connections and additional problems relevant to the mathematics they teach.

Common Core State Standards for Mathematics

The choices of what mathematical content and practices to include in this book—as well as what tasks, strategies, and approaches to teaching and assessing to include—were all made in light of the Common Core State Standards. This is true not only for the content standards linking operations and algebraic thinking but also for the standards on base-10 numbers, fractions, geometry, and measurement and data. If I had cited the pertinent CCSSM content or practice standard each time it was being modeled, there would have been too many Common Core references. Hence, I reserved citations for use only with the most challenging ones.

> Fact: The standards do accommodate and prepare students for Algebra 1 in 8th grade by including the prerequisites for this course in grades K–7.
>
> —www.corestandards.org/about-the-standards/myths-vs-facts

My Premises

As you read through and engage in this book's explorations, you will no doubt notice the following premises, which have held true throughout my career:

Premise 1: We must desire to engage with mathematics. When mathematics is explored in ways that reveal its usefulness, its beauty, and its humanity, teachers and students alike develop a motivation and desire to engage with mathematics—on emotional and intellectual levels—two critical ingredients for a positive and rewarding mathematical experience.

Premise 2: We need to know much more than what we teach. Teachers are professionals. They understand that they must know much more than what they teach. I have shared this diagram with every teacher I've worked with as a representation of my strong belief in Premise 2.

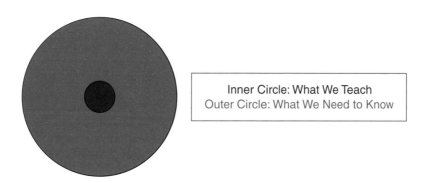

Inner Circle: What We Teach
Outer Circle: What We Need to Know

    A broad lens on learning enables teachers to build intelligently on students' existing foundations and erect new foundations for future study. A rich repertoire of knowledge empowers teachers to welcome rather than fear incisive questions, help *all* students grow in their knowledge, and inspire students with fascinating new mathematics.

> Teachers with higher content knowledge are not only more apt to teach mathematics in a manner that is compatible with learning algebra but are also more inclined to hold their students to higher standards. . . . Not surprisingly, the quality of mathematics teaching depends on the teachers' knowledge of the content.
>
> —Joy Darley and Barbara Leapard (2010, p. 185)

Premise 3: We must have a profound understanding of the mathematics we teach. The traditional U.S. curriculum has been characterized as "a mile wide and an inch deep," because it traditionally attempted to "cover" so many topics while never "uncovering" any one topic in great depth. Consequently, an in-depth knowledge of the mathematics taught is often lacking. *Planting Seeds* helps remedy this situation.

Premise 4: If we are too comfortable, then we are not growing. If teachers become too comfortable with what they are teaching and how they teach it, they become set in their ways, and growth stagnates. Leaving the comfort zone now and then is positive and productive. Discomfort leads to change, change begets growth, and growth engenders new learning and excitement. As you delve into this book, you may feel a bit uncomfortable at times. Think of it as your own professional development, your adventure into new and stimulating mathematical territory, where one day you will be able to lead your students with confidence, mindfulness, and knowledge.

Premise 5: Raise the performance bar, and students will rise to meet you. "American students have not been succeeding in the mathematical part of their education at anything like a level expected of an international leader" (National Mathematics Advisory Panel, 2008, p. 3). A main goal of the Common Core State Standards is to raise the level of mathematics education, described by some as two years behind international counterparts (Greenberg, 2008). I strongly believe *all* students should have the right to learn high-level mathematics. If you think the level of *Planting Seeds* is too advanced for your students, rather than worrying about what they *won't be able* to do, honor them with the belief that they *will be able* to think. When students sense your confidence in them, they develop self-confidence and rise to meet your expectations.

> We have learned that children are capable of mathematical insights and mathematical invention that exceed our expectations....The question of the expectations we knowingly or unknowingly set for our students is nowhere more crucial than in the gateway area called algebra.
>
> —Joan Ferrini-Mundy, Glenda Lappan, and Elizabeth Phillips (1997, p. 282)

My Hope

For too many students, mathematics begins—in the world of arithmetic—as a meaningless set of numerical procedures, and then becomes—in the world of algebra—a meaningless set of symbolic procedures. It is my sincere hope that *Planting Seeds* will offer readers more breadth and depth in the mathematics they already know and new insights into algebra's many faces: algebra as generalizing arithmetic; algebra as problem solving; algebra as examining structure; algebra as modeling real-world situations; and algebra the study of relationships between quantities that change. After reading this book, you will no longer think of algebra as *separate from* the mathematics you teach. This separation was typical of traditional curricula that long deprived students of deep mathematical thinking in the elementary grades and impeded them from learning algebra with understanding in the later grades. I trust you will see algebra not just as a garden of ideas but as a garden in full bloom awash with vibrant colors.

> If I had to explain algebra to a student, I would say: "Think of all that you know about mathematics. Algebra is about making it richer, more connected, more general, and more explicit."
>
> —Ricardo Nemirovsky, as quoted by Erick Smith (2008, p. 133)

EXPLORATION I

Geometry, Measurement, and Data

An Algebraic Perspective

Geometry and algebra are not just two subjects that appear throughout the curriculum; they are also distinct ways of thinking about mathematical ideas.

—Thomas Banchoff (2008, p. 99)

Photo by Jim Conner and Kathleen Watt

RATIONALE FOR EXPLORATION I

- Seeing algebraic thinking, discoursing, and doing in a context of geometry, measurement, and numerical data. This includes thinking about the general when working with the specific and interacting with multiple representations: concrete manipulatives, drawings or pictures, tables of numbers, words and graphs.

- Developing friendliness with one of the world's most famous numbers, π.

- Understanding π as a relationship. Most teenagers and adults have no conceptual understanding of π as a relationship between two quantities. Students in grades 3–5 can understand a multiplicative relationship of "a little more than three times longer" or "about three times longer" between two lengths when the relationship is modeled in ways that make sense to them.

- Avoiding rote memorization. Students who engage in Circling Circles, through the actions of measuring, computing, discussing, comparing, and analyzing, will not need the following mnemonics, which are void of any mathematical sense making: "One can tell from afar that a circle's $2\pi r$; one can find with great care that a disc is πr^2!"

- Seeing how calculators can be used to introduce a notion to come (nonrepeating and nonterminating decimals) in a way that intrigues students and causes them to wonder.

- Connecting fractions with decimals and seeing them as two forms of a same number, just as water and ice in science are two forms of H_2O.

- Rising to a higher level of geometric thinking. Students in grades 3–5 are expected to move beyond Van Hiele Level 1 and gradually rise to Level 2; that is, they move from visualizing and naming 2-D and 3-D shapes to seeing these shapes as bearers of properties they can articulate.

1

Circling Circles

The Lesson (Grade 3)

A close examination of algebra's origins reveals two roots—*arithmetic* and *geometry*, hence the powerful interrelationship between arithmetic, geometry, and algebra. In recent work by advocates of teaching algebra in the early grades, much has been written about the connections between arithmetic and algebra (Carpenter, Franke, & Levi, 2003; Carraher, Brizuela, & Schliemann, 2007; Russell, Schifter, & Bastable, 2011). My contention is that not enough has been written about the privileged relationship between *geometry* and algebra. Geometric concepts are as vital as numeric ones, and their links with algebra are tangible in ways that numerical concepts are sometimes not. Children in grades 3–5 are still in the concrete operational stage, according to Piaget's theory of cognitive development. So the concrete experiences of working with shapes—manipulating, tracing, drawing, measuring, discovering properties, examining characteristics, and noticing patterns—are important components of children's mathematics education.

Experiences with geometry develop students' spatial sense. This includes spatial intuition and spatial perception, two potent tools according to Fields Medal recipient Sir Michael Atiyah. They are the reason

> geometry is actually such a powerful part of mathematics—not only for things that are obviously geometrical, but even for things that are not. We try to put them into geometrical form because that enables us to use our intuition: our intuition is our most powerful tool. (Atiyah, 2001, p. 5)

Children come to school with intuitions about, and insights into, 2-D and 3-D shapes, and with ideas about their properties and interrelationships. Coupled with their intuitive knowledge is children's natural interest in things geometric: They are attracted to and intrigued by squares, circles, and triangles, fascinating and familiar shapes in their geometric world. The *Circling Circles* Exploration offers opportunities for cultivating algebraic reasoning through the exploration of the most perfect, plane, closed curve called the circle, considered by ancient and modern cultures the symbol of the human psyche, the unity of heaven and earth, the inclusivity of the universe, and much more.

The two-day lesson recounted below took place in a third grade classroom of an elementary school I had been working with for three years. Our common goals were to deepen teachers' content and pedagogical knowledge of mathematics and to create a culture in which teachers and students valued, discussed, and enjoyed meaningful mathematics, both in and out of the classroom.

REFLECT . . .

[Friedrich Froebel's] philosophy was clear: if children could be stimulated to observe geometric objects from the earliest stage of their education, these ideas would come back to them again and again during the course of their schooling, deepening with each new level of sophistication. The rudimentary appreciation of shapes and forms . . . would become more refined as students developed new skills in arithmetic and measurement and later in more formal algebra and geometry.

—Thomas F. Banchoff (1990, p. 11)

Setup

On a winter morning, the lesson was intended to model Common Core mathematical practices (NGA/CCSSO, 2010). I chose *Circling Circles* because it incorporates several: Modeling with mathematics, using appropriate tools strategically, looking for and making use of structure, and looking for and expressing regularity. Regarding content, while the lesson clearly is about geometry, it also features algebraic concepts as well as algebraic ways of reasoning, talking, and doing. Just as in the field of mathematics, where algebra is enhanced by geometry and geometry is expressed through algebra, this lesson interweaves both ways of knowing.

The third-graders were quietly waiting. Seated in groups of two or three students, each pair or trio had a bag with all the necessary manipulatives (Figure 1.1).

Ms. Flores, a caring and dedicated teacher, welcomed me back to her classroom. The Hula-Hoop I had requested was hidden under her desk. Inspired by my theatre experience, I enjoy adding elements of surprise or suspense to my teaching, whenever possible. It was 10 o'clock, and I was granted a full hour.

FIGURE 1.1 Manipulatives needed for the lesson

Photo by Didier Rousselet

Discussion

1. Exploring Circles

In my lesson opening, I wanted to ascertain students' ideas about circles: "What can you tell me about circles?" "It's like a ball," began Daniel. Following suit, Daniel's peers soon had a list of circular objects cascading onto the white board: bicycle wheels and car tires, CDs and DVDs, soccer balls and basketballs, jar lids, checker pieces, plates, a roll of tape, coins, and more (Figure 1.2). We listed these contributions under the heading "Circular (Round) Objects," highlighting that *circus* and *circle* have the common root *circ* from the fact that original circuses had circular arenas for human and animal performances.

FIGURE 1.2   Examples of circular (round) objects

Photo by Didier Rousselet

Dimension

I drew students' attention to the different dimensions of the listed objects. They knew the term *3-D* from movies, so we connected the letter *d* to the word *dimension.* They agreed that CDs and coins are *flat* and could live in *Flatland*. Since they hadn't heard of that word, I held up the famous little book of the same title by English schoolmaster Edwin Abbott (1992). "In this Romance of Many Dimensions (the book's subtitle), the inhabitants of Flatland are line segments and polygons," I explained. Acknowledging her students' apparent interest, Ms. Flores promised to order the book so they could read it later. We returned then to our circles.

Soccer balls and basketballs on the other hand are definitely 3-D objects. They cannot live in Flatland, because they have "thickness." They live in *Spaceland*, also coined by Abbott. We reviewed the word *sphere* for a 3-D, hollow, inflated ball like the classroom globe or a beach ball. And we learned the word *disk* for a 2-D or flat, circular object, almost like a CD or DVD except with neither thickness nor a hole at the center.

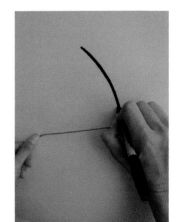

FIGURE 1.3   Drawing a circle with marker and string

Photo by Didier Rousselet

Definition

Just as the 2-D Square was the main character in the book *Flatland*, the 2-D Circle was the protagonist of our lesson. "I can see you know lots of circular objects. Now, can someone explain what a *circle* is?" As they pondered how to put their thoughts into words, I pulled out of my bag of props a prepared piece of string with a black marker attached to one end: my handmade compass. Then I drew a point on the board, labeled it CENTER, and holding the free end of the string at *that* point with my left thumb, I drew a circle with the marker in my right hand (Figure 1.3). Another perplexity arose: Was the circle the black ring only, or the ring *plus* the enclosed circular region of the white board?

To resolve the quandary, we accessed the online dictionary, Math is Fun, on the interactive white board and looked up the definition of the word *circle:* "A 2-dimensional shape made by drawing a curve that is always the same distance from a center" (www.mathsisfun.com/definitions/index.html).

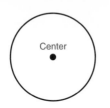

FIGURE 1.4 A circle and its center

The class accepted that the circle was therefore "the black ink only," as one student put it, *not* the enclosed circular disk, nor the point called *center of the circle* (Figure 1.4). "Is that the same for triangles?" inquired bright-eyed Disha. "Excellent question! You took the words right out of my mouth!" I exclaimed. Disha was a math lover and a high-level thinker. Drawing a triangle on the board and shading it in, I explained: "Even though we often refer to *all of this* as a triangle, *mathematically* a triangle is only the three connecting line segments, not the shaded region inside." That was news to some students.

RECOGNIZE . . .

A geometric object is a mental object that, when constructed, carries with it traces of the tool or tools by which it was constructed.

—Nathalie Sinclair, David Pimm, & Melanie Skelin (2012, p. 8)

2. Posing the Problem

"I brought a problem for you today about circles; are you ready to solve it?" They were. "Before I state the problem, I have a warm-up question."

Modeling With a Square

Ms. Flores assisted me by holding up another prop: a square picture frame. I took out a precut piece of string, equal in length to the side length of the square frame. Modeling a side length, I placed it atop the frame, stretching it from corner to adjacent corner, and asked, "How many times do you think this piece of string fits *around* the square frame?" Several hands shot up. I called on Paula: "Four times," she answered. "Who agrees?" I continued. More hands went up. "Who can convince us all that it's four times?" I carried on. "It's four 'cause they're four equal sides," explained Emma. It sounded convincing. I nevertheless modeled the *perimeter*, as I had the side length, by wrapping a longer string tightly *around* the frame and cutting off a piece equal in length to the frame's perimeter. We compared lengths: Indeed, the short string fit four times "inside" the long one. I marked the perimeter string to model that it contained four side-length strings (Figure 1.5).

FIGURE 1.5 Materializing the square frame's side length and perimeter with string

(a) Side-length string

(b) Perimeter string

Modeling With a Circle

It was time to bring out the Hula-Hoop. The kids got excited. Some of them wanted to show me how well they could Hula-Hoop. I promised they could do so *after* the lesson. Extra incentive to dive into our problem.

Diameter. We pretended the hoop was as thin as the black circle drawn on the white board. The students understood that real-world circles must have thickness; otherwise they would be too fragile to hold. Manipulatives are never perfect, but it suffices to point out their limitations and then proceed. Children are experts at pretending. Plus, they love to indulge teachers. "Any idea what the *diameter* of a circle is?" I began. Some knew the word but couldn't define it. "Breaking down the word, *dia* means "going through or across" in Greek, and *meter* means "measure." So the diameter is the *measure* of *what*, going *through what*?" I asked, as I turned to the circle on the board to hint at the center point. Some caught on. "The *center?*" asked Alexander? "Correct. But *what* goes through the center?" I pressed. "A piece of string?" added Alexander. "Yes, a taut piece of string we'll call a *line segment*," I explained further. "So the diameter is a line segment through the center of a circle that touches the circle at both ends," I clarified.

As Ms. Flores held the Hula-Hoop firmly, I stretched a piece of string across the hoop, through its invisible center, and touched the hoop at both ends with my index fingers and thumbs. We estimated the center's location, aided by a visual clue: The diameter had to divide the circle into *two equal semicircles* (Figure 1.6). Students helped me with their view of the hoop from a distance. I finally cut off a piece and held it up saying, "This is a representation of the Hula-Hoop's diameter. We'll call it our 'diameter string.'"

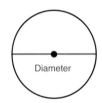

FIGURE 1.6   A circle and its diameter

The Question

"And now for my question: How many diameter strings would we need to encircle the Hula-Hoop? In other words, how many times do you think the diameter fits along the perimeter of this circle?" Before I could explain that the perimeter of a circle has a special name, Kindra corrected me, "You mean the *circumference*?" "Absolutely," I intoned with praise, "the distance *around* a circle is called the *circumference*—another word starting with *circ,* right?" No doubt Cindy Neuschwander's math adventures of Sir Cumference were popular in Ms. Flores's class (Neuschwander, 1997).

Student conjectures ranged from 2 times to 5 times. Ms. Flores pulled up the prepared chart on the interactive board and tallied their conjectures by counting raised hands for each category (Table 1.1). There were more 3s and 4s than there were 2s and 5s.

Not surprisingly, only whole numbers were uttered. After all, the students were only beginning to learn that numbers called *fractions* live between numbers 0 and 1 on the number line, and between other consecutive whole numbers as well. Moreover, the answer to the warm-up question on the perimeter of a square was the whole number 4.

TABLE 1.1   First chart used to tally student conjectures

How many diameter strings fit around the Hula-Hoop?			
2 times	3 times	4 times	5 times

Does the Size of the Circle Matter?

Before I sent them off in small groups to explore the problem, I surveyed one more thing: "Do you think the number of times the diameter fits around a circle will change if the circle gets bigger or smaller?" All but one student opined that the answer

TABLE 1.2 Second chart used to tally student conjectures

What do you think?	
I think the answer is the same for all circles	I think the circle size matters: larger circles give greater answers.

depends on the circle size, namely, that in larger circles the answers would be greater than in smaller circles. We tallied those responses as well, admiring Jason's daring to be the sole tally mark in the first column (Table 1.2).

3. Measuring to Find Out

Measuring With String

Students removed scissors, string, marker, and pencil from their bags, as instructed. Each group received a different-size circular object and the same instructions (Figure 1.7; see Appendix, page 205, for student worksheet). The eight circular objects handed out were lids ranging in size from 3 to 29 cm in diameter.

FIGURE 1.7 Circling circles instruction sheet (Part I)

Circling Circles (Part I)

Names: _____ _____ _____ _____

Prediction: Before measuring, discuss the number of times *you think* the diameter will fit around the lid. Agree on a number and write your group's prediction here _____.

Tasks: Decide who will do Steps 1, 2, 3, and 4.

Step 1: Cut a piece of string equal in length to the diameter of the lid.

Step 2: Cut a piece of string equal in length to the circumference of the lid.

Step 3: Use the marker to mark the number of times the short piece of string fits inside the long piece of string.

Step 4: Talk to each other and share your thoughts. Choose one idea and write about it on the back of this paper. It can be a question, an observation, a conjecture, a picture, or something else.

We read the directions together. "Thumbs up if they are clear; thumbs down if you need help understanding something." Ms. Flores and I attended to those in need while the others got to work. One group worked on Ms. Flores's wastepaper basket (35-cm diameter) and another on my child-size Hula-Hoop (71-cm diameter). Students assigned to the basket were instructed to measure the container's rim, at the opening. That required dexterity, as did measuring the contour of the Hula-Hoop!

Almost all groups found that the diameter fit "three times and a little more" around their circular objects. The majority marked their strings as shown in Figure 1.8 (b), and a few as shown in Figure 1.8 (c).

That the diameter length would fit inside the circumference length *the same number of times for all circles* was "awesome" for some and "cool" for others. One child—a little man in a boy's body—who loved big words called out, "astonishing!" The discovery of the invariant ratio between circumference and diameter in *all* circles was a true "aha moment" for the class, as almost all students had conjectured higher ratios for larger circles.

FIGURE 1.8   Materializing the lid's diameter and circumference with string. The intervals between consecutive tick marks in (b) and (c) represent the lengths of the diameter string.

(a) Diameter string

(b) Circumference string (a little more than 3 diameters)

(c) Circumference string (exactly 3 diameters)

Ratio. We didn't use the word *ratio*. Instead I chose the word *relationship*. While the circle sizes varied, we found that the *relationship* between the length of the diameter and the length of the circumference remained the same. Ms. Flores's students had discovered an important property of circles in the same way that early civilizations had, namely, by noticing that a rope around the periphery of a circle equaled just over three lengths through its center. That discovery marked the beginning of the four-million-year story of pi; it also marked the end of our *Circling Circles* Exploration, Part I. My third-graders were tired but looking forward to further investigation on Day 2.

REMEMBER . . .

From the very beginning of his education, the child should experience the joy of discovery.

—Alfred North Whitehead (1916, p. 1)

Measuring With a Metric Tape

Circling Circles Part II, which took place the following day, began with a hands-on exploration. Students used their metric measuring tapes and followed a second set of instructions (Figure 1.9; see Appendix, page 205, for student worksheet). Again we read the instructions aloud and provided clarification. We reviewed a centimeter–body connection: "A centimeter is about as wide as a third-grader's pinky finger (at the top), and an inch is about two pinky fingers."

Uncertain about the students' grasp of the millimeter tick marks on the metric tapes, I told them to record the whole-number centimeter measurement nearest to the length they measured. However, if the measurement fell halfway between two consecutive centimeter measures, they were to record the *larger of the two* numbers. (In other words, they would round up). Ms. Flores and I roamed the room, assisting students who called for help. When all groups were finished, we recorded their data in a class table in the order in which they raised their hands (Table 1.3). Students accepted the use of *D* and *C* quite naturally.

FIGURE 1.9   Circling circles instruction sheet (Part II)

Circling Circles (Part II)

Names: _____   _____   _____   _____

Tasks: Decide among yourselves who will *estimate* (Steps 1 and 3), *measure* (Steps 2 and 4), and *write* (Step 5).

Step 1: *Estimate* the length of the diameter (the longest distance **across**): _____ cm

Step 2: Now use the metric tape to *measure* the length of the diameter: _____ cm

Step 3: *Estimate* the length of the circumference (the distance **around**): _____ cm

Step 4: Now use the metric tape to *measure* the length of the circumference: _____ cm

Step 5: Talk to each other and share your thoughts. Choose one observation or reaction and *write* it on the back of this paper.

Delving Deeper

4. Representing With Numbers and Words

Saying It With Numbers

Once the measurements from all groups were displayed, I invited observations on the numerical data. More specifically, I asked the students to focus on how the numbers in the right column compared to the numbers in the left column. As with any group of students, comments ranged from lower-level, specific remarks such as, "Group H's numbers are backwards [referring to 29 and 92]," to higher-level, more general observations such as Paula's comment: "If you take the first number and multiply by three, you sometimes get the second number," noticing the pairs (5, 15) and (6, 18). Asked to give examples, she obliged me, "Five times three is fifteen, and six times three is eighteen." "Any others?" I inquired. "No," she replied. "What about the other pairs of numbers," I asked Travon, confident I could forge ahead with his help, having overheard his conversation with his partner. Eloquently he proceeded, "Well, if you multiply by three, you *almost* get the second number," with a nice long drawl punctuating "almost." "What do you mean by 'almost'?" I continued. "You get a little bigger . . . like, um, three times three is nine but it's ten. Four times three is really twelve, but it's thirteen, and, um . . . thirteen is a little bigger than twelve." I recorded Travon's reasoning (Figure 1.10).

TABLE 1.3   Class data table

Group	Diameter Length across (in cm) D	Circumference Length around (in cm) C
A	3	10
B	4	13
C	7	22
D	11	35
E	6	18
F	8	26
G	5	15
H	29	92
I (Hula-Hoop)	71	227
J (wastebasket)	35	112

Observing Regularity in *All* Rows. Not convinced that all students could work out mentally the relationship between the double-digit numbers, I called on Robin for further clarification: "Can you show the class that the same relationship holds between the two measurements found by Groups D and H?" Robin rose to the call: "Eleven times three is thirty-three—that's easy—and thirty-five is a little bigger," she explained, borrowing the phrase "a little bigger," used by Travon and recorded on the board. Displaying her amazing number sense, Robin continued: "Well, twenty-nine is close to thirty, and ninety-two is close to ninety, and three times three is nine—oh, no, I mean, thirty times three is ninety." Again, for the purpose of clarity, I recorded Robin's thinking right under Travon's, hoping the regularity in the data would emerge for *all* students (Figure 1.11).

FIGURE 1.10 Travon observes that circumference measurements are "a little bigger" than three times diameter measurements.

$D = 3$	$C = 10$	$3 \times \mathbf{3} = 9$ / 10 is a little bigger than 9
$D = 4$	$C = 13$	$4 \times \mathbf{3} = 12$ / 13 is a little bigger than12

FIGURE 1.11 Robin observes that the relationship between circumference and diameter is approximately the same for several pairs of two-digit measurements.

	$D = 3$	$C = 10$	$3 \times \mathbf{3} = 9$ / 10 is a little bigger than 9
	$D = 4$	$C = 13$	$4 \times \mathbf{3} = 12$ / 13 is a little bigger than12
	$D = 11$	$C = 35$	$11 \times \mathbf{3} = 33$ / 35 is a little bigger than 33
	$D = 29$	$C = 92$	
	↓	↓	
Estimating:	Close to 30	Close to 90	$30 \times \mathbf{3} = 90$ / 92 is a little bigger than 90

Together we examined the data in the last two rows of the table and confirmed the *almost*-tripling relationship between D and C in *all* rows.

By now, everyone could see the relationship between the numerical measurements of diameter and circumference from the class data table, but clearly *not everyone* had made the connection between this numerical relationship and the string experiment from Day 1. This was evidenced by the Eureka wave that spread across the room following Lynnette's exclamation, "Oh, neat, that's just like the string!" Eager to have everyone share in the joy of this connection, I purposely pursued, perplexed, "What do you mean?" "The long string was almost like three times the short string, but a little more!" Which just goes to show us teachers that sometimes what we *think* is implicit needs to be made explicit. With their sometimes-unexpected comments and often-amazing questions, students give us all the ingredients to make a good lesson . . . provided we remain attentive listeners!

Saying It With Words

I explained to the class why Groups E and G got a relationship of *exactly* three to one. In a perfect world, they too would have obtained *a little more than* three. Students need to know that any data set contains measurement errors, and that, in particular, our investigation was subject to human error in measuring, reading, and recording; imperfection in measuring instruments; effects of rounding numbers up or down; thickness of the Hula-Hoop and basket; and other factors. But, these errors were normal and by no means minimized the importance of their discovery.

On Day 1, through the concrete string experiment, students touched upon the discovery through visualization. On Day 2, producing classroom data through measurement revealed the same discovery, but his time through the language of numbers. Now, their next task was to translate their discovery into the language of words—into English. Instructions were clear: Their sentences had to include the words *diameter* and *circumference* and had to describe a property of *all* circles. To add incentive, I shared the fact that the first recorded work in mathematics—the Rhind Papyrus, currently in the British museum—contained mathematicians' fascination with this same property of circles. And that was about 1650 BCE, more than 3,500 years ago, in Egypt!

After a few minutes, students volunteered to read their generalizations out loud. Ms. Flores selected five of them for their originality and copied them verbatim from slate to board (Table 1.4). Although Sentence 2 didn't comply with the directions, it helped visualize the string experiment from Day 1. These verbal representations reinforced the observed relationship between the diameter and circumference of all circles: big, small, *all*. They also inspired the less verbal students to carve out their own formulations.

TABLE 1.4   Verbal representations of the diameter-to-circumference relationship

Examples of Verbal Representations
1. When you take a circle and mezur the diameter you get the circomfrence times 3 but thers a bit more.
2. If you walk round a circle it's like a little more than 3 times if you walk through the centr.
3. The diametr string of a circel needs three to go round the circumference.
4. 3 times the diameter plus a wee bit more is the sircumference
5. diameter + diameter + diameter = circumference almost

Multiplication–Division Connection

I projected my next slide onto the board, adding a new, empty column to the right of our class data table. It was titled "$C \div D$ or $\frac{C}{D}$." Using their TI-108 calculators, the students divided C by D. My goals for them were to have fun dividing with calculators, to expose them to decimals in a novel way, and to observe the inverse relationship between multiplication and division.

The excitement over using calculators (to divide, no less!) was coupled with the puzzlement caused by the digit strings of variable lengths. The ten group recorders called out the numbers appearing on their calculators. Ms. Flores entered them into the last column of the table (Table 1.5), diligently transcribing all digits called out. Two groups had inadvertently reversed dividend and divisor, but they quickly caught on.

Curiosity engendered comments such as, "They all start with a three," and "Some are short and some are long!" and questions such as "Are the longer ones bigger?" This wonderful question from Lynnette brought a smile to my face; listening to children's math talk invites us inside their minds and reminds us how they think. The question prompted me to draw a magnified interval of the tape measure on the board and show that all the quotients found, while in *appearance* very different, live close to one another on the number line (Figure 1.12 red segment). It was new to many students that the small tick marks between

TABLE 1.5 Students use the division key on four-function calculators to find $C \div D$

Group	Diameter/D Length across (in cm)	Circumference/C Length around (in cm)	$C \div D$ or $\frac{C}{D}$
A	3	10	3.3333333
B	4	13	3.25
C	7	22	3.1428571
D	11	35	3.1818181
E	6	18	3
F	8	26	3.25
G	5	15	3
H	29	92	3.1724137
I (Hula-Hoop)	71	227	3.197183
J (wastebasket)	35	112	3.2

three and three-and-a-half were labeled 3.1, 3.2, 3.3, and 3.4. But it made sense. Also, they easily accepted "3.0" as an alternative name for "3," as it logically fit into the sequence, 3.0, 3.1, 3.2, 3.3, 3.4, 3.5 . . . Third-graders have plenty of time to deepen their understanding of decimals in grades 4 and 5, but visualizing them on the number line from early on is crucial.

FIGURE 1.12 All quotients in Table 1.5 live within the small red interval on the number line.

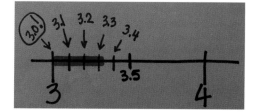

Having established "a little more than three" first with the string experiment and second in the multiplicative relationship between D and C (Table 1.3), some students were not surprised when encountering it again, especially those who understood that division is the inverse of multiplication— "like subtraction and addition," said Madison. But, while this is important, I chose to move on to demystifying this mysterious number.

5. Representing With Pictures and Symbols

Pi Talk

Hoping the students were clear on the existence of human error in measurement, as discussed, I posed a question—albeit a low-level, yes-no question—to the entire class to double check: "How many of you think that in a perfect world we should have all found the same number?" The majority of hands sprang up. "Any idea what that number would be, Lamar?" I asked pointedly, secretly knowing from Ms. Flores of his fascination for pi. "A little more than three?" he replied. "Absolutely. But do you know a special number that begins with three and has many digits beyond the decimal point?" I persisted. "Pi?" he asked excitedly, clearly never having connected pi to circles. I pressed a little further,

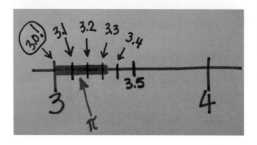

FIGURE 1.13   Locating pi inside the interval of quotients computed by the students

"What number is pi?" "Three point one, four, one, five, nine, two, six, five, three . . . " he answered, impressing students and teachers. "Excellent!" cried Ms. Flores, so proud of her student." I carried on in admiration, "Wow! That's indeed the number you *all* would have found in a perfect world." Unable to contain his enthusiasm, Lamar blurted out, interrupting me, "Pi has a million numbers. My Dad taught me." Feelings of wonderment could be seen, felt, and heard.

To wrap up our "pi talk," we pulled up the "100,000 Digits of Pi" website (www.geom.uiuc .edu/~huberty/math5337/groupe/digits.html) and scrolled down. The students were mesmerized. The hardest concept to grasp was that *more and more* digits did not signify a *bigger and bigger* number. "Is pi way bigger than all the quotients we found?" I inquired. "No!" said Kayla, assertively. "Do you agree with Kayla?" I asked Gabe, who was daydreaming. "I don't know," he replied, pretending to be reflecting. "Then call on someone to help you understand why this number, with so many digits, is *not* a huge number," I persevered. Gabe called on our Number Devil. Once again, Robin met the challenge with confidence, "Because it starts with three and then there's a one, so it's smaller than three two five (meaning 'three *point* two five')!" "Good thinking! No matter how many digits there are—even a million—pi lives between 3.1 and 3.2, like the four other numbers we found with our calculators," I said, pointing to numbers such as 3.1818181 in our table. "So 3.25 and 3.3333333 are *bigger* than pi!" I reiterated, indicating pi's relative location inside our interval with an arrow (Figure 1.13).

I didn't worry whether this concept was clear; over the following two years, the students would grow deeper roots of understanding of decimals.

REALIZE . . .

One can get a tremendous amount of mileage out of a continuing discussion on the estimation of π, from the first time a kindergarten student realizes that the belt around a can reaches a little more than three times across the top, to second-semester calculus where one studies integrals for arc length.

—Thomas F. Banchoff (1990, p. 35)

Saying It With Pictures

For the final task, students had a choice: Those who wanted to engage their creative *artistic* talents joined Group 1. Their task? To "say it with pictures"; namely, to draw a picture representing what they learned about diameter and circumference in all circles. Ms. Flores provided these students with drawing supplies and assistance. Group 2, a smaller group of math aficionados, opted to use a different creative talent: *abstract thinking*. Their task? To "say it with symbols"; namely, to write an equation relating C, D, and π. (Students learned the symbol for pi from the website.) They worked with me.

Ms. Flores handed out colored paper, colored pencils, and crayons. She also allowed students to use slates and colored dry-erase pens if they preferred. She suggested tracing a lid's contour if their representation needed a circle. Once they understood the assignment, students were on their own, guided solely by their imagination and creativity.

Student-Created Pictorial Representations. Students were clearly inspired by the prior day's actions of cutting diameter and circumference strings, comparing them side by side like line segments, and marking the diameter-string units inside the circumference strings. Consequently, most pictorial representations depicted these actions. Max and Danica's pictures, faithfully reproduced here, are representative of two variations on the "linear string theme" observed (Figure 1.14).

FIGURE 1.14   Reproductions of sample student drawings of the *D*-to-*C* relationship. (a) Max's drawing includes both diameter and circumference lengths and their relationship; (b) Danica's drawing shows the circumference string as composed of three diameter strings and gives a quasisymbolic equation.

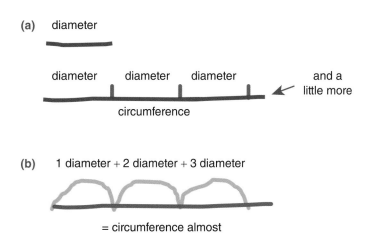

Only one student, Gabe, depicted the visual "wrapping" of the diameters *around* the circumference of a circle, which had been verbalized and modeled by the teacher but not enacted by the students. Figure 1.15 is a reproduction of his clever rendering. As the saying goes, this picture is worth a thousand words. Gabe's drawing not only enlightens the viewer but also reveals the significant learning that took place in two days. Recall that only one day earlier, the children had guessed that the diameter would wrap around a circle two, three, four, and five times. Gabe's rendition was a reminder for me not rush to conclusions about daydreamers. After all, 17th century French mathematician René Descartes claimed that analytic geometry flashed before him in a dream, and 20th century Indian mathematician Srinivasa Ramanujan that new mathematical ideas came to him during meditation!

Saying It With Symbols

After two days of using *C* and *D* as shorthand notations for circumference and diameter, students were comfortable with their meanings. "It's like our initials instead of our

FIGURE 1.15   Author's reproduction of Gabe's pictorial representation that vividly conveys the fact that it takes three diameters—plus a little "xtra"—to wrap around the circumference.

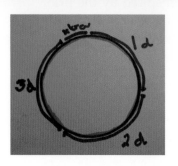

names," offered Disha as a lovely analogy during our small-group discussion about symbols. Less obvious to these second-semester third-graders was the meaning and use of the recently acquired symbol, π. "It's actually a number close to 3—between 3.1 and 3.2 to be exact—with millions of digits beyond the decimal point; since it's impossible to say or write the entire number, we use π for short." That was my attempt at explaining pi to young children. Some students seemed comfortable with this abstraction; others less so. Writing number sentences was common in Ms. Flores's class, but writing symbol sentences was less so.

Teacher-Guided Symbolic Representations. To guide them on the final stretch, I returned to the verbal representations on the board (Table 1.4) and had them pick the ones they found easiest to translate into equations. "3 times the diameter plus a wee bit more is the sircumference" and "Diameter + diameter + diameter = circumference almost" were their choices. Both were partially in equation form, as the first contained "is" and the second an equals sign. For lack of time, I focused on the first sentence, which they seamlessly converted to, "3 × D + aweebitmore = C." "So three times D doesn't quite equal C, right?" I said. They acquiesced. Nudging them further to the finish line, I inquired, "So

FIGURE 1.16   Symbolic representations of the *D*-to-*C* relationship

$$\pi \times D = C \qquad 3^+ \times D = C$$

what could we multiply D by to get C *exactly*?" "Pi?" guessed Disha, with a radiant smile. I felt it was more of a guess than an understanding, but, after all, she was only in third grade! We accepted her proposition, and she proudly wrote our final equation on the board (Figure 1.16). I added the equation $3^+ \times D = C$ next to it, adding, "'Three plus' will be our secret code to remember that pi is *a little more than* three, OK?" They smiled in agreement. In time, both equations will merge and π will take on meaning. But for now, the *about-3 relationship* between D and C was what mattered.

Closure

Ms. Flores and I brought closure to the *Circling Circles* Exploration by having the two groups visit each other's work and learn from their peers' representations. In the final whole-group discussion, students took turns verbalizing what they had learned. The actions of circling, stretching, cutting, comparing, measuring, computing, tracing, drawing, and writing were now stored in their bodies' memory banks. In addition, students had cultivated habits of mind essential to mathematics, including conjecturing, discerning, comparing, explaining, discovering, verbalizing, representing, generalizing, and even symbolizing. By acting, thinking, and talking like young mathematicians, they had planted the seeds of a fundamental concept that in a couple of years would lead to the algebraic notions of ratios, proportional relationships, and linear functions. The mysterious number pi—and its relationship to circles—had begun to be demystified.

Sandra had not forgotten: "Can we do the Hula-Hoop now?" "Certainly!"

2
Behind *Circling Circles*
Algebra Connections

Astudy on the history of algebra and its implications for teaching (Katz, 2007) outlines the four main conceptual stages in algebra's evolution:

1. The *geometric* stage, where the concepts of algebra are geometric;

2. The static *equation-solving stage*, where the goal is to find numbers satisfying certain relationships;

3. The *dynamic function* stage, where motion is an underlying idea; and finally,

4. The *abstract* stage, where mathematical structure plays the central role. (p. 185)

All along, from the first traces of algebraic thinking in Babylonian mathematics, algebra has been closely related to numbers. That connection has survived to this day in the *generalized-arithmetic* approach to introducing algebra, one of the five common curricular approaches mentioned in the introduction to this book.

In the *geometric* stage, numbers and measurements were conceived geometrically (Figure 2.1). The ancient Greeks used geometric diagrams or constructions to solve real problems. The *geometric algebra* they gave us survived through the 9th century CE.

FIGURE 2.1   Linear, square, and cubic measures represented geometrically

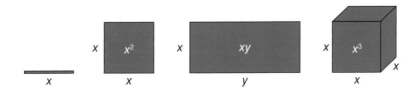

The milestone book on solving equations by Persian mathematician Al Khwarizmi (c. 820 CE) moved algebra into the *equation-solving* stage, which lasted 800 years. Its impact on school mathematics was such that most adults today who've taken algebra think of it as synonymous with solving equations for *x*.

In the 17th century, new interests moved algebra even further: Johann Kepler wanted to understand the paths of planets (Figure 2.2) and Galileo Galilei the paths of projectiles (Figure 2.3). Focus shifted from finding single solutions of isolated equations to studying entire curves. The curves in Figure 2.3 are graphs of *functions*, or relationships between varying quantities that change: height of football over time. Such relationships were at the heart of the *dynamic function* stage.

FIGURE 2.2   Path of a planet around the sun

FIGURE 2.3   Heights of a football projected at different initial angles

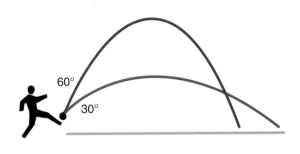

Finally, by the dawn of the 20th century, the emphasis on finding the underlying structures (or patterns) of mathematical objects or phenomena gave birth to *abstract algebra*. The Common Core mathematical practice, "Look for and make use of structure" originates here. For example, children can notice that $2 \times n$ is the structure of all even numbers, and $2 \times n + 1$ is the structure of all odd numbers (Neagoy, 2012) (Figure 2.4).

Remnants of all four stages are present in today's school algebra. Retracing the historical path of a mathematical topic sheds light on the path of a child's learning of that topic. In the case of algebra, going from concrete (number and shape) to abstract (variable, function, and structure) is the logical progression. Cumulatively, the explorations in this book address all aspects of early algebra. Exploration I alone offers multiple lenses on algebra in the early grades, including modeling, understanding number, quantitative reasoning, functional thinking, and multiple representations of functional relationships.

FIGURE 2.4   (a) Even numbers have algebraic structure $2 \times n$. For example, $8 = 2 \times 4$. (b) Odd numbers have algebraic structure $2 \times n + 1$. For example, $9 = 2 \times 4 + 1$.

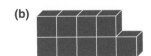

Because teachers need various illustrations of algebraic thinking, talking, and doing before fostering them in their students, this chapter revisits each section of Chapter 1, identifies important mathematical ideas in grades 3–5, and makes the algebra connections explicit. The primary focus is the mathematics, but suggestions are also made for interacting with the mathematics in meaningful ways.

RESEARCH . . .

We suspect the successful weaving of an algebra strand throughout the K–12 curriculum will depend on the fluidity with which teachers are able to move back and forth between algebraic representations and representations expressed through natural language, diagrams, tables of values, and graphs.

—David Carraher and Analúcia Schliemann (2010, p. 29)

CHAPTER 2

THE BIG IDEAS OF

- Invariance, meaning distinguishing what varies from what remains the same. Geometrically, the circles change size, but the diameter-to-circumference relationship remains *invariant* (unchanged). Numerically, the D and C measurements vary, but their ratios, $\frac{C}{D}$, remain equivalent or *invariant.*

- The difference between *additive thinking* and *multiplicative thinking*, and the cultivation of the latter starting in grade 3. Multiplicative thinking is the foundation for the concepts of fraction, ratio, percent, proportion, the operations of multiplication and division, and proportional and linear relationships—the core of beginning algebra.

- The importance of *modeling* throughout mathematics, in all content areas and at all grade levels.

- *Multiple representations* of the concept of a ratio, one of several meanings of the symbol $\frac{a}{b}$ to be developed staring in grades 3–5.

- The need for more focus on *quantitative reasoning* (comparing additively or multiplicatively two or more numbers or quantities) rather than on isolated *numerical computations*.

- The importance of pausing, zooming out, and reflecting: cultivating the habit of mind of *generalizing*, with words, pictures, numbers, equations, and graphs.

Discussion

1. Exploring Circles

The role of circles in our history, culture, and language not only is fascinating but provides some fun trivia as well. Mankind has been captivated by circles and spheres since before recorded history. The circle is considered nature's most perfect natural shape, just as the square is considered the most perfect human-made shape. Studying the assumed spherical planets and their assumed circular orbits gave rise to the science of *astronomy*; and studying the circular ripples on water's surface caused by the drop of a pebble played a role in the advent of the mathematics of instantaneous change, also known as *calculus*. Mankind's fascination with circles is reflected in the wealth of idioms containing the word: "It's a vicious circle," "We've come full circle," and "He can run circles around his brother." A well-known idiom to math lovers is "trying to square the circle," meaning trying to solve an impossible problem. This idiom refers to a problem posed by ancient Greek geometers. In 1882, this famous problem was proved impossible to solve!

The number pi (π) has puzzled mathematicians, artists, and others for nearly 4,000 years. "Probably no symbol in mathematics has evoked as much mystery, romanticism, misconception and human interest as the number pi (π)" (Blatner, 1997, p. 1). Most people who've completed middle school mathematics associate pi with circle formulas, may know it's about 3.14, and probably know its symbol, but rarely can they "see," with their mind's eye, the simplicity of its meaning. Hence the importance of *Circling Circles*!

Dimension

Classical Meaning of Dimension. In the third century BCE, the ancient Greek mathematician, Euclid of Alexandria, stated the dimensions of three spaces in his axioms, or self-evident truths requiring no proof. A *line*, he said, is a "breathless length," because it has neither width nor depth—just length. Therefore it is *one*-dimensional. A plane surface, simply called a *plane*, materialized in our world by the surface of a white board, a computer screen, or a page in a book, has both length *and* width and is therefore *two*-dimensional. Lastly, the *space* we live in—the easiest for children to comprehend because it's *their* world—has length, width, and depth and is therefore *three*-dimensional. Following Euclid's reasoning, it's easy to deduce that a *point* has neither length, nor width, nor depth and is therefore *zero*-dimensional. These spaces are known as *Euclidean spaces*.

FIGURE 2.5   The coordinates of P and O are (3) and (0), respectively.

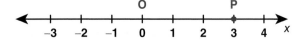

Modern Meaning of Dimension. "The seventeenth century witnessed a truly important wedding, far more than the union of royal dynasties . . . algebra and geometry became one (Stein, 1996)." *Algebraic* geometry, the brainchild of French mathematicians René Descartes and Pierre Fermat, is known today as *analytic* or even *Cartesian* geometry, named after Descartes. Analytic geometry radically changed the way mathematicians conceive of dimension. In this modern view, the dimension of a space or object is defined by the number of *real numbers* needed to locate a point in that space. To locate a point on a line, we need one number: Call it the *x-coordinate*. In Figure 2.5, point P is denoted by the *x*-coordinate (3), and point O, the selected origin of the line, by (0).

FIGURE 2.6   The coordinates of P and O are (3, 2.5) and (0, 0), respectively.

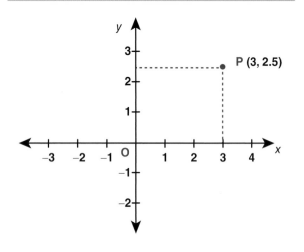

Two numbers, called the *x*- and *y-coordinates*, are needed to locate a point on any surface. In Figure 2.6, the number pair (3, 2.5) denotes point P, and (0, 0) the origin O of the plane. As a *real*-world application, locating a ship out at sea requires two coordinates, *longitude and latitude*, which give the ship's distance from the prime meridian (virtual *y*-axis) and the equator (virtual *x*-axis), respectively.

Finally, in the space inside a sphere or a cube, or simply in our everyday space, three numbers are required to locate a point: the *x*-, *y*-, and *z-coordinates*. In Figure 2.7, the triple (3, 4, 2) denotes point P, and (0, 0, 0) the origin O of the space. To visualize P's coordinates, start with the point (*x, y*) = (3, 4) on the plane of this page (the *xy*-plane); move two units away from the page *toward* you, along the *z*-axis. While the reasoning in analytic geometry is different from that of classical geometry, both systems arrived at the same dimensions: one for lines (straight or curved), two for surfaces (flat or curved), and three for any portion, bounded or boundless, of Spaceland, as Abbott called it in his famous book titled *Flatland* (1992).

Dimension of Geometric Attributes. In grade 3, students begin to develop a conceptual understanding of area and perimeter and acquire basic skills for computing perimeters and areas of simple figures (CCSS.Math.Content.3.MD and CCSS.Math.Content.3.G). By the end of grade 5, students must understand basic geometric attributes in order to "solve real-world and mathematical problems involving area, surface area, and volume" in grade 6 (CCSS.Math.Content.6.G). The emphasis in grades 3–5 is more on conceptual understanding and visualization. But grade 5 students are expected to know perimeter and area formulas for rectangles and volume formulas for rectangular solids. The concept of attribute dimension is the same for all shapes. Here is a nice way to visualize attribute dimension in grades 3–5:

1. The *perimeter* of a polygon, or the *circumference* of a circle—materialized by a piece of string that outlines the figure—can be stretched out like a line segment and is therefore *one*-dimensional. The word *perimeter* is used for both the contour *and* its length. Note that a polygon or a circle itself is *two*-dimensional, because *it lives in a plane*.

2. The *area* of a polygon or a disk—materialized by the region enclosed by its boundary—is a "piece" of a plane (or Flatland) and therefore *two*-dimensional. The word *area* is

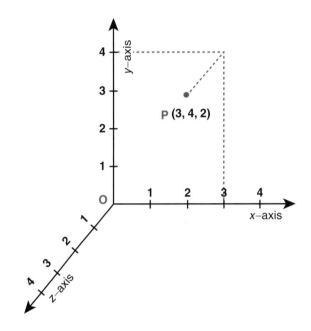

FIGURE 2.7 The coordinates of P and O are (3, 4, 2) and (0, 0, 0), respectively. Only the positive half-lines of the axes are shown here.

TABLE 2.1 Dimensions of attributes of perimeter (circumference), area, and volume

1-Dimensional	2-Dimensional	3-Dimensional
The *perimeter* of a square	The *area* of a square	The *volume* of a cube
The *circumference* of a circle	The *area* of a disk	The *volume* of a sphere

used for both the region and its measure. The area of a rectangular floor, for example, can be visualized by the amount of thin tiling needed to cover it. In this case, both geometric shape and area are *two*-dimensional.

3. The *volume* of a 3-D shape—materialized by the space enclosed by its surface area—is a "piece" of space (or Spaceland) and is therefore *three*-dimensional. The word *volume* is used for both the space and its measure. The volume of a cube or sphere can be visualized by the amount of water or sand needed to fill it. Here again, both the geometric shape and its volume are *three*-dimensional.

In summary, perimeter lives on a line, area lives in a plane, and volume lives in space! See Table 2.1 examples.

Algebra Connection

- **National Mathematics Advisory Panel Report.** The NMAP (National Mathematics Advisory Panel, 2008) identified three "critical foundations of algebra": (1) fluency with whole numbers, (2) fluency with fractions, and (3) particular aspects of geometry and measurement. Under the third, the panel argued, "Students should be able to analyze the properties of two- and three-dimensional shapes using formulas to determine perimeter, area, volume, and surface area" (p. 18). The foundations for these concepts are laid in grades 3–5. What's the connection with algebra? Read on!

- **Whole-Number Exponents.** Exponents, such as 10^2 (for 10×10) or 10^3 (for $10 \times 10 \times 10$) are an important part of algebraic notation. Children begin using them in late elementary school: "Use whole-number exponents to denote powers of 10" is a grade 5 expectation (CCSS.Math.Content.5.NBT.A.2). From the start, exponential notation should make sense. One way to cultivate sense making is by associating the symbolic notation with a concrete representation. The connection to geometric attributes of length, area, and volume—for the first three whole-number exponents—is a powerful one (Figure 2.8). Use manipulatives to make these power-of-10 measures come to life. Your students will never wonder in middle school why x^2 is called "x-squared" or why x^3 is called "x-cubed"! I still recall the elation of a kindergarten teacher upon making the connection between x^3 and *the volume of a cube with edge length x*. "It's so obvious now, but I can't believe I never learned this before!" she commented. This disconnect between algebra and geometry exists at *all* grade levels.

FIGURE 2.8   Length, area, and volume can be used to give meaning to whole-number powers of 10.

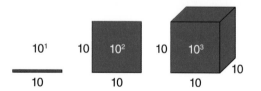

- **Algebraic Formulas in Middle School.** As students get more sophisticated in writing algebraic formulas for perimeter, area, and volume of shapes, they realize the logical connection between *dimension* (of the geometric attribute) and *degree* (of the algebraic expression). In the case of a single variable, like s, s^2 and s^3, the degrees are 1, 2, and 3 respectively. In the case of two or more variables, the connection between dimension and degree still holds. For instance the *area* of a rectangle is *length* × *width* or $lw = l^1w^1$. Adding the exponents (1 + 1) yields a degree of 2 for the expression. Similarly, the volume of a rectangular box, *length* × *width* × *height* or $lwh = l^1w^1h^1$, has degree 3 (1 + 1 + 1). This is a beautiful connection between algebra and geometry that often gets lost. Table 2.2 illustrates this connection in three attributes, perimeter, area, and volume.

TABLE 2.2   Equality between geometric attribute dimension and algebraic expression degree

	Side length s	Dimensions l, w	Side length s	Dimensions l, w	Edge length s	Dimensions l, w, h
Geometric Attribute	Perimeter	Perimeter	Area	Area	Volume	Volume
Dimension	1	1	2	2	3	3
Algebraic Expression	$4 \times s$ $4s^1$	$l + w + l + w$ $2 \times (l^1 + w^1)$	$s \times s \qquad s^2$	$l^1 \times w^1$	$s \times s \times s \qquad s^3$	$l^1 \times w^1 \times h^1$
Degree	1	1	2	2	3	3

REMEMBER . . .

Our modern way of referring to . . . x^2 or x^3 as "x square" and "x cube" still reminds us of their embedded concrete beginnings. Our modern language hangs behind the relics of its past revealing thereby the monomials' [meaning x^2, x^3] original geometric-spatial origin.

—Luis Radford (2009, p.17)

Definition

Nathalie Sinclair (Sinclair, Pimm, & Skelin, 2012, p. 8), makes a powerful statement about the construction of geometric objects: "A geometric object is a mental object that, when constructed, carries with it traces of the tool or tools by which it was constructed."

A Dynamic Construction. For this reason, I consciously chose a dynamic creation of a circle. It involved the choice of some point (the center), a fixed piece of string (the radius), and a tip of a pen in motion, which produced an infinite set of points (the circle). Had I pulled up a ready-made, perfectly round, static circle, no mental "video" would have been created. This mental imagery, replayed over and over, both concretely and abstractly, is a foundation for the eventual construction of a formal definition of circle in middle school. "Geometric images provide the content in relation to which properties can be noticed, definitions can be made, and invariances can be discerned" (Sinclair et al., 2012, p. 8). Properties noticed or verbalized in this dynamic creation included the following: (1) A circle is a 2-D figure, because it lives in a plane; (2) a circle has a fixed, or invariable, radius; (3) a circle has infinitely many radii; (4) the diameter is the longest distance across a circle; and (5) the points that compose a circle are equidistant from the chosen center. We will see later that these properties will help generate and understand the algebraic equation of a circle.

Common Core Math Standards for Grades 3–5 and Van Hiele Levels. The research by two famous Dutch educators on geometric thinking, known worldwide as the Van Hiele theory (Crowley, 1987), has been the most influential work in American geometry curricula since the 1950s. The Van Hiele model identifies five levels of understanding spatial concepts children go through as they mature in geometric thinking: visualization, analysis, informal deduction, deduction, and rigor. The levels, not age-dependent as are Piaget's cognitive development stages, describe ways of thinking rather than amounts of knowledge. Careful analysis of the Common Core State Standards for Mathematics (CCSSM) (NGA/CCSSO, 2010) for grades 3–5 reveals a shift toward greater emphasis on Level 2. "At this level, students begin to appreciate that a collection of shapes goes together because of properties. Ideas about an individual shape can now be generalized to all shapes that fit that class" (Van de Walle & Lovin, 2006, p. 182). For example, they may say that all rectangles have two congruent diagonals or that all circles have infinitely many diameters. "Progress through the levels is more dependent on instruction received than on age or maturation" (Crowley, p. 5). Thus, in order to prod students from the beginning level of recognizing an isolated figure on the basis of its appearance, toward the more sophisticated level of analyzing shared properties of classes of figures (such as squares or circles), we must provide stimulating experiences in which they actively engage in constructing, drawing, measuring, describing, comparing, questioning, verbalizing, and more (Crowley, pp. 8–10). Ideally, students should be at Level 2 by grade 5, with some still at Level 1 and others already at Level 3.

Algebra Connection

- **Invariance and Generalization.** Geometers look for invariance. Regarding shapes, for instance, they look for those properties of a class of shapes that do not change such as color, size, texture, position, or other empirical characteristics do. For example, *all* squares have four equal sides *and* four equal angles. Algebraists look for generalization. Regarding whole numbers, for instance, they look for properties of operations on those numbers that don't depend on the numerical values of particular numbers. For example, addition is commutative because $n + m = m + n$ holds for *all* whole numbers m and n. "Geometry is not so much a branch of mathematics but a way of thinking that permeates all branches," say some math educators (Jones, 2010, p. 213). "Algebra is seen as a 'style of mathematical thinking' . . . that cuts across content areas and unifies the curriculum," say others (Smith, Silver, & Stein, 2005a, pp. xiv–xv). Clearly, both mathematical languages have in common the search for invariance and generalization. Ideas about invariance and generalization are implicit in elementary curricula but rarely explicitly addressed by teachers. Generalizing is a human tendency, and children are not excluded. Shifting from making statements about specific numbers or shapes to entertaining general assertions about them is quintessential to algebraic thinking. We must therefore cultivate the habit of mind, in our students and ourselves, to search for the general in the particular.

- **Algebraic Definition of a Circle.** In geometry, there are two ways of defining a figure: "defining by saying what must be done to bring the figure into existence (*defining by genesis*) and defining by specifying the particular property that must be true for every instance of that figure (*defining by property*). Naming is often related to definition and can reflect one or the other of these means of defining" (Sinclair et al., 2012, p. 58). In *Circling Circles*, I modeled "what must be done to bring a circle into existence," and we discussed some properties. In the process of discussing, students named, spoke, said, verbalized, stated, gestured, and explained—key to algebraic discourse in the early grades. Over time and with maturity, the mental video on circle construction evolves into the polished *verbal* *definition*: "A set of points equidistant from a chosen point called the center." Over more time and with further sophistication, the verbal definition evolves into a *symbolic equation*, arrived at through the initial conceptual understanding. In high school, students will encounter the general equation for a circle with radius r and center $(0, 0)$: $x^2 + y^2 = r^2$ (Figure 2.9).

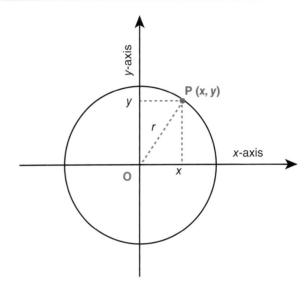

FIGURE 2.9 $x^2 + y^2 = r^2$ is the general equation of circles centered at the origin with radius r.

2. Posing the Problem

Modeling

In mathematics, three meanings of *model* or *modeling* come to mind:

1. Modeling Tools or Models. Mathematical tools or manipulative materials that help teachers convey a mathematical concept to students, such as base-10 blocks for place value or Cuisenaire rods for fractions, are often called models. In *Circling Circles*, the piece of string wrapped around the square frame or circular lid served as a model for perimeter and circumference. Manipulative models, pictures or diagrams, and spoken or written words in natural language are some of the ways in which young children represent and convey their mathematical ideas. In Sections 4 and 5 of this chapter, we revisit the central role of representations in early and later algebra.

2. Mathematical Modeling. Mathematical modeling refers to the specific process of investigating a problem, situation, or phenomenon in the real world. It involves four steps: First, identify the problem of interest (real world). Second, abstract the "mathematical skeleton" of the problem, and express it in mathematical language; this is called the *mathematical model* (mathematical world). Third, find the solution(s) to the mathematical model (still in the mathematical world). Fourth, "go back" to the real world, apply the solution to the original problem, and make adjustments to the purely mathematical solution(s), if necessary, so that the real-world solution makes sense (Figure 2.10).

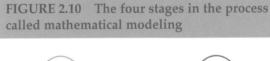

FIGURE 2.10 The four stages in the process called mathematical modeling

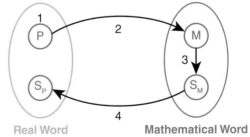

Real Word   Mathematical Word

3. A Mathematical Model. A mathematical model, denoted by M in Figure 2.10, is the mathematical representation of a real-world problem. It is expressed in the form of one or more algebraic equations or functions. Think of it as the shorthand notation of the real problem expressed in words. In *Circling Circles*, upon measuring the circumferences and diameters of multiple real-world circles, we concluded, "The circumference (C) of any circle is a little more than three times its diameter (D)." The *mathematical model* for this relationship is $C = 3^+ \times D$ or, precisely, $C = \pi \times D$.

Algebra Connection

• **Modeling Is Center Stage.** A prime characteristic of human beings is our perpetual desire to understand and explain our world. Nearly every explanation of our past or present, and any prediction of our future, involves quantitative attributes: length, area, volume, mass, temperature, pressure, time, revenue, cost, profit, population, and so on. These quantitative attributes are modeled with numbers and variables, and relationships among quantities are modeled with equations. Much of the mathematics used today to describe, explain, or forecast was developed as a direct result of modeling real-world phenomena. For these reasons, mathematical modeling is fundamental not just to secondary mathematics but to elementary mathematics as well. One of four big ideas in the grade 3–5 algebra standard reads, "Use mathematical models to represent and understand quantitative relationships (National Council of Teachers of Mathematics [NCTM], 2000, p. 158). The fourth Common Core Mathematical Practice (CCSS.Math.Practice.MP4) is "Model with mathematics." In grades 3–5, students learn that mathematical models have both descriptive and predictive power. For example, $C = 3^+ \times D$ or $C = \pi \times D$ *describes* the relationship found between C and D. It can also be used to *predict* the value of C for any given D, or vice versa. In preparation for formal equations, students explore concrete, pictorial, numerical, tabular, and graphical representations of quantitative relationships. These ideas are developed later in the students' mathematical education.

The Question

"How many diameter strings do you think we need to encircle the Hula-Hoop? In other words, how many times do you think the diameter fits along the perimeter of this circle?" We will focus on two big ideas here: additive versus multiplicative thinking, and quantitative reasoning, both prominent in the CCSSM.

Additive Thinking. "How long is this pool?" or "How tall is that building?" or even "How far to Uncle George's house?" are questions young children ask way before they develop the concept of *linear measure*. Questions regarding length, height, and distance pertain to *linear* measure, as their answers can be visualized as portions of a straight line, or, as I fancy saying, their answers *live on a line*. *Circling Circles* capitalizes on children's natural curiosity about measurement. The question posed in the lesson involved a comparison between two lengths, the diameter and the circumference. In geometric *comparison* of linear measurements, a strong tendency exists among teachers and students alike to pose and answer questions *additively*. A typical *additive comparison* question is, "How much taller is Diego than Andrea?" It suggests the following thinking: "How many inches (or other units) must I *add* to Andrea's height to get Diego's height?" Young children often find the solution by counting up, while teachers often model the problem with subtraction. Whether using addition (counting up) or subtraction (its inverse), this problem exemplifies *additive thinking*. Mathematics educators have called attention to the urgent need to cultivate *multiplicative thinking* in the elementary grades (Guershon & Confrey, 1994), especially in grades 3–5, when students are developing an understanding of multiplication's manifold representations and interpretations.

Multiplicative Thinking. A perfect illustration of the pull toward additive reasoning is the way fifth- or sixth-graders commonly reason through the following problem:

The standard bathrooms in Hotel NB are supplied with 3 plastic toiletry bottles—shampoo, conditioner, and body lotion—and 7 towels—two large, two small, two washcloths, and one bath mat. For the Collins yearly family reunion, Grandma Nancy booked several standard rooms in the hotel. The relatives counted a total of 15 toiletry bottles in their combined bathrooms. How many towels are there in their combined bathrooms?

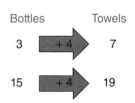

FIGURE 2.11   Common (but incorrect) additive thinking used to solve proportional situations

Bottles		Towels
3	+ 4	7
15	+ 4	19

I have given this problem to many a rising sixth-grader and the common thinking is: "7 is 4 more than 3, and 19 is 4 more than 15; so the answer is 19." They write down 3 bottles and 7 towels, look for their *difference* ("4 more" or "4 less"), and then conclude that the same difference must exist between 15 bottles and the answer, consequently 19 towels (Figure 2.11).

A remedy to this "one-way mathematics" is to present students with *multiplicative comparison* situations in their earliest experiences with measurement, namely, linear measurement. "How many diameter strings do you think will encircle the Hula-Hoop?" is an example of multiplicative thinking in a geometric comparison context. "How many *times* does the diameter fit along the perimeter of the circle?" is explicitly suggestive, for it exploits the word *times,* associated with multiplication. Ask multiplicative comparison questions when studying other quantitative attributes such as time, money, volume, or temperature: "How many times more money is a dollar than a quarter?" or "In the month of October, how many times colder is the average temperature in Fairbanks, Alaska, [25°F] than the average temperature in Aruba [83°F]?" [Answers: "four times" and "almost three-and-a-half times," respectively.] Don't let non-whole-number answers deter you from exploring such questions with young children. Such answers reveal real-world situations and offer opportunities for estimating and rounding to the nearest whole.

Algebra Connection

*   **The Prominence of Multiplicative Thinking.** Multiplicative reasoning is at the heart of any work with ratios, rates, and proportions. "Proportionality is an important integrative thread that connects many of the mathematics topics studied in grades 6–8 (NCTM, 2000, p. 217), the prealgebra or algebra years for all students. The traditional, procedural approach to solving the bottle–towel problem is to create the proportion $\frac{3}{7} = \frac{15}{x}$ and to *cross-multiply.* In other words, find the value of x that makes the "cross products" $3 \times x$ and 7×15 *equal.* The value 35 is the only solution for x. But, as students move on to high school, rules like "cross-multiply to solve proportions" and "invert and multiply to divide fractions" become shrouded in the same mystery. Unable to make sense of these *rules,* students gradually abandon sense making and surrender to memorizing procedures. To prevent this unfortunate yet common state of things, cultivating *multiplicative reasoning* early is key. Applying it to the bottle–towel problem entails the following thinking: The numbers of bottles and towels are related in an unchanging way: 3 bottles to 7 towels, 6 bottles to 14 towels, et cetera. We wish to preserve this 3-to-7 relationship—or *ratio*—as the number of bathrooms increases. We observe that 15 is *5 times* 3, which means there are *5* bathrooms. Therefore, computing *5 times* 7 yields the correct number of towels, 35. Students in grades 4 and 5, who learn fraction multiplication, can understand the diagrammatic explanation in Figure 2.12.

• **The Importance of Quantitative Reasoning.** The quantitative attributes, or quantities for short, studied in grades 3–5 are length, area, volume, weight, time, temperature, angle, and money. Two quantities of the same nature can be compared in terms of greater than (>), less than (<), or equal to (=). We can make additive or multiplicative comparisons, such as "about three years older," or "about three times greater than," (e.g., *Circling Circles* lesson). When measuring is possible, we can compare two quantities more precisely by considering their numerical values assigned by the process of measurement. When we think quantity, we usually think *measurable* quantity. Indeed, "Quantities are attributes of objects or phenomena that are measurable. It is our *capacity* to measure them—whether we have carried out those measurements of not—that makes them quantities" (Smith & Thompson, 2008, p. 101). Why is quantitative reasoning considered such "an important part of the development of a deep understanding of algebraic ideas" (Blanton, Levi, Crites, & Dougherty, 2011, p. 39)? Focusing on relationships between real-world quantities rather than on computations with numbers disconnected from concrete situations helps students make sense of their experiential world while providing a foundation for developing the algebraic reasoning needed to describe and represent these real-world relationships. We need a better balance between *number and operating on numbers,* on one hand, and *quantity and reasoning about quantities* on the other—in the elementary grades—if students are to experience a more meaningful engagement with algebra later on.

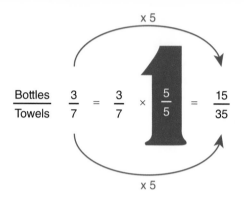

FIGURE 2.12   The 3-to-7 and 15-to-35 bottle-to-towel "relationships," or ratios, are equivalent. An equation between two equivalent fractions or ratios is called a *proportion*.

3. Measuring to Find Out

Students' experience with measurement in grades 3–8 typically begins with introductions to nonstandard and then standard units of measure. The sequence quickly proceeds to learning *algebraic formulas* for the basic geometric attributes of perimeter, area, and volume, most of which are memorized rather than understood (e.g., the formulas in Table 2.2). When students proceed too quickly to calculations on algebraic formulas for geometric relationships, they stop thinking about the *geometric* meaning, and then gradually they stop *thinking* altogether. Laying an informal foundation for a deeper understanding of circumference was a motivation behind the *Circling Circles* lesson.

REASON . . .

If the connections between algebraic thinking and geometric thinking are emphasized each time they arise, then students can approach each new topic with greater understanding and with greater confidence.

—Thomas Banchoff (2008, p. 110)

Measuring With String

Visualizing πd in Grades 3–5. Sometimes two quantities of the same nature are impossible to *compare*: the heights of two buildings on different streets or the distance one swims on two different days. Unable to lay them side-by-side, we resort to a third quantity of the same nature called a *unit of measure*. In our lesson, we did this in two ways, first an informal one then a formal one. The informal approach mirrored exactly what Euclid did with numbers and quantities in the third century BCE; namely, he represented the quantities with line segments. In our lesson, line segments were materialized by pieces of string which, when stretched out, resemble portions of a line. In their first task, students used string D as their *nonstandard* unit of measure and counted how many D units were needed to cover string C. In other words, students *evaluated* C by comparing it with a chosen unit of measure called D. By definition, this is what is means to *measure*.

Algebra Connection

- **Structural Similarities in Measuring.** As mentioned in the introduction to this book, secondary algebra instruction nowadays takes different approaches. One approach is "algebra as the study of structure." The idea here is that mathematics is a highly interconnected subject with patterns and regularities governing seemingly disconnected content areas. As a formal language, algebra is perfectly suited to expressing and representing these patterns and regularities (or structures) symbolically. A main objective of *early* algebraic thinking, as in all of mathematics, is cultivating the habit of mind to "look for and make use of structure," the seventh Common Core Mathematical Practice (CCSS.Math.Practice.MP7). In all actions of measuring itself, we find structural similarities. Measuring is the process of assigning numbers to objects.[1] The process consists of three steps:

1. Assign the number 1 to a selected unit of measure, nonstandard or standard;

2. "Cover" the object to be measured by copies of this unit; and

3. Record the measurement as a *number* and a *unit*.

The number of copies needed to cover the object may not be a whole number, as in *Circling Circles*. "The mathematics student who understands this principle—as a general property of many important measurements—has acquired insight into the connection between real situations and quantitative models" (Fey, 1990, p. 90)

- **Measuring and Multiplicative Comparisons.** The process of measuring requires multiplicative thinking in two ways. First, in unit conversion, students "use their knowledge of relationships between units and their understanding of multiplicative situations to make conversions, such as expressing . . . 3 feet as 36 inches" (NCTM, 2000, p. 172). Indeed, if 1 foot is 12 inches, then 3 feet is 3 *times* more, or 36 inches. (For students using U.S. math curricula, additional conversions are required between United States customary units and metric units.) Second, the measuring process itself is multiplicative. Calculating the area of a 30-in. by 60-in. rectangular desktop in 3-in. by 5-in. index cards means figuring out how many *times* the index card or *unit* fits inside the large rectangle. A tessellation of the desktop with 10×12 identical index cards, or $120 \times (1\,\text{card})$, models the process and

---

1. In this discussion, it is understood that some *attribute* of the object is being measured.

FIGURE 2.13   (a) A 30-in. by 60-in. desktop area measured in 3-in. by 5-in. index cards (120 units); (b) a 2-in. by 3-in. business card area measured in 3-in. by 5-in. index cards ($\frac{2}{5}$ of 1 unit)

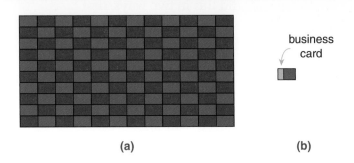

business
card

(a)   (b)

solution (Figure 2.13, a). A 2-in. by 3-in. business card, on the other hand, would require only a fraction of one 3-in. by 5-in. index card, $\frac{2}{5} \times (1\,\text{card})$ to be exact (Figure 2.13, b). This last example gives meaning to fraction multiplication, an important argument for making quantitative reasoning an arena for burgeoning algebraic ideas.

Measuring With a Metric Tape

Students in grade 3 are expected to "solve real world and mathematical problems involving perimeters of polygons, including finding the perimeter given the side lengths" (CCSS.Math.Content.3.MD.D.8). Yet, in the 2007 National Assessment of Educational Progress (NAEP) exam, known as the "U.S. Report card," only 43% of *fourth*-graders answered the following question correctly:

> A stop sign has 8 sides of equal length. Ryan knows that the length of each side is 10 inches. Explain how Ryan can find the perimeter (distance around) of the sign. What is the perimeter of the sign? [Answer: _____ inches.]

Why is measurement so hard for children? First, process-to-object theorists (Sfard, 1991) suggest that process-based thinking *must precede* object-based thinking. Process entails carrying out a procedure, the action of doing something such as measuring. When a learner becomes fluent in a process and is able to consider it *without* the need to perform it, a shift occurs in the nature of her knowledge: "Encapsulation" of the *process* into an *object* of knowledge (concept) is said to occur. Second, among the big ideas in measurement concept development, math educators (Van de Walle & Lovin, 2006) stress the importance of "understand[ing] how measurement instruments work so they can be used correctly and meaningfully" (p. 252). Combining the views of researchers and educators, and applying them to the concept of perimeter, young children must *carry out the process* of measuring perimeter by actually running a tape measure along the outer edge of "flat" objects and making sense of their readings. Only then will the concept of perimeter take root.

Algebra Connection

At the start of this chapter, we mentioned the 17th-century merging of algebra and geometry into analytic geometry. Here we revisit the geometry–algebra connection to make more sense of analytic geometry.

• **From Geometry to Algebra.** From the analytic geometry perspective, measurement is less about magnitudes and their measurable attributes and more about the act of *turning shapes into* numbers, variables, and/or equations—in short, *turning geometry into algebra*. In the previous Algebra Connection section, we saw that the process of measuring assigns numbers to objects. Take a cube, for example, with edge length 2 in. Its attributes are expressed in *numbers* (and units). Using these numbers, we create numerical equations:

1. Edge length: $E = 2$ in.

2. Face area: $F_A = 4$ sq. in.

3. Total surface area: $S_A = (6 \times 4)$ sq. in. or $S_A = 24$ sq. in.

4. Volume: $V = 8$ cu. in.

Given a *general* cube with edge length x measured in *any given unit*, its attributes are written as *algebraic expressions*—which are generalizations across *all* cubes. Using these expressions, we create algebraic equations:

5. Edge length: $E = x$

6. Face area: $F_A = x^2$

7. Total surface area: $S_A = 6x^2$

8. Volume: $V = x^3$

In grades 3–8, students derive more and more sophisticated formulas (equations) for perimeter, area, and volume of two-dimensional (Figure 2.14) and three-dimensional shapes.

FIGURE 2.14   Area formulas for (a) a rectangle with dimensions b and h (grades 3–5), and (b) a triangle with the same dimensions (grades 6–8). Geometric visualization helps explain why one area is half the other.

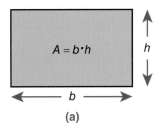

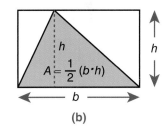

(a)   (b)

Delving Deeper

4. Representing With Numbers and Words

The word *representation* refers to both a *process* and a *product*: the act of representing *and* the state of being represented. The NCTM ranks *representation* among its five essential process standards and states, "The ways in which mathematical ideas are represented is fundamental to how people can understand and use those ideas" (2000, p. 67). The CCSSM build upon the NCTM standards by incorporating all forms of representation in both mathematical content and practice.

Saying It With Numbers

Using a spreadsheet with three columns (Group, D, and C) allowed us to record the class numerical data and make them visible and accessible to all students for the ensuing discussion. The integration of electronic technologies into the learning and teaching of secondary school algebra is commonplace today. Technological tools facilitate verbal (words), numerical (data tables), graphical, and symbolic representations. Early algebra research has shown the advantages of exposing children to these four core forms early on, in addition to the gestural, verbal, concrete, pictorial, and iconic representations that students naturally use to explain their thinking.

Algebra Connection

• **Two-Column Data Tables.** Studies show that young students, when given a two-column table of numbers representing a relationship between varying quantities, naturally look *downward* to find patterns (Warren, 2008), a manifestation of additive thinking.

The arbitrary (not ascending) order of the data in Table 1.3 in Chapter 1 (shown in Table 2.3 here) discouraged the *vertical* analysis and forced students to examine the data *horizontally* to discern a regularity in the numbers. (Chapter 5 describes in more detail the cognitive difference between *looking across* and *looking down* columns of related data.) As explained earlier, the question formulation further helped students focus in the "about three times" multiplicative relationship between diameter and circumference.

FIGURE 2.15 The *C*-lengths (yellow) and *D*-lengths (green) evolve from lengths to numbers

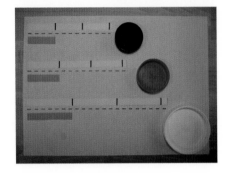

Photo by Didier Rousselet

TABLE 2.3 Data from Table 1.3

Group	*D*	*C*
A	3	10
B	4	13
C	7	22
D	11	35
E	6	18
F	8	26
G	5	15
H	29	92
I (Hula-Hoop)	71	227
J (wastebasket)	35	112

• **The Concept of Ratio.** (In this discussion, we round pi to 3, which you can do with your students, as did the ancient mathematicians!) The purpose of the tabular representation was for students to see the diameter–circumference relationship, previously discovered by hands-on comparison of two lengths (Figure 2.15), in a new way: through *numbers*. The prior physical manipulation inspired them to notice the 1-to-3 numerical relationship.

While the word *ratio* frightens many people, it is precisely what students found: a *relationship* between two quantities that compares their *relative* counts or measures. On a field trip with 3 chaperones and 30 students, the *C*-to-*S* ratio is 3-to-30 or 1-to-10. A vinaigrette made with 2 parts vinegar and 3 parts oil has a *V*-to-*O* ratio of 2-to-3. Students will eventually learn the symbolic notations, $\frac{x}{y}$ and $x:y$, for ratio. The order of the numbers is critical: The *first* quantity in the spoken language corresponds to the *numerator* or *first* term of these notations, respectively. One important property to remember is that *one part of a ratio relates to the other part by multiplication* (Figure 2.16, red arrows). Another is that t*he ratio remains unchanged as the numerical values of both parts change by the same factor* (Figure 2.16, blue arrows). Since $\frac{D}{C} = \frac{1}{3}$, if the diameter of some circle is 15, its circumference is 45. Figure 2.16 shows the two ways of obtaining 45, thus illustrating the two properties of ratio.

FIGURE 2.16 Two multiplicative properties of ratio

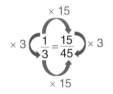

Saying It With Words

Verbal representations, like pictorial and symbolic ones, bring up an important duality in representations: The *student-invented* ones versus the *teacher-presented* ones. Many educators make a case for the importance of allowing young students to develop their own representations, on the way to acquiring *classical* mathematical representations—classical at the present stage of mathematics' evolution (Kamii, Kirkland, & Lewis, 2001). In *Circling Circles*, students invented many verbal and pictorial representations, not all of which could be related here. The tabular and symbolic ones were teacher-presented.

Algebra Connection

- **The Role of Language.** Language plays a crucial role in the development of algebraic thinking. It is one of many means to express generalization. "Generalizing is never distinct from the language by which the *result* of the activity—generalization—is expressed or represented. Generalizations may be expressed in a number of ways—through natural language, through algebraic notation using letters as variables, or even through tables and graphs" (Blanton et al., 2011, p. 9). Salim's verbal representation stating, "3 times the diameter plus a wee bit more is the sircumference," (Table 1.4, #4) is saying in natural language something similar to what the equation $C = \pi \times D$ is saying in symbolic algebraic language. Keep in mind that up until the 17th century, *symbolic* algebra, as we know it today, did not exist. It was *rhetorical* algebra for centuries, algebra expressed in natural language. It progressively evolved toward *syncopated* algebra, a hybrid between rhetorical and symbolic. Finally, the symbols of today's algebra were agreed upon in the mid-1600s and have remained practically unchanged for 350 years. At every stage, however, algebra was capable of expressing powerful ideas. We must therefore allow children to follow the natural evolution of algebraic thinking: from words to symbols.

5. Representing With Symbols and Graphs

Pi Talk

Algebra Connection

- **Uses of Letters.** There are multiple uses of letters in algebra. For instance, a letter can be an *unknown* or a *variable*. Solving for x in the equation $x + 2 = 6$ yields *one* specific solution, namely, 4. In this case, x is called an unknown, a value that becomes *known* after some symbol manipulations. On the other hand, in the equation $C = \pi \times D$, C and D represent variables, quantities that take on a *range* of values, often an infinite number of values. The equation expresses a specific relationship between the varying quantities. A letter can also denote a *constant*, a quantity that does *not* vary but has a fixed value. Evidence from the literature shows that the symbol π was chosen in the early 18th century to denote the irrational[2] number equal to the quotient $\frac{C}{D}$, the object of our study. Most probably π, the Greek equivalent to our letter *p*, was chosen because it is the first letter of the word περιφέρεια, Greek for *periphery*.

Saying It With Symbols

Devising symbolic equations for the relationship between D and C was the most challenging part of our lesson, partly because it was at the end of two intense days of mathematical work, and partly because students were not accustomed to writing with symbols. But that is not to say that young students cannot understand the use of symbols.

---

2. A rational number can be written as a fraction, $\frac{a}{b}$, in which a and b are integers, and $b \neq 0$. An irrational number cannot; in its decimal form, the decimal part is neither terminating nor repeating.

Algebra Connection

• **Getting to Know Symbols.** Research shows that young students can make sophisticated use of symbols, ones *they choose* and find logical, such as the first letters of words in a problem. Teachers should cultivate the use of symbols, whenever appropriate, so that symbols may become *friendly* to students. By addressing the problem, "There were 4 boys and 13 girls playing in the yard. How many children were there all together?" students can develop the habit of writing "4 + 13 = 17 *as well as* equations such as "B = 4," "G = 13," and "B + G = 17," alongside the numerical equation. In my own K–12 education in French schools, we were often asked to give both a "literal" solution (using letters) and a "numerical" solution (using numbers) to a problem. This made for a natural transition from arithmetic to algebra.

Saying It With Graphs

Rearranging the diameter and circumference data from Table 1.3 with the help of a spreadsheet, we obtained ordered pairs of numbers (*D*, *C*) (shown in the blue columns of Table 2.4).

• **From Algebra to Geometry.** We saw that the act of measuring turns shapes into numbers (for particular shapes) or algebraic expressions (for general shapes). Conversely, *plotting* turns numbers or algebraic equations into shapes—in short, *turns algebra into geometry*. Consider a two-dimensional space (a plane). Students in grades 3–5 study properties of plane figures and, by grade 5, learn to plot ordered pairs of numbers in the *xy*-plane (CCSS.Math.Content.5.G.A). Plotting the ordered pairs (3, 10), (4, 13), (5, 15), (6, 18), (7, 22), (8, 26), we notice that these points seem to line up (Figure 2.17). Clearly, they are not perfectly aligned due to measurement and graphing errors. More will be said of *linear* relationships in Exploration II, but this example suffices for now to illustrate that pairs of numbers, when plotted, can "turn into" a shape—in this case, *a straight line*. Students learn in middle school that nonvertical straight lines passing through the origin are graphs of proportional relationships, a subfamily of linear relationships, central to all first-year algebra curricula.

TABLE 2.4 Numerical entries from Table 1.3 rearranged in ascending order

Group	Diameter	Circumference
A	3	10
B	4	13
G	5	15
E	6	18
C	7	22
F	8	26
D	11	35
H	29	92
J	35	112
I	71	227

Closing Thoughts

With the *Circling Circles* lesson, seeds of proportional thinking had been planted in Ms. Flores's class. It will be years before the seeds of thought enter the realm of awareness, and even longer before they come to fruition. But when these students enter pre-algebra in middle school, they will recall their physical actions of circling circles with "a little more than three diameters." It will help them make sense of the circumference formulas. And when they learn new algebraic formulas for other geometric shapes, they will remember visualizing 1-D space as straight lines inhabited by outstretched pieces of string, or line segments; 2-D space as *Flatland,* planes inhabited by shapes like squares and circles; and 3-D space as *Spaceland*, their real world. In the long run, these conceptualizations will help them understand the connections between algebraic formulas and geometric dimensions. And finally, when they take their first algebra course—three, four, or five years down the road—and graph their first linear function of a proportional relationship between two variables, they may draw on their memories of physically placing their *D*- and *C*-strings on the horizontal and vertical axes respectively, to give meaning to *x*- and *y*-coordinates (see *Next Steps*, Chapter 3). These memories will help them make a connection between proportional relationships and straight-line graphs through the origin, a connection some eighth-graders don't make.

FIGURE 2.17   Plotted ordered pairs (*D*, *C*) form a "straight line" in the 2-D plane

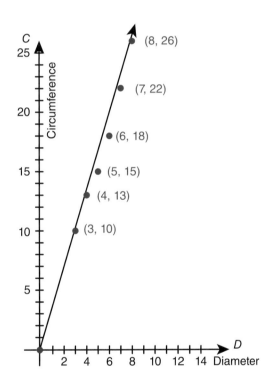

3
Beyond *Circling Circles*

More Problems to Explore

Answers and explanations to the nontrivial questions in this chapter can be found in the Appendix, page 189.

I. Next Steps

1. Rationale

In second grade, students learn to represent whole numbers as lengths on horizontal or vertical number lines, labeled with tick marks corresponding to whole numbers (CCSS.Math.Content.2.MD.B.6). In fifth grade, students learn to plot points, represented by ordered pairs of numbers, such as $(5, 2)$ or $\left(\frac{1}{2}, -3\right)$, on a two-dimensional Cartesian coordinate system defined by two perpendicular axes, both labeled with tick marks corresponding to the integers (CCSS.Math.Content.5.G.A.1 and 5.G.A.2). In the Next Steps Exploration, string lengths marked on 2-D paper materialize the x- and y-coordinates of points in a plane, a nice prelude to the abstract concept of *a point in 2-D*.

2. Data

A few days after I conducted the *Circling Circles* Exploration with Ms. Flores's class, she carried out the Next Steps. She divided her class into seven groups. She had saved the diameter and circumference string pairs from the *Circling Circles* Exploration, but used only seven of them, assigning one to each group. Table 3.1 lists the data used, gathered by original groups C, D, E, F, G, H, and J. Measurements are rounded to the nearest centimeter and rearranged in ascending order.

On a wall, Mrs. Flores taped a large sheet of paper with a horizontal axis labeled D (diameter) and a vertical axis labeled C (circumference). Both axes were marked in centimeters.

3. Instructions

The following instructions should be modeled for students with one string pair.

1. Begin at the origin, O, move to the right the length of your *diameter string* and mark the point as DX on the D-axis: D for diameter and X for your initial. For example, Ty's diameter would be marked as DT (Figure 3.1). Then remove your diameter string.

2. From the point DT, on the D-axis, move straight upward the length of your *circumference string* and tape it to the paper. Then, mark the point CX on the C-axis corresponding to the height of the circumference string: C for circumference and X for your initial. Ty's circumference is CT. Finally, make a dot at the tip of the circumference string: that's *your* point. Ty's point for instance is CT cm *north* of the horizontal D-axis and DT cm *east* of the vertical C-axis (Figure 3.1).

4. Observations

After all students had marked their DX and CX lengths and taped their circumference string to the chart, students were surprised to discover yet another regularity; this time it was not a numerical one but a graphical one: All their points seemed to line up (Figure 3.2). To verify, Ms. Flores asked Tom to connect the seven points with line segments. They seemed indeed to form a straight line (more or less). Rachelle asked, "Does it go through O?" Tom extended the line, and the group consensus was that "it probably does."

The follow-up exploration sparked off more questions:

- It looks like the points line up. Why?
- It looks like (0, 0) lines up with the rest. Why?
- What might other points on the line represent?

More questions to ponder, more connections to establish, more meanings to find! In middle school, students learn that the slope of this line is π, the geometric representation of the equivalent ratios: $\frac{Cx}{Dx} \approx \frac{Cy}{Dy} \approx \frac{Cz}{Dz} \ldots \approx \pi$. (Here we assume precise measurements.)

TABLE 3.1 Diameter and circumference measurements in centimeters

	G	E	C	F	D	H	J
D	5	6	7	8	11	29	35
C	15	18	22	26	35	92	112

FIGURE 3.1 Ty's diameter (green) and circumference (red) strings. After the point was marked, the green string was removed.

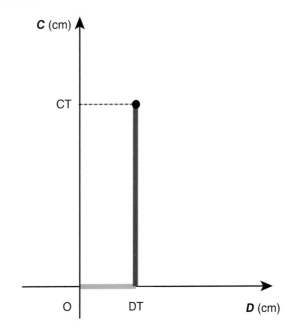

FIGURE 3.2   2-D graph of seven diameter–circumference string pairs

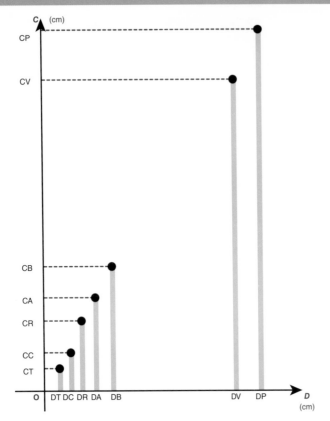

II. For Your Own Learning

1. Pi Is Not Just About Circles

People usually associate π with circles and spheres, just as mathematicians did up to the 17th century, when π wandered beyond the world of geometric shapes.

Statistics

The number π figures in the algebraic equation of the common bell-shaped curve attributed to German mathematician Carl Friedrich Gauss (1777–1855).

Probability

Suppose you dropped a needle of length l on a floor with alternating black and white stripes of equal width l. The 18th-century French mathematician Comte de Buffon proved that the probability of the needle landing on *both* colors is $\frac{2}{\pi}$. Students can repeat this experiment by dropping 100 toothpicks, each equal in length to the width of the floor stripes, and computing the ratio $\frac{\#\ toothpicks\ on\ both\ colors}{100}$. They will find that about 65% of the toothpicks land on both colors. This result is indeed very close to $\frac{2}{\pi} \cong 0.64$. Students can research the amazing story of Buffon's needle.

Infinite Series (Calculator Exploration)

A sum such as $1 + 2 + 3 + 4 + \dots$ is called an infinite series, because it has an infinite set of terms. The famous infinite series $\frac{1}{1} - \frac{1}{3} + \frac{1}{5} - \frac{1}{7} + \frac{1}{9} - \frac{1}{11} + \ \dots$ is attributed simultaneously to three mathematicians—German, Scottish, and Indian. The sum of the series equals $\frac{\pi}{4}$. For an approximation of π, multiply the sum obtained (using at least 15 terms) by four!

Key to the Universe

A 2006 film shows Japanese engineer Akira Haraguchi reciting 100,000 digits of π in 16 hours, with five-minute breaks every two hours. That's about two digits per second! Through memorizing digits of π, Mr. Haraguchi seeks life's eternal truth, he explains. Only a few digits are necessary for most calculations, yet scientists and laypeople have competed to find more digits of the world's most famous ratio. American computer scientist Alexander Yee and Japanese engineer Shigeru Kondo reached 12 trillion digits in December 2013!

Fascination

Over more than two millennia, from 250 BCE—when Greek mathematician Archimedes first discovered a mysterious connection between circumference and area of circles—to this day, the fascination for π has remained alive. This fascination moved Hannah Stein to write a beautiful poem for her husband Sherman K. Stein (Figure 3.3). A rich resource for interested students is *The Joy of π* (Blatner, 1997), a jewel of a book.

The study of circles and spheres, with π at center stage, like the study of numbers, is one of a few topics that unite classical and modern, concrete and abstract mathematics.

2. Correct Geometric Terminology

Do you use the phrase, "six-sided die?" Don't worry if you do; everyone does, in speech and in print. Mathematicians sometimes do as well. It begs the question, though, "What is a 'side' in 3-D?" Mathematically, the term *side* in fact has no meaning: in a 3-D space, there are edges and faces but no sides. *Side* is used for the outer edges of a *polygon* in 2-D. Correct use of vocabulary helps students now and in formal geometry later (Figure 3.4).

It is important to observe a parallel:

- The square, a *two*-dimensional object, has components of dimension *d less than* 2: Its vertices are *zero*-dimensional, and its sides are *one*-dimensional.
- Likewise, the cube, a *three*-dimensional object, has components of dimension *d less than* 3: Its vertices are *zero*-dimensional, its edges *one*-dimensional, and its faces *two*-dimensional.

FIGURE 3.3   Excerpt from *Loving a Mathematician* by Hannah Stein to her husband Sherman Stein

. . . I used to think Pi
was just a way of measuring circles.
You tell me now that Pi lurks
in gaseous, in liquid universes
where there are no circles, where rings
couldn't form if I dropped a pebble.
For there are no pebbles either—
no discs no balls no equators—
only pure structure.
It's true, you say,
that Pi always turns up,
like an old irrational uncle
who's been traveling around the country
doing card tricks. But circles
are only one of his arts:
Pi rolls his thumb through the ink
of odd numbers; from his hiding place in
square roots under square roots like
a wagonload of deviant potatoes
Pi intones: *dividing by*
a squared prime
has nothing to do with roundness.

Source: "Loving a Mathematician" by Hannah Stein, from *Strength in Numbers* by Sherman Stein

---

FIGURE 3.4   Terminology for the components of 2-D polygons and 3-D polyhedra

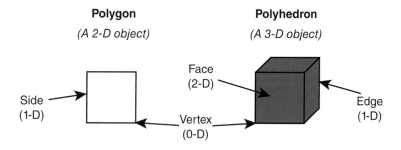

- The same holds for the tesseract, also known as the 4-cube, the *fourth*-dimensional analogue of the square and cube: Its components are of dimensions 0, 1, 2, and 3. All cubes of dimension greater than three are called *hypercubes*. They fascinate children.

3. A Square Is a Special Rectangle

"A square is a special *rectangle*." You have probably made this statement a hundred times if you've been teaching for a while. Is it correct? Undeniably. But I find it interesting that, in my entire career as a professional-development provider, which has included many a classroom visit, I have never heard the analogous statement, "A square is a special *rhombus*." Somehow, in the elementary classroom culture, the properties of squares we discuss with students are skewed in favor of rectangles. Revisiting these properties (Figure 3.5), we see that a square is just as much *a special rhombus* as it is *a special rectangle*; for to be a square, a parallelogram must have two properties:

1. Four equal sides, *and*

2. Four equal angles (therefore four *right* angles. Students will learn that the sum of all angles in a quadrilateral is 360°. Thus, four equal angles implies $\frac{360°}{4} = 90°$)

Since most students answer "four equal sides" when asked the definition of a square—and often forget property #2, and since a rhombus has four equal sides, seize that opportunity to make students aware of the fact that a square is therefore a *special* rhombus as well.

> **FIGURE 3.5** Squares have symmetric relationships with both rhombi *and* rectangles.

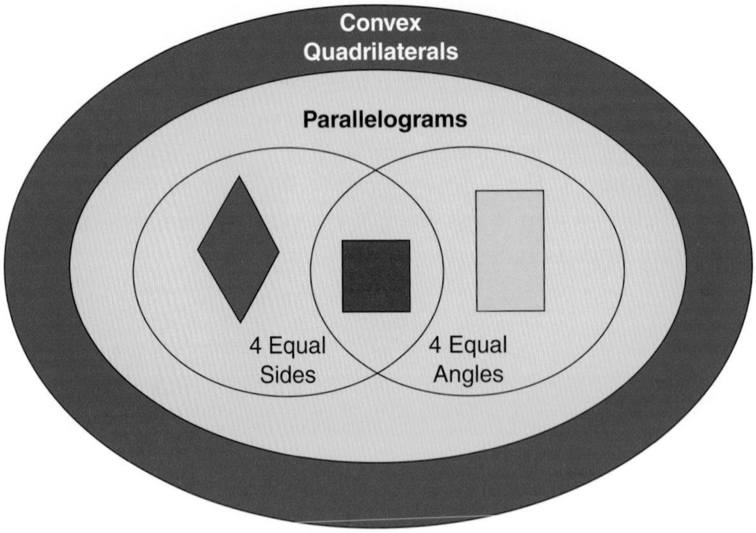

III. For Your Students' Learning

A central part of early algebraic thinking is observing and articulating properties of operations, a cornerstone to elementary mathematics. Similarly, a central part of geometric thinking—at Van Hiele Level 2—is observing and articulating properties of figures, a cornerstone of elementary geometry. Both ways of thinking are about noticing connections, patterns, relationships, and the beginnings of generalizations. As the opening quote of Exploration I says so accurately, "Geometry and algebra are ... distinct ways of thinking about mathematical ideas."

1. Fix One and Vary the Other

An important conceptual understanding that serves students through calculus—with its optimization problems—is the ability to differentiate between perimeter and area. The Common Core State Standards for Mathematics (CCSSM) (3.MD.D.8) and the National Council of Teachers of Mathematics (NCTM) standards both highlight this:

> Students in the elementary grades can explore how changing an object's attribute affects certain measurements. For example, cutting apart and rearranging the pieces of a shape may change the perimeter but not the area. In the middle grades this idea can be extended to explorations of how the surface area of a rectangular prism can vary, as the volume is held constant. Such observations can offer glimpses of sophisticated mathematical concepts such as invariance under certain transformations. (NCTM, 2000, p. 45)

Fixed Area

Using square tiles or grid paper, make a rectangle of a given area, say, 48 square units. With the same set of tiles, symbolizing the invariant area of 48 square units, create other rectangles (Figure 3.6). With each new rectangle, record width, length, area, and perimeter (Figure 3.7). What do you notice? When is the perimeter the smallest? When is it the

FIGURE 3.6   Rectangles with equal areas but different perimeters

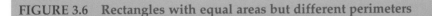
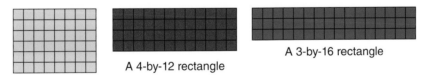

A 4-by-12 rectangle

A 3-by-16 rectangle

A 6-by-8 rectangle

largest? Repeat this exercise with other numbers of tiles. Older students can experiment with prime numbers of tiles and generalize for *all* prime numbers.

Real-World Context. A big family reunion is coming up, and you've been asked to help arrange 24 small square tables into one large table so that everyone can sit together. There are three conditions: (1) All tables must be used, (2) neighboring tables must be joined along entire sides, and (3) exactly one person can be seated along a side of a square table. Explore and draw different arrangements, listing the number of people each can seat. Which one can seat the most people? Which one can seat the least? Make your final choice, and explain you reasoning for choosing that arrangement over the others.

FIGURE 3.7   Record of rectangles with constant area 48 and varying perimeters

W	L	A	P
6	8	48	?
4	12	48	?
3	16	48	?
.			
.			
.			

FIGURE 3.8   Record of rectangles with constant perimeter 36 and varying areas

W	L	P	A
2	16	36	?
6	12	36	?
·			
·			
·			

Fixed Perimeter

Problem. Charmaine wants to build a rectangular pen for her new pet in her back yard. She has 36 meters of fence. Help her figure out the dimensions of the largest possible pen she can build using all 36 meters. Record your answers in a table (Figure 3.8). After finding several options, make at least two observations about your data. Finally, make a recommendation to Charlene and defend your decision.

String, square tiles, and grid paper are available for your use in addressing this problem.

Challenge. Take a rectangular sheet of paper. Measure its length and width, and compute its perimeter and area with your calculator. Imagine different "nibbles" you could remove.

1. Can you cut out a nibble such that the perimeter increases? Decreases? Remains equal?

2. Can you cut out a nibble such that the area increases? Decreases? Remains equal?

2. Visualizing Equivalent Fractions

Another important concept that takes root in grades 3–5 is the notion of *invariant ratio*. In *Circling Circles*, students found an invariant ratio among the circumference-to-diameter relationships for all their circles. But the word *ratio* is more a middle school term. In the upper elementary grades, the concept of invariant ratio appears in the guise of equivalent fractions, equal quotients, and multiplicative comparisons, all of which were addressed in *Circling Circles*. This exploration offers another opportunity to see equivalent fractions in a new light.

1. Pick two rows of the multiplication table, for instance the 2- and 3-tables (Figure 3.9).

FIGURE 3.9   Rows 2 and 3 of the multiplication table

X	1	2	3	4	5	6	7	8	9	10
1	1	2	3	4	5	6	7	8	9	10
2	2	4	6	8	10	12	14	16	18	20
3	3	6	9	12	15	18	21	24	27	30

2. Create the corresponding fractions or ratios $\frac{2}{3}$, $\frac{4}{6}$, $\frac{6}{9}$, and so on. Review, through inquiry, the multiplicative relationships among this family of fractions. Students may be surprised to find equivalent fractions lurking inside multiplication tables.

3. Using inches or centimeters, have students construct paper rectangles of dimensions 2-by-3, 4-by-6, 6-by-9 . . . one rectangle per fraction (Figure 3.10). (*Note*: Use

the terms *short side* and *long side* so students don't always associate "width" with the shorter side of a rectangle.)

4. **Discussion.** Probe for students' understanding of the *meaning* of the constant quotient or ratio "1.5." One student might formulate it this way: "If you take half of the short side (Ss) and times it by three, you get the long side (Ls)." An older student may put it this way: "The long side is one-and-a-half times the length of the short side."

5. **Algebraic Formulation.** Attempt to symbolize and generalize students' observations. After writing numerical equations for the first several rectangles, the hypothetical students above may come up with generalizations of the following sort, *for all the* rectangles: $\frac{1}{2}$ of $\text{Ss} \times 3 \rightarrow \text{Ls}$, and $\text{Ls} = 1.5 \times \text{Ss}$, respectively. This provides a nice opportunity to revisit equivalent expressions, namely, $\frac{1}{2} \times 3$ is equivalent to 1.5.

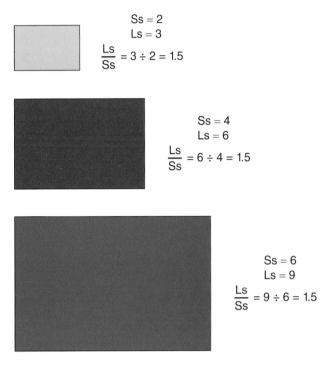

FIGURE 3.10   Three members of the family of rectangles with an invariant Ls-to-Ss ratio of 3-to-2

$\text{Ss} = 2$
$\text{Ls} = 3$
$\frac{\text{Ls}}{\text{Ss}} = 3 \div 2 = 1.5$

$\text{Ss} = 4$
$\text{Ls} = 6$
$\frac{\text{Ls}}{\text{Ss}} = 6 \div 4 = 1.5$

$\text{Ss} = 6$
$\text{Ls} = 9$
$\frac{\text{Ls}}{\text{Ss}} = 9 \div 6 = 1.5$

6. **Number, Algebra, and Geometry Converge.** Suppose a student piles up the rectangles from smallest on top to largest on the bottom, and, while lining up Ls and Ss neatly, exclaims, "The diagonals are all the same!" Anticipate such teachable moments and be prepared: Hand out rectangular grids with the same units (inches or centimeters). Have students plot the ordered pairs (Ss, Ls) in the Cartesian plane (Figure 3.11). The points line up and indeed the diagonals live on the line!

Like *Circling Circles*, this exploration has many facets: equivalent fractions, invariant ratios, geometric shapes, and algebraic expressions, all of which culminate in a series of colinear points in the Cartesian plane. By no means will students grasp all. But exposure to these notions provides grounding metaphors from which will emerge the concepts of *similarity* and *proportionality* in the middle years. Similarity of shapes, with its roots in classical geometry, is a fundamental idea of the mathematics of space. Young children experience these notions intuitively when playing with miniature planes or dolls, objects with real-world proportions but on different scales. The notions become formalized in secondary mathematics. The final image of a line is empowering to students. It will be engraved in their mind's eye when they learn the notion of slope, a cornerstone of algebra. Here, it is the visual embodiment of the invariant ratio $\frac{3}{2}$ or 1.5. Indeed, the slope of the line is $\frac{3}{2}$ or 1.5, and its equation is $y = \frac{3}{2}x$, or $y = 1.5x$.

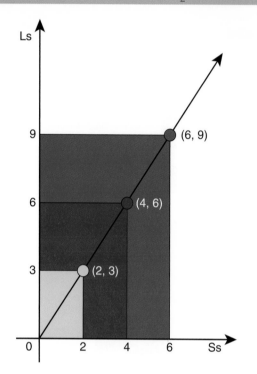

FIGURE 3.11 **Graphical representation of rectangles with invariant Ls-to-Ss ratios of 3-to-2. The slope of the line is $\frac{3}{2}$ or 1.5.**

3. The Circumference of the Earth (Calculator Exploration)

Have students estimate the diameter segment of the earth, the distance of the virtual line segment passing through the earth's center and connecting two points on the globe (approximately 8,000 mi or 12,800 km). If Internet access is available, have them research this distance and compare their findings to their estimations. Next, applying what they learned in *Circling Circles*, ask them to approximate the circumference of the earth. (*Note*: The measure of the earth's circumference around the equator is a bit longer than the one through the poles, interesting information to share with students.)

Follow-Up Research

Eratosthenes' Computation. In the 3rd century BCE, the Greek mathematician Eratosthenes realized the first true measure of the earth's circumference. We marvel today at the accuracy of his measurement. Have students research what it was and how he figured it out. He is also famous for the *Sieve of Eratosthenes*, a simple algorithm for finding all prime numbers. Grade 5 students should investigate it.

4. A Tennis Can: Taller or Fatter?

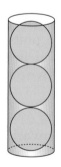

Allow some time to pass after the *Circling Circles* lesson. Bring a regular tennis ball can to class, and set it on your desk. Wait for questions, and then suggest, "Let's take a vote: Before we measure, let's estimate: Which is longer, height or circumference? They could also be equal." Most people, when asked the first question, say the height is longer. But when offered the possibility they're equal, many people switch their vote to equality. Next, have students use their tape measures to check. They will discover that the can's circumference is greater than its height (Figure 3.12). If no one makes the connection with what was previously learned, draw a vertical section of the can through the middle and have an inspired student explain why. (The *height is exactly* $3 \times D$; the circumference is *a little more than 3 diameters*, or $\pi \times D$).

5. Seeing Relationships

Volumes of cones and cylinders are the material of middle school geometry. But relationships and connections students can see now will help them in building, understanding, and remembering the formulas they will learn. The first relationship is between *regular polygons* and the *circle*. As the number of sides in a regular polygon increases, the polygon more closely resembles a circle (Figure 3.13). In Figure 3.13, the side lengths are decreasing, but you can have students construct consecutive regular polygons with *equal* side lengths, symbolized by equal-length straws. For teachers only, and for simplicity, I will use mathematical language here: "The *limit* of an *n*-sided polygon, as $n \to \infty$, is a circle," where "$n \to \infty$" means "as the number *n* approaches infinity."

Prisms and Pyramids

An informal definition of a prism is a polyhedron made of two *n*-sided polygonal faces in parallel planes (often called the bases), joined by *rectangular lateral faces* (Figure 3.14). Pyramids are analogous except for the fact that one base (say the "top" base) is a point, called the *apex*. Here *triangular lateral faces* join the base to the apex (Figure 3.15). Both prisms and pyramids are named after their bases: If the base is a hexagon, we call it a hexagonal-base or simply a hexagonal prism or pyramid. It is easy to see, if we focus on the *n*-sided polygonal base, that as $n \to \infty$, the *limit* of the prism is the cylinder and the *limit* of the pyramid is the cone. (*Note*: All prisms, pyramids, cylinders, and cones are assumed to be *right*. *Oblique* solids are not studied in the early grades.)

FIGURE 3.12   Investigating the dimensions of a tennis ball can during a parent math academy session

Photo by Charo Rodriguez

FIGURE 3.13   The limit of a regular *n*-sided polygon, as $n \to \infty$, is a circle.

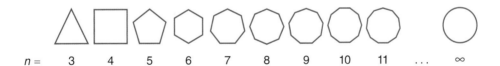

$n =$ 3   4   5   6   7   8   9   10   11   . . . ∞

FIGURE 3.14   As $n \to \infty$, the limit of an *n*-sided polygonal prism is the cylinder.

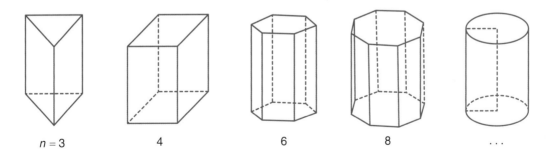

$n = 3$ 4   6   8   . . .

The algebraic mindset looks for and sees relationships such as the one between *n*-sided regular polygons and the circle, and connections between parallel families of objects such as prisms and pyramids. Let us foster habits of mind that seek out such relationships.

FIGURE 3.15   As $n \to \infty$, the limit of an n-sided polygonal pyramid is the cone.

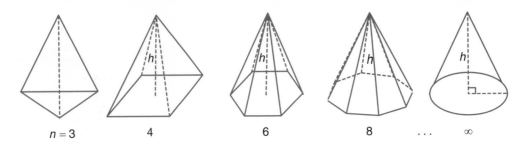

$n = 3$ 4   6   8   . . .   ∞

6. A Pattern of Nonoverlapping Triangles Inside Polygons

Have students draw a series of five or six polygons with consecutive numbers of sides. They need not be regular polygons. Name one vertex point on each A (Figure 3.16). Name the other points B, C, D. . . . Next, in each polygon, draw all possible diagonals from A to other vertices, and notice the number of nonoverlapping triangles formed. If $n = 3$, no diagonals are possible, and thus there is only one triangle, the starting one. Observe the relationship between the number of sides, n, and the number of triangles created, T. Express it verbally. Predict how many triangles are in a dodecagon ($n = 12$) or an icosagon ($n = 20$). Write the relationship symbolically. (*Note*: This relationship is a building block of the formula for the number of degrees in a polygon. Seeing triangles inside polygons now will help students make sense of the formula later.)

FIGURE 3.16   Polygons with consecutive numbers of sides

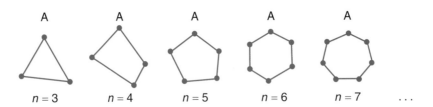

$n = 3$ $n = 4$ $n = 5$ $n = 6$ $n = 7$ . . .

7. How Does It Change?

1. Draw a line segment of length $l = 3$ *linear* units. Double its length. What is the length now? How has it changed? Answer with words, drawings, and symbols.

2. Draw a rectangle of length $l = 3$ *linear* units and width $w = 2$ *linear* units. What is the area of the rectangle in *square* units? Double length *and* width. What is the area now? How has it changed? Answer with words, drawings, and symbols.

3. Draw a rectangular prism of length $l = 3$ *linear* units, width $w = 2$ *linear* units, and height $h = 4$ *linear* units. What is the *volume* of the prism in *cubic* units? Double length, width, *and* height. What is the volume now? How has it changed? Answer with words, drawings, and symbols. (Use connecting cubes to build these prisms.)

Repeat this exercise, changing *doubling* to *tripling*. Can you predict what will happen if you *quadrupled* the dimensions in each case. Can you generalize?

8. More Connections Between Polygons and Circles

Students are well aware of the relationship between the green and yellow pattern blocks (Figure 3.17a). Offer them a new context in which to rediscover this same relationship. Using play coins of one size, have them "pack" the coins together as tightly as possible on their desks. Ask, "How many coins does each coin touch? They will have found what is known as *hexagonal packing*. Why? Because the centers of the *six* coins surrounding any one coin form a hexagon (Figure 3.17b). Also, the centers of any *three* tangent (touching) coins form an equilateral triangle. Six of these equilateral triangles are inside each hexagon. Connect the center of the hexagon to its vertices to check. French mathematician Joseph-Louis Lagrange (1736–1813) proved that hexagonal packing is the *densest* circle packing in a plane. It has many applications in our 3-D real world, both at the human and atomic scales.

FIGURE 3.17   (a) Pattern blocks; (b) circle packing in a plane modeled by coins on a desk.

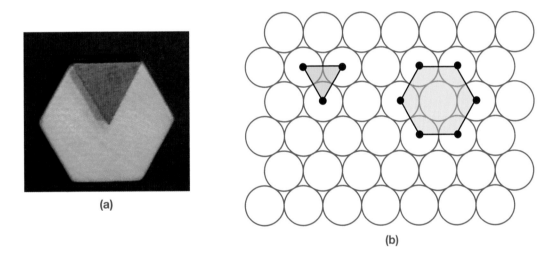

(a)

(b)

9. Practicing With Numeric and Algebraic Expressions

1. Draw a square of side length 5 cm. How will you use the number 5 to find the perimeter P? Write a *numeric* expression describing this process. Now suppose the side length of a square measures s cm. How will you use the number s to find the perimeter? Write an *algebraic* expression for the perimeter P.

2. Draw a rectangle of length and width 5 cm and 7 cm, respectively. How will you use the numbers 5 and 7 to find the perimeter P? Write a *numeric* expression describing this process. Now suppose the length and width of a rectangle measure l cm and w cm, respectively. How will you use numbers l and w to find the perimeter? Write an *algebraic* expression for the perimeter P.

3. Repeat questions 1 and 2, replacing the word *perimeter* with *area*.

10. Visualizing Unit Conversion

Linear Measure

Draw a 3-cm line segment as seen through a magnifying glass ("zoom in"). How long is this line segment in millimeters (mm)? Explain using your drawing. Repeat the question with a 3-foot line segment (this time, zoom out). How long is it in inches?

Area Measure

Draw a 3-cm by 4-cm rectangle as seen through a magnifying glass (zoom in). What is the area of this rectangle in *square* centimeters (sq. cm)? What is the area of this rectangle in square millimeters (sq. mm)? Explain your second answer two different ways, using your drawing. Repeat the question with a 3-ft by 4-ft rectangle (this time, zoom out). Find the area in *square* feet (sq. ft) and *square* inches (sq. in.). Explain your second answer two different ways, using your drawing.

EXPLORATION II

Patterns and Functions

What's Their Connection to Algebra?

We have found that students are not only capable of deeper functional analysis than previously thought, but that the genesis of these ideas appears at grades earlier than typically expected. In particular, we have found that the types of representations students use—the progression of mathematical language in their descriptions of functional relationships, the ways students track and organize data, the mathematical operations they use to interpret functional relationships, and how they express covariation and correspondence among quantities—can be scaffolded in instruction beginning with the very earliest grades, at the start of formal schooling.

—Maria Blanton and James Kaput (2011, p. 5)

RATIONALE FOR EXPLORATION II

- Mathematics is the science of *patterns*.

- Mathematicians and scientists study phenomena of *change*—over time or space—in multiple contexts. Students study change in the explorations of patterns and functions.

- The concept of *function* is one of the most—if not *the* most—important concept in mathematics. In the 21st-century *function-based* approach to algebra, functions are central to algebra.

- Students and teachers alike must see the connection between patterns and functions: Most patterns can be transformed into functions.

- By exploring patterns, students develop the habits of mind to notice, express, and analyze *regularities* in their world and in their minds. In grades 3–5, students are expected to venture beyond repeating patterns and explore growing patterns.

- Asking, "What do you see?" focuses on pattern *structure*. Asking, "What comes next?" focuses on the power of patterns to predict what lies ahead. The answers to both are connected.

- *Functional thinking* is par excellence a form of algebraic thinking in grades 3–5.

- Function tables expose students to the concept of *variable*—in a concrete way—as a quantity that changes or *varies*. While letters are used for both, the concept of a variable is different from the concept of an *unknown*.

4

Fancy Fences

The Lesson (Grades 4–5)

Despite the grouping of "patterns" and "functions" under the rubric "algebra" in national and state standards documents and prevailing mathematics curricula, the underlying mathematical connection between pattern and function, or between function and algebra, is not always clear. Math educator Erick Smith agrees: "The relationship among patterns, functions, and algebra is not necessarily obvious. . . . Elementary school teachers may create rich classroom experiences around patterns, yet not have a sense of how this topic ties into the ongoing mathematical development of their students, much less into the topic of functions" (Smith, 2003). He goes on to say that, similarly, middle school teachers may not have a sense of how the notion of function relates to students' later understanding of algebra or calculus. The need for illumination is especially felt among elementary school teachers, who introduce only the rudiments of the function concept to their students and may not see how it is a major link in the "pattern → function → algebra" chain. *Fancy Fences*, a lesson on growing patterns, sheds light on some of the implicit links. Chapter 5, the analysis of the lesson's algebraic landscape, reveals them explicitly. Exploration II is dedicated to the teachers who have asked me over the years to address this topic. Their insightful questions were my inspiration.

REFLECT . . .

What humans do with the language of mathematics is to describe patterns. Mathematics is an exploratory science that seeks to understand every kind of pattern—patterns that occur in nature, patterns invented by the human mind, and even patterns created by other patterns. To grow mathematically, children must be exposed to a rich variety of patterns appropriate to their own lives through which they can see variety, regularity, and interconnections.

—Lynn Arthur Steen (1990, p. 8)

Setup

On a two-day spring visit to a small Florida elementary public school, we were scheduled to work on patterns and functions in a 4th–5th-grade combo class. The students were seated in groups, four in all, with craft sticks, 12-inch rulers, and pattern blocks at each table (see Figure 4.1). I met with the class both days, giving us the luxury of deep exploration. On Day 1, we laid the groundwork and revisited familiar patterns in unfamiliar contexts or representations. The longer period on Day 2 allowed students to tackle a more challenging lesson, *Fancy Fences*, from many angles. Mr. Ramsey, a young, ambitious teacher and a lover of mathematics, was determined to change the math culture, not just in his class but also in the entire school. He had enjoyed our work together during my fall visit and had asked for "more instructional tasks that lead to *further* explorations." He wanted to learn more about inquiry, classroom discourse, model building, and the use of technology. He invited me to lead the lesson but was there to coteach or assist.

Background. For years prior to Mr. Ramsey's arrival, most students at this school had lacked an appreciation for mathematics. Math lessons had generally followed a machine-like pattern: Homework correction, followed by teacher presentation of new material, followed by student seatwork on practice problems. This unthinking approach shaped the students' ideas about mathematics as something *done to* them, something requiring little human interaction, something deficient of sense making. Mr. Ramsey and I were trying to help these students experience mathematics as a human activity involving intellectual habits of mind, such as asking questions, and emotions, such as excitement about discovering unexpected connections. The road ahead was long, but we were on the path.

FIGURE 4.1   Manipulatives needed for the lesson

Lesson Tool Box

- *Craft sticks*
- *12-inch rulers*
- *Pattern blocks (triangles, squares, and hexagons)*

Discussion

1. Day 1: Groundwork

Querying About Patterns

On the first day, we had a lively group discussion about patterns. As always, I begin with a question to peer into the minds of students, to learn as much as possible about what they already know, and to build on that prior knowledge. "Why do we study patterns?" was the opening question. A wide range of answers ensued, from providing examples ("red, white, blue, red, white, blue, red, white, blue . . . "; "2, 4, 6, 8, 10 . . . ") to making a philosophical reflection, "The cycle of life is a pattern." They realized patterns were all around them, in numbers, words, art, dance, music, science, math—in short, everywhere!

"So *what is* a pattern?" was my second big question. There was a class consensus on the definition of pattern as "something that repeats." Students were able to distinguish between *repeating* patterns and *growing* patterns without difficulty. They could also discern the *repeating unit* of a repeating pattern, such as "red, white, blue" in the above example, but they were unsure how to define a growing pattern, aside from the fact that it "gets bigger." The explorations ahead were designed to refine their ideas about growing patterns, appropriate for grades 3 and up (see *Planting the Seeds of Algebra, PreK–2,* Exploration III for repeating patterns). Students would connect shape to number, notice and describe relationships between changing quantities, generalize and represent relationships, discover links among different representations, and experience variables informally. Having cited both natural patterns, such as butterfly wing designs, and human-made patterns, such as a poem's rhyming words, I rewarded students with a slide show of pattern pictures (Figure 4.2).

FIGURE 4.2   Natural patterns: (a) spiral-shaped fossil and (b) sand ripple patterns. Human-made patterns: (c) the Library of Alexandria ceiling (Egypt) and (d) mosque floor tiles

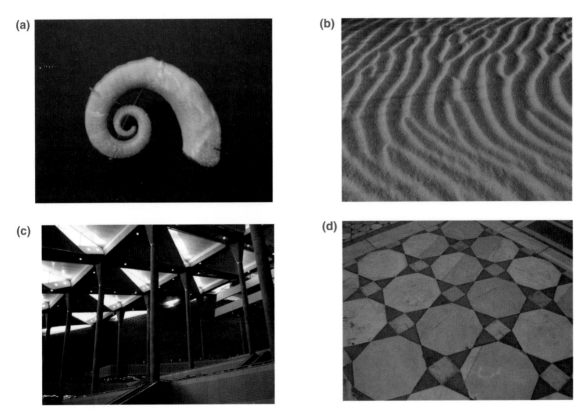

Photo (b) © Holger Karius/Dreamstime

Growing Patterns I

The first exploration consisted of constructing regular polygons (triangles, quadrangles, pentagons, hexagons) with craft sticks and examining the relationship between the number of polygons constructed and the number of sticks needed to construct them. Each group was assigned a different polygon. Figure 4.3 shows the first part of the *triangle* exploration (worksheets for all four explorations can be found in the Appendix, starting on page 206). As expected, two tendencies were observed: First, students focused on the *number of sticks* sequence, in isolation, since they recognized them as multiples of 3, 4, 5, or 6, respectively. In doing so they reasoned *recursively*, meaning they saw each term as the previous term increased by a same, repeating number, *the constant increment*. Taking the triangle, for example, verbal descriptions included, "it keeps adding three" "they're going up by three," and "they're multiples of three."

FIGURE 4.3   Part I: Creating triangles with craft sticks

Exploring Growing Patterns
Grades 3–5

Part I: Creating Triangles With Craft Sticks

1. Make a few equilateral triangles using craft sticks:

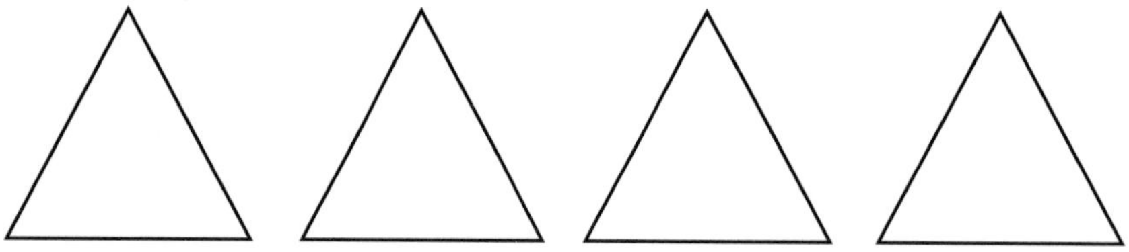

2. How many sticks are needed to make

   1 triangle? _____ 2 triangles? _____ 3 triangles? _____ 4 triangles? _____

3. What do you notice about the number of triangles? What about the number of craft sticks?

   _____

   _____

   _____

   _____

4. Notice the relationship *between* the number of triangles *and* the number of craft sticks needed to make them. List three different ways you could **represent** this relationship:

   _____

   _____

   _____

   _____

Second, when asked to focus on the *relationship* between the two sets of numbers, displayed in a function table (also called in-out or input-output table), student responses mostly exhibited *covariational thinking*, again consistent with the research literature. This means that students mostly analyzed the table by *looking downward*, considered the two columns of numbers *in parallel*, and described each one recursively. Briyanna's response is representative (Figure 4.4). She ends with, "I noticed the relationship of the numbers," but there was no indication of her noticing the "times-3" relationship *between* the number of triangles and the number of sticks. The range of ability was significant, as seen in two extreme responses to the question, "Suppose you used 102 craft sticks to build equilateral triangles. How many triangles did you build?" "Ja'Nae, who found the times-3 triangles→sticks relationship, used division, the *inverse* of multiplication, to find 34 triangles (Figure 4.5a); Michael on the other hand drew 102 sticks, circled three by three, and counted 34 groups (Figure 4.5b). While it was time consuming, his method worked for him.

FIGURE 4.4   Briyanna's response to the *relationship between* number of triangles and number of sticks

5) Here is a **tabular representation:** continue the patterns for a few more rows.

Number of Eq. Triangles	Number of Craft Sticks	In this box, describe the patterns you see. In your own words, tell me at least three things you noticed.
1	3	1) On the said number of eq. triangles that the are add one.
2	6	
3	9	
4	12	2) On the said number of craft sticks I noticed they are adding 3
5	15	
6	18	
7	21	3) I noticed the relationship of the numbers.
8	24	
9	27	
10	30	

FIGURE 4.5   Student responses to the same question, illustrating a range of ability

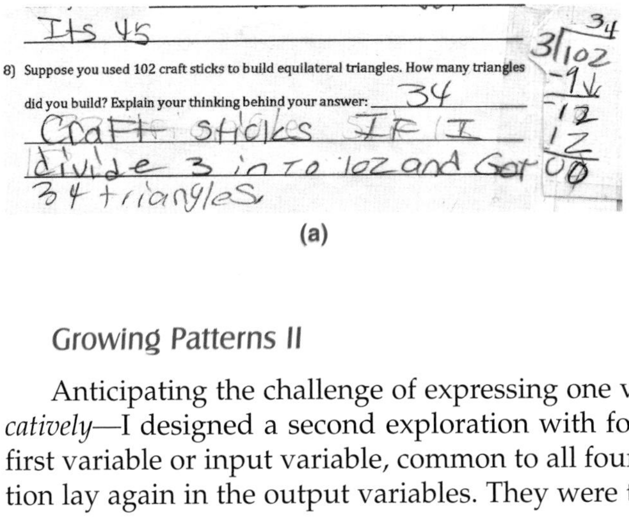

Its 45

8) Suppose you used 102 craft sticks to build equilateral triangles. How many triangles did you build? Explain your thinking behind your answer: **34**

Craft sticks if I divide 3 into 102 and got 34 triangles.

$$3\overline{)102}$$

(a)

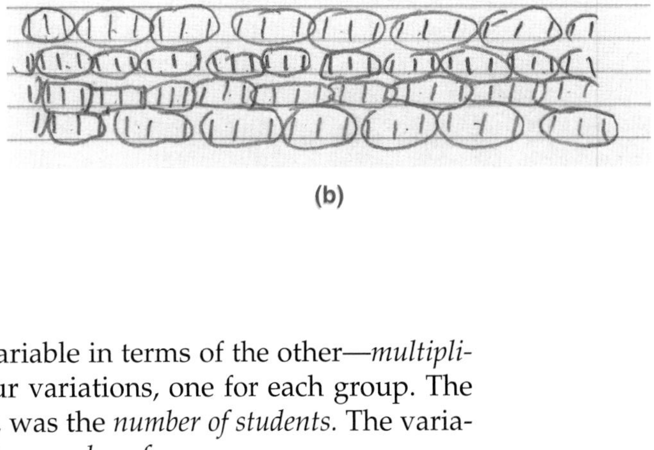

(b)

Growing Patterns II

Anticipating the challenge of expressing one variable in terms of the other—*multiplicatively*—I designed a second exploration with four variations, one for each group. The first variable or input variable, common to all four, was the *number of students*. The variation lay again in the output variables. They were the *number of*

1. Eyes and noses;

2. Eyes and ears;

3. Eyes, ears, and noses; and

4. Eyes, ears, and hands.

Students found it more natural to *connect* the two variables in these relationships. The human body context of the second set of explorations at first concealed their similar

FIGURE 4.6   Tynetta's response to # of students → # of eyes and ears

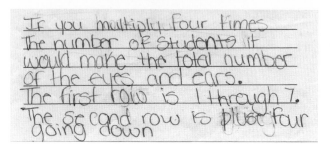

> If you multiply four times the number of students it would make the total number of the eyes and ears. The first row is 1 through 7. The second row is plus four going down

FIGURE 4.7   Destiny's additive thinking in *looking across*

1) Continue the patterns you see, for a few more rows, and explain your thinking

Number of Students	Total Number of Eyes + Ears	Explain your Thinking (Meaning, how did you find it?)
1	4	By adding 3
2	8	By adding 6
3	12	By adding 9
4	16	By adding 12
5	20	By adding 15
6	24	By adding 18
7	28	By adding 21

mathematical structure: For example, the functional relationship[1] between a number of quadrilaterals and the corresponding number of craft sticks is the same as the one between a number of students and their combined eyes and ears (times 4). Tynetta, a mature fifth-grader, was the first to set the tone for multiplicative thinking. The others followed suit. She wrote and read out loud, "If you multiply four times the number of students it would make the total number of the eyes and ears." She was proud of her discovery, sensing from her teachers' pregnant smiles that she was onto something important. Her additional comments confirmed her difficulty in letting go of additive thinking: "The first row is 1 through 7. The second row is plus four going down" (Figure 4.6). In both sentences, she obviously meant *column*, not *row*.

A shift was taking place from covariational thinking to *correspondence thinking*. The latter requires *looking across* a function table. Students began looking across, line by line, in order to discern an unchanging or *invariable* functional relationship between the two changing quantities called *variables*. The first is known as the *independent* variable; the second is the *dependent* variable, as its value depends on the value of the first variable. But students need many experiences before correspondence thinking becomes reflex. Destiny's paper confirmed this: She did analyze the function table looking across, but rather than noticing the invariable *multiplicative* relationship "times 4," she compared the number pairs *additively*, row by row (Figure 4.7). Ah, the beauty of teaching! Ah, the power of student thinking! Ah, the wonder of the unexpected! This was a nice reality check.

Day 1 Wrap-Up

By the end of Day 1, the four groups' results were on the board for all to contemplate. Students saw connections *among* the four problems in each exploration—"times 3," times 4, "times 5," and "times 6"—and *between* the two sets of explorations:

1. Number of craft sticks in *n* triangles ↔ number of eyes and noses on *n* students

2. Number of craft sticks in *n* quadrilaterals ↔ number of eyes and ears on *n* students

---

1. Some elementary math textbook series use the words *function* and *function table* early on. Others just use *relationship* and defer the use of the term *function* to middle school. Chapter 5 addresses the definition of function and students' common misconceptions of function.

3. Number of craft sticks in n pentagons $\leftrightarrow$ number of eyes, ears, and noses on n students

4. Number of craft sticks in n hexagons $\leftrightarrow$ number of eyes, ears, and hands on n students

We wrapped up the Growing Patterns exploration with a fun and surprising graphical representation of the times tables (see Figure 4.8b for "times 4"). Plotting ordered pairs of numbers as points in a coordinate plane, while part of the Florida Math Standards, was relatively new to some students. Mr. Ramsey used a free digital graphing tool that he had downloaded to his computer. Students had fun entering the different sets of number pairs, such as (0, 0), (1, 4), (2, 8), (3, 12), (4, 16) and so on for "times 4" and were surprised to see the points line up. Mr. Ramsey connected the points with a straight line to confirm they were truly colinear, but he specified that the multiples of 4 occurred at the points, directly "north" of 0, 1, 2, 3, 4 . . . on the horizontal axis (Figure 4.8b). Students commented that all times-tables lines started at (0, 0). I asked them why. "Because zero times anything is zero," answered Daisha. For each of the four multiplicative cases—3, 4, 5, and 6—students now had a number of representations:

- Two *verbal* descriptions of real-world problem situations,
- A concrete *geometric* illustration with craft sticks,
- A *tabular* display of the number pairs in the form of a function table,
- A familiar *numerical* display in the form of a multiplication table (Figure 4.8a), and
- A new *graphical* display in the form of colinear plotted points (Figure 4.8b).

FIGURE 4.8   The "times 4" traditional table (a) and graph (b)

×	0	1	2	3	4	5	6	7	8	9	10
0	0	0	0	0	0	0	0	0	0	0	0
1	0	1	2	3	4	5	6	7	8	9	10
2	0	2	4	6	8	10	12	14	16	18	20
3	0	3	6	9	12	15	18	21	24	27	30
4	0	4	8	12	16	20	24	28	32	36	40
5	0	5	10	15	20	25	30	35	40	45	50
6	0	6	12	18	24	30	36	42	48	54	60
7	0	7	14	21	28	35	42	49	56	63	70
8	0	8	16	24	32	40	48	56	64	72	80
9	0	9	18	27	36	45	54	63	72	81	90
10	0	10	20	30	40	50	60	70	80	90	100

(a)

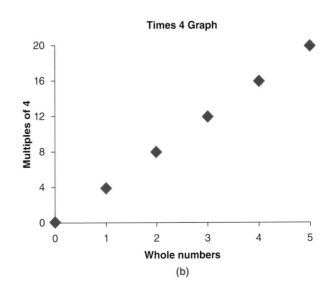

(b)

"Times tables" had taken on a new life. Did we think the students had understood deeply the harbingers of functional thinking? Of course not! But active engagement had been achieved, and the groundwork had been laid for deeper understanding to occur.

> ### RESEARCH . . .
>
> It is the ability to make translations among and within . . . several modes of representation that makes ideas meaningful to learners. . . . Moving among notations allows access to these different aspects of a mathematical concept, becoming more powerful through the links established among representations.
>
> —Barbara M. Brizuela and Darrell Earnest (2008, p. 276)

2. Day 2: Pattern Block Fences

Growing Patterns III

On the second day, Mr. Ramsey and I decided to keep the group arrangements from the previous day. The dynamics proved to be productive, partly because the students were used to working together and partly because Mr. Ramsey had selected a diversity of thinkers for each group. The exploration of the day consisted in constructing fences of increasing lengths with pattern blocks. Each group was assigned a *unit* polygon (Figure 4.9). By appending successive copies of the same unit polygon to the initial one, students were to create a growing pattern of fences. Figure 4.10 shows two of the four growing patterns of *shapes*: the first five iterations of the square fence (a) and the first five iterations of the pentagon fence (b). Similar fences were constructed with successive triangle or hexagon units. In all fences, adjacent polygon units had to share *an entire side*.

FIGURE 4.9 Unit polygons for fence constructions

Triangle   Square   Pentagon   Hexagon

The focus of the day was on the perimeter: observing how it grows in length as the number of unit polygons increases. Measured in *linear* units, the successive perimeters were to be expressed in whole numbers. These increasing perimeter lengths generated from a sequence of polygon fences would exemplify a growing pattern of *numbers*. Each fence sequence alone was interesting in itself, but we were curious to see what similarities and differences students would observe among *all four* patterns of fancy fences by the end of class. Furthermore, the *Fancy Fences* explorations would provide material for follow-up lessons. The popular fancy fence was the pentagon fence (Figure 4.10b), perhaps because it was the only two-colored fence, perhaps because it resembled most the traditional picket fence. In any case, they renamed it the "house fence."

Guiding Questions

The questions posed contained two easy ones everyone could answer and two higher level ones requiring algebraic thinking. They were stated as follows:

1. Describe, in as much detail as you can, how the perimeter changes as the number of *your* unit polygons increases.

2. Find the perimeters of *your* 5th and 10th fence. Can you find them a second way?

3. How many of *your* unit polygons are in a fence of perimeter 62? (*Note:* The unit of measure for the perimeter is discussed below.)

4. Without counting the outer edges of a fence, or adding downward in your function table, can you figure out a way to *predict* the perimeter of a fence with *any number* of unit blocks?" This is called finding the *function rule.*

Use words, blocks, diagrams, tables, graphs, and/or equations to express your ideas.

FIGURE 4.10   First five iterations of the square fence (a); first five iterations of the pentagon/house fence (b)

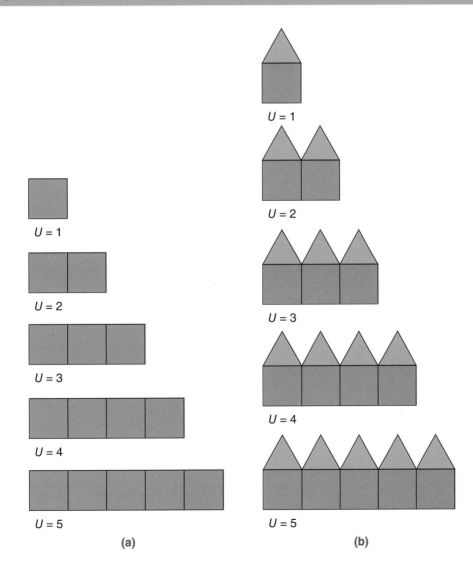

U = 1	*U* = 1
U = 2	*U* = 2
U = 3	*U* = 3
U = 4	*U* = 4
U = 5	*U* = 5
(a)	**(b)**

Understanding the Problem. In the case of the triangle, square, and hexagon, it was clear that all sides were equal. But the group building the house fence made a few quick discoveries. First, they hadn't thought of the traditional house-shape as a pentagon, because they had always worked with regular pentagons, they said (Figure 4.11). Second, they discovered by comparing edges that the green triangle and orange square had equal side lengths. Therefore, *their* unit pentagon, like all the other unit polygons, also had *equal* sides, even though it was not a *regular* pentagon (as it *didn't* have *equal interior angles* as well). Finally, they taped the two blocks together to remind them that the green triangle and orange square *combined* formed their *unit polygon*.

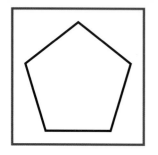

FIGURE 4.11
Regular pentagon

Defining the Unit of Measure for Perimeter. "All the pattern blocks are one inch!" cried out Jamal, who was busy comparing the pattern-block pieces on his table to each other and to a 12-inch ruler. "You don't mean 'they *are* one inch,' do you?" interjected Mr. Ramsey. "I think you mean all their outer edges are one inch long, right?" he added. Jamal smiled with acknowledgment. His statement was true, since the red trapezoidal pattern blocks, with *unequal* edges, had been purposely excluded from the pattern blocks on their tables. *All* pattern blocks had one-inch side lengths indeed. We now had the *unit of measure*—namely, *inches*—for our upcoming perimeter measurements, albeit a second use of the word *unit* in this exploration. We reviewed both uses: The first (unit polygons) to build the fences, the second (inches) to measure their perimeters. Mr. Ramsey made one final clarification for the whole class: "We count only *outside* edges to get the perimeter, right? Not the *inside* edges of blocks that are neighbors." They were now on their own.

3. Functional Thinking

Recursive Thinking

Mr. Ramsey and I were the guides on the side, offering assistance whenever asked and providing helpful hints as needed. At first, students were busy building their first few fences, counting the number of sides, and recording the perimeter values—in a row or a column. All groups were examining the increments between these successive values to detect a pattern and find the next term. Again, they exhibited recursive thinking.

Covariational Thinking

Problem Setup. In this third episode of growing patterns, we had not provided a specific format for data recording. We left it up to the students to decide how to organize their data. After reminding students to consider *both* sequences of values, namely, the unit numbers *and* perimeter lengths, we noticed all groups made function tables to record their first iterations. They were familiar with them, plus we had reviewed them the day before. But there were discrepancies among the tables nevertheless. In the left column, two groups listed the first five counting numbers for the fence numbers, one drew the first five fence diagrams, and one combined both, as illustrated in Figure 4.12. Atop the first column, three groups wrote "Unit Squares," "Number," and "Fence," respectively. The fourth group left it blank. For the sake of uniformity, and honoring student choices, everyone adopted "Number of Unit Polygons" for the first variable (independent variable), thereby combining the two student ideas, "Number" and "Unit Squares" (Figure 4.12). The word "Perimeter" figured atop the right column at all tables, correctly denoting the second variable (dependent variable). Directions to investigate the pattern of *growing perimeters* were clear. Students henceforth adopted their preferred terms: *input* for the number of unit polygons used and *output* for the perimeter of the resulting fence.

Problem Approach. Students discussed and marked constant changes from row to row in their function tables. Two groups, the triangle-fence group and the house-fence group, clearly demonstrated covariational thinking as they marked not only increments in the perimeter column but in the unit polygon column as well, thus considering the change of both variables *simultaneously*. Students were advised to insert a + sign before their 1s to indicate *increasing* values (Figure 4.13). The triangle group was visibly puzzled by the +1 increments in *both* columns. "They're both like counting numbers," commented Solomie to her team members. Demystifying the parallel constant change of +1 was for later. For now we wanted to capitalize on the perimeter growth patterns.

Revisiting the Definition of a Pattern. "Yesterday, you all agreed that a pattern is 'something that repeats'; your perimeter values *don't* repeat but grow larger. So what makes this a pattern?" I queried. Larah stated the connection in this way: "The perimeter keeps going up by the same number, plus four, plus four, plus four—the plus four repeats." A fifth-grader's description of *constant change*. "Well said, young lady!" exclaimed Mr. Ramsey. She, like others, observed a constant change by examining the number patterns recursively, from the covariational approach.

Correspondence Thinking

Students found Questions 1 and 2 straightforward. Question 3 was tricky. By the end of the group-work phase, some students were tackling Question 4, the hardest of all. Within two of the four groups, there were hints of "correspondence

FIGURE 4.12 Triangle fence function table

Number of Unit Polygons	Perimeter of Fence
1	3
2	4
3	5
4	6
5	7

FIGURE 4.13 Triangle fence perimeters exhibit a constant change of 1

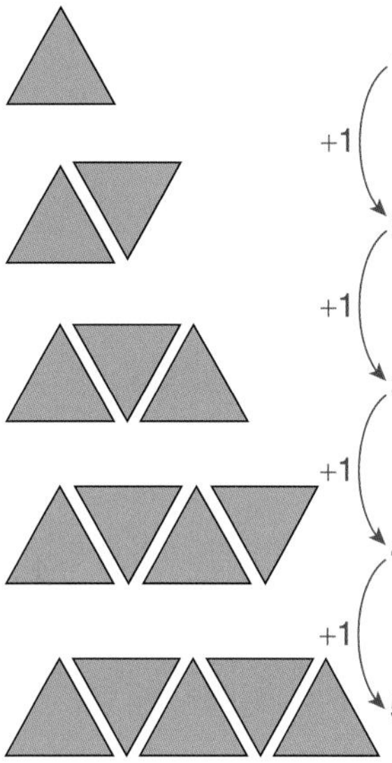

Number of Unit Polygons	Perimeter of Fence
1	3
+1	+1
2	4
+1	+1
3	5
+1	+1
4	6
+1	+1
5	7

thinking": thoughtful attempts to identify a generalized expression that outputs the fence perimeter for any given input number of unit polygons. Several students needed help. We attended.

TABLE 4.1	Stages in Raven's thinking about the house fence, from arithmetic to algebra		
# Unit Polygons	Times 3		Perimeter
1	3	+ 2 →	5
2	6	+ 2 →	8
3	9	+ 2 →	11
4	12	+ 2 →	14
5	15	+ 2 →	17

An Enlightening Exchange. While observing the house-fence group, I was intrigued by scribbles on a scrap paper. On it were written, in column form, the first five multiples of the number 3 (3, 6, 9, 12, 15) and the symbol/numeral combination +2. "Who wrote this?" I inquired. "I did," said Raven, "but it's not right," she added. *"What's* not right?" I pursued. "It's not times three." *"What is not* times three?" I insisted. "The perimeter," she answered. I pointed to her crossed out +2, adding, "Why did you write plus two?" Placing the times-3 column beside her group's perimeter column (as shown in Table 4.1), she explained, "It's like times three, but it's two more, so it doesn't work." The previous day's work had apparently left her with the erroneous impression that correspondence relationships had to be *exact* multiples. "By your observation, what would the perimeter of the 30th house-fence be?" I carried on. "Ninety-two inches." "What about the 100th fence? "Three-hundred and two," she answered, her face beaming with the sudden realization she had found a strategy that worked. Raven had found a *general expression,* "× 3 followed by + 2" for the perimeter of *any* pentagon fence. Since this was an advanced group, I gave them a question to ponder: "Using *U* for *any* number of units and *P* for the fence perimeter, can you write an expression, with words and/or symbols, stating the relationship you just described?"

READ . . .

In grades 3–5, students should investigate numerical and geometric patterns and express them mathematically in words or symbols. They should analyze the structure of the pattern and how it grows or changes, organize this information systematically, and use their analysis to develop generalizations about the mathematical relationships in the pattern.

—National Council of Teachers of Mathematics (2000, p. 159)

Delving Deeper

4. Class Sharing

"I can attest that my field is really about ideas above anything else," says mathematician and novelist Manil Suri (2013, p. A23). The best part of a math lesson, in my opinion, is when students formulate their ideas for the benefit of others, and often for their own benefit. Listening, with a keen ability to peer into another's mind and grasp a different point of view, is as important an art of communication as is the art of clearly articulating one's own view.

It was time for a blackboard splash.[2] Mr. Ramsey divided the blackboard into four sections so that each group would have enough space to display its findings. As instructed at the outset of the lesson, each group of problem solvers had appointed a recorder, a communicator, a prop manager, and one or more evaluators. The recorders came up simultaneously to write down their group's collective results; they were followed by the communicators, who came up, one after the other, to explain their group's thinking as clearly as possible; they were assisted by the prop managers, who modeled with blocks whenever necessary. The evaluators listened attentively from their seats to assess whether explanations were clear.

Photo by Jim Conner and Kathleen Watt

Question 1: Analysis of Perimeter Change

Everyone observed that as the number of unit polygons increased by 1, the perimeter also increased by a constant value:

- 1 for the triangle fence
- 2 for the square fence
- 3 for the house fence, and
- 4 for the hexagon fence.

As on the previous day, students exhibited covariational thinking. The groups expressed it in different ways: "The units and the perimeters go up the same—it's plus one, plus one, plus one . . . for both" said Daniel (referring to the triangle fences). Angela was more articulate; referring to the house fence, she said "Each time we added a block to the fence, the perimeter got three bigger." "Any thoughts about why you found the numbers you did?" I probed. Mystery. But mystery is good. It's stimulating. Didn't Einstein say, "The most beautiful thing we can experience is the mysterious?" They began searching, but no one could verbalize the reason on the spot. To be continued.

Question 2: Perimeter of Fences #5 and #10

All students found correct perimeter values for their respective fence #5 by building the first five fences and counting sides. For the tenth fence, answers varied. One group said, "We timesed our fifth line by two and then we checked but it didn't work." They had applied their discovery from the previous day to a situation that was *not* proportional. Students were getting a first taste of a nonproportional relationship of constant change—without knowing it. The observation was rich with mathematics, so we decided to address it at a later date (see Chapter 5 for discussion on proportional reasoning). The triangle group explained, "We started with three and we counted by one: four, five,

---

2. I have employed this instructional technique for years but only recently read, in a math education journal article, the phrase *blackboard splash.* It is a powerful metaphor, and I regret that I was unable to track down the article in order to give credit to the author who coined it.

six . . . [nine counts] . . . until we got to the twelve." Interesting that they hadn't seen the simple +2 relationship from their data table: 10 + 2 = 12 (Figure 4.12). Grasping a correspondence relationship requires a cognitive leap. That group wasn't there yet. The lesson here for us teachers? Students don't always see what we expect them to!

An Interesting Error in Perimeter #10. The hexagon-fence group erred in their reasoning, albeit an interesting reasoning. Martín said his group figured out the 10th perimeter using a "neat way," without actually building the 10th fence. They subtracted 1 for each of the nine junctures of the 10 hexagons, thus obtaining 6 x 10 – 9 = 60 – 9 = 51 inches. Samuel, an attentive evaluator from another group, jumped in, "You're supposed to take away *two* where they join, so it's minus 18, not minus 9." This observation helped Martín see that the 10th hexagon-fence perimeter is in fact 42 (60 – 18), not 51 (60 – 9) (Figure 4.14). Once these corrections were made on the board (Table 4.2), a pattern of perimeter values emerged. "Oh neat, it goes 12, 22, 32, 42!" exclaimed Tynetta. "It's like counting by 10s." Carmen added, "The others go by 5s." Indeed, the sequence of perimeter values for fences #5—namely, 7, 12, 17, and 22—increase by 5. More questions to ponder later. The beauty of the blackboard splash: These class reactions would not have happened without it!

FIGURE 4.14   Student-provided correction of hexagon-fence #10 perimeter: 10 × 6 – 9 × 2 = 42

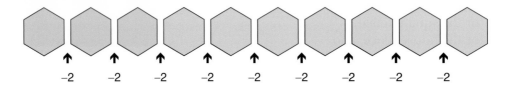

The method of subtracting two inches for every pair of sides "that touch on the *inside*" ignited gray matter, moving some students further along the path toward generalization. Despite their incorrect *numerical* answer (51), I commended the hexagon group for their *algebraic* thinking, for their thinking about structure: from the geometric structure of the fence to the mathematical structure of the perimeter function rule. They were thinking *algebraically* about the perimeter without actually counting all sides.

TABLE 4.2   Student answers to Question 2, including correction made in last column

	Triangle-Fence Group		Square-Fence Group		House-Fence Group		Hexagon-Fence Group	
Specific *P* **values (inches)**	5th	7 in	5th	12 in	5th	17 in	5th	22 in
	10th	12 in	10th	22 in	10th	32 in	10th	42 in

Question 3: The 62-Inch-Long Perimeter

"How many of *your* unit polygons are in a fence with a perimeter of 62 units?" proved to be too ambitious a question, the result of wanting to do too much in two days. In the previous day's explorations, where the correspondence relationships were simple multiples of 3, 4, 5, or 6, students could see—once Ja'Nae reminded everyone—that "division goes backwards" (Figure 4.5a). On Day 1, in Growing Patterns I and II, students were able to solve questions in both directions:

1. Given an input value, you *multiply* by a factor, say 4, to find the output value, and inversely,

2. Given an output value, you *divide* by a divisor, say 4, to find the input value.

This was a nice application of the inverse relationship between multiplication and division. But in Growing Pattern III, the relationship was subtler. Some students first divided by the correct factor and *then subtracted* 2, an understandable error. Since this question was too complicated to resolve in a limited amount of time, we set it aside to be revisited (see Chapter 5 for strategies in tackling Question 3). We moved on to Question 4.

Question 4: Strategies Toward Generalization

The answers to Question 4, "Can you figure out a way to *predict* the perimeter of a fence with *any number* of unit blocks?" confirmed that children are capable of sophisticated thinking.

Arithmetic to Algebra. Raven came up to the board to explain the pentagon group's thinking, which she had already shared with me. They had applied themselves to express their finding symbolically. She stated it in this way: "You take any units you want. You can call it *U*. You just multiply by 3, but then you have to add 2 to make it work." With a little nudging from her team, Raven translated her English sentences to a verbal-symbolic hybrid expression, "*U* × 3 plus 2 gives *P*." Mr. Ramsey, nonintrusively, added another line right under hers: "*U* × 3 + 2 → *P*," and said, "Just think about that and see if it makes sense." To the reader, perhaps the second statement seems obvious. But to a fourth- or fifth-grader, the cognitive change can be significant. Also significant are the ensuing changes that will gradually occur through the end of middle school, as shown in Figure 4.15. The last form is the *standard* form used in secondary school for linear relationships or functions. Former algebra students remember this equation, but often forget its meaning.

> **FIGURE 4.15   Gradual evolution toward *standard form* of linear function**
>
> $$U \times 3 + 2 \rightarrow P$$
> $$\Downarrow$$
> $$U \times 3 + 2 = P$$
> $$\Downarrow$$
> $$P = U \times 3 + 2$$
> $$\Downarrow$$
> $$P = 3 \times U + 2$$
> $$\Downarrow$$
> $$P = 3U + 2$$
> $$\Downarrow$$
> $$y = mx + b$$

Geometry to Algebra. A very different strategy unfolded when Donnell came up to share the thinking of his group, the square-fence group. "I think we got it!" He began excitedly. "We got another way," he continued. Assisted by his prop manager, he brought up 10 squares with him, placed them on the teacher's desk, and made a long rectangular fence. As he traced the two long edges of the fence with his finger, one after the other, he said, "There's 10 inches up here (top) and there's 10 inches down here (bottom). Then you add these 2 here (left end and right end). That's 22 inches (Figure 4.16a)." Sensing where he was going, and proving to the class he hadn't counted edges, I interjected, "What about the *hundredth* fence?" "It'll be 202," he retorted with confidence. Donnell's approach needed some elaboration for his peers. Donnell's group, like Raven's, had found a generalized strategy allowing them to generate the perimeter of *any* fence. He analyzed the *geometric structure* of a "square-fence" of any length and decomposed the perimeter into four parts: two long sides that vary—top and bottom, and two short sides that always measure one inch each—left and right. Without using symbolic notation, but only natural language and convincing gestures, he described the correspondence rule, or the *function rule*, for P as $2 \times U + 2$ (Figure 4.16b), where U can be any number of units.

FIGURE 4.16   Diagrams capturing the stages in Donnell's thinking, from geometry to algebra

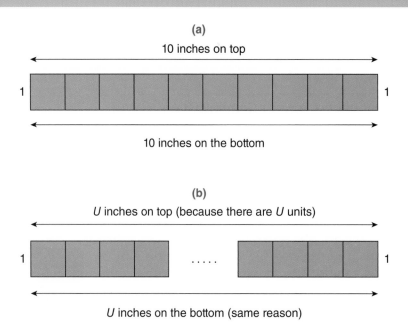

As expected from our observations of the groups' work, only two groups strategized toward a generalization for the perimeter of *any* fence and attempted to articulate it. Table 4.3 summarizes the four group responses to challenging Question 4.

TABLE 4.3   Author's summary, from field notes, of group answers to Question 4

	Triangle-Fence Group	Square-Fence Group	House-Fence Group	Hexagon-Fence Group
Strategy used toward generalization	Saw that P is "2 more than" U	Saw it in the **geometric** structure of any long fence	Saw it in the function-table **numerical** values	Saw a way to generalize for the 10-hexagon fence (despite error)
Function rule for any fence #	Did not attempt to generalize for *any* fence #	Gave a **verbal-gestural description** of a general rule	Generated a **verbal-symbolic** hybrid **equation** $U \times 3$ plus 2 gives P	Did not attempt to transfer finding to *any* fence #

5. Reflecting on the Work

Embryonic Symbolic Thinking

Photo by Jim Conner and Kathleen Watt

The gradual progression from English words to the use of symbols in the class discussion and on the board recording happened organically, led by Raven, who set the example in her presentation. Her choice of using *U* for unit and *P* for perimeter, a kind of shorthand notation, seemed logical to her peers and was accepted by them without hesitation. It became the established choice in the classroom discourse. Also, arrows rather than equals signs were used for functional relationships between inputs and outputs. They conveyed both action and direction.

A Pattern of Patterns

We concluded the two-day intense exploration by focusing students' attention on the pattern of patterns that had emerged. To this end, we projected onto the white board a recapitulating chart, prepared in advance, with four two-column tables. Using the symbolism students had adopted, Mr. Ramsey and I added the constant changes in red to each *P*-column, and listed the function rules at the bottom (Table 4.4). Seeing the *Fancy Fences* function tables side by side enabled students to reflect on their own work in light of one another's work. Each *Fancy Fences* pattern was now an element inside a new, greater pattern, for which Tameika coined "a pattern of patterns." We gave them time to absorb

TABLE 4.4 Out of the four function rules emerged a new pattern.

Triangle-Fence Group			Square-Fence Group			House-Fence Group			Hexagon-Fence Group		
U	*P*		*U*	*P*		*U*	*P*		*U*	*P*	
1	3	+1	1	4	+2	1	5	+3	1	6	+4
2	4	+1	2	6	+2	2	8	+3	2	10	+4
3	5	+1	3	8	+2	3	11	+3	3	14	+4
4	6	+1	4	10	+2	4	14	+3	4	18	+4
5	7	+1	5	12	+2	5	17	+3	5	22	+4
⋮			⋮			⋮			⋮		
× 1 + 2 $U \longrightarrow P$			× 2 + 2 $U \longrightarrow P$			× 3 + 2 $U \longrightarrow P$			× 4 + 2 $U \longrightarrow P$		

the pattern of patterns and reflect for a moment. "The last two days, you worked on *teacher* questions. Tomorrow, we'll work on *student* questions," announced Mr. Ramsey, inviting questions. Students asked all sorts, some superficial but others quite observant. Before the class ended, Mr. Ramsey recorded (with some editing) three pointed questions:

1. "If the red numbers (the constant changes) are all "+", why is it "×" in the rule?" (For example, the house-fence perimeters change by + 3, but the rule is × 3 + 2.)

2. "Why do all rules have a + 2?"

3. "Would the pattern keep on going if we used octagons or even bigger shapes?"

Closure

Mr. Ramsey and his fourth- and fifth-graders had their work cut out for the next few days. So many questions to ponder, and student questions to boot! His students had been very gracious in welcoming me to work with them. I expressed my appreciation for their thoughtfulness, curiosity, and time on task. In closing, I recommended, in the follow-up explorations, they not lose sight of the concrete pattern-blocks-building experience whence their patterns originated. "Don't forget the connection between the geometric structure of the fences you built with blocks and the algebraic structure of the equations on the board: Seeing the geometry with your eyes will help you see the algebra with your minds."

RECOMMEND . . .

We advocate here a habit of mind, not just curricular materials, whereby teachers understand both how to transform and extend their current resources so that the mostly arithmetic content of the elementary grades can be extended to opportunities for pattern building, conjecturing, generalizing, and justifying mathematical relationships and how to embed the mathematics within the kinds of socio-mathematical norms that allow children to build mathematical generality.

—Maria Blanton and James Kaput (2011, p. 21)

5
Behind *Fancy Fences*
Algebra Connections

The overarching goal of this chapter is to make explicit the connections between *patterns* and *functions*, and their connection to *algebra*. First a historical note about each.

Patterns of all kinds affect our lives: political, economic, circadian, meteorological, and health patterns to name a few. To effectively understand and control the changing world we live in, we must be attentive to patterns of change, learn to discern them, and use them to make predictions. Mathematics as a major field of study is defined in the 21st century as *the science of patterns*. "The recognition and analysis of patterns are important components of the young child's intellectual development because they provide a foundation for the development of algebraic thinking," says an expert in the mathematics education of children (Clements, 2004, p. 52).

The concept of **function** has evolved significantly during the more than 300 years of its history. It emerged as a mathematical object with the advent of calculus. In essence, it is a special type of relationship between two sets of variables. German mathematician Gottfried Leibnitz first coined the term *function,* and Swiss mathematician Leonard Euler later introduced the notation "$f(x)$," for "function of x," still in use today. About 100 years ago, the international mathematics community decided that functions, until then reserved for university study, would become part of the secondary mathematics curriculum. Deemed fundamental to all of mathematics, functional relationships between quantities recently became part of the elementary school mathematics curriculum as well (NCTM, 1989, 2000; NGA/CCSSO, 2010).

Finally, there is **algebra**. Algebra has a longer history than function, evolving through four major stages since its earliest traces in Babylonian mathematics (see the introduction to Chapter 2). Like functions, it had long been the privilege of university study. About 200 years ago, it entered the U.S. high school curriculum. In the first yearbook of the National Council of Teachers of Mathematics (NCTM), which included surveys of high school mathematics from 1900 to 1925, David Eugene Smith described students' attitude toward algebra:

> Valuable as the teacher might feel it to be, the majority of the pupils looked upon it as a fairly interesting way of getting nowhere. (Smith, 1926, p. 20)

You may think not much has changed over the past 100 years. Indeed, the 20th-century emphasis on procedural methods over conceptual learning contributed much to the negative attitudes toward algebra, persisting to this day. In an attempt to remedy this mathematical and cultural situation, NCTM made algebra a preK–12 content standard, in which patterns and functions converge in meaningful ways from the start.

Given the significance of function in mathematics, this chapter is replete with foundational notions of a child's ascent toward understanding the concept. While it is impossible to address all aspects of this concept, a selection of the most important ones follows.

CHAPTER 5

THE BIG IDEAS OF

- Studying patterns cultivates students' *inductive reasoning*. Inductive reasoning leads to *generalization*. Without generalization, there is no algebra (or mathematics).
- Exploring patterns refines students' ability to discern structure. Repeated addition of a constant change leads to *linear* functions, the most basic family of functions in algebra. The graphs of linear functions are straight *lines*.
- A function is a special kind of relationship between two sets: Each element of the input set is paired with *exactly one* element in the output set. Any pattern can be transformed into a function by pairing counting numbers with pattern elements.
- A big idea of functions is the notion of *stasis* and *change*. Stasis refers to what is, what remains unchanged, or what remains *invariant*. Change obviously refers to what *varies*. We must address both and contrast the two when analyzing functions.
- Function tables are child-friendly representations. In examining function tables, students exhibit and develop two important ways of thinking *functionally: recursive* or *covariational* thinking (looking *down* the tables) and *correspondence* or *rule-wise* thinking (looking *across* the tables). The first focuses on what changes, the second on what remains *invariant*.
- Students should explore multiple *representations* of functions: concrete manipulatives that model the function, words that describe the problem or situation, tables that organize inputs and outputs in columns or rows of numbers, equations that relate input and output variables, and (for students in grade 5 and some in grade 4) graphs in a 2-D plane.
- Grades 3–5 students need not be proficient with symbols when expressing functional relationships between input and output variables, such as "Input x 3 = Output" or "$3I = O$." They can describe relationships using words, numbers, diagrams, and so on.

REFLECT . . .

Mathematics, the science of patterns, is itself changing. For the sake of our future we must harness mathematics to the patterns of change. And to do that we must change the way that mathematics is taught, to create a new generation able to perceive and manipulate new patterns.

—Ian Stewart (1990, p. 216)

Discussion

1. Day 1: Groundwork

Querying About Patterns

The three main reasons for studying patterns in mathematics are

- Patterns are all around us,
- The human brain is hardwired to discern patterns, and
- Mathematics is the science of patterns.

Patterns All Around. Patterns arise from the world we live in or the worlds that inhabit our minds. They can be helpful in understanding real-world phenomena—such as voting patterns based on demographics, or purely recreational to entertain us—such as the color patterns in the code-cracking Mastermind for Kids game. Children encounter patterns from infancy in sounds, in lights, and in their daily routine. They are attracted to color and shape patterns, letter and number patterns, word and action patterns, and sound and movement patterns. In time, they learn to distinguish between repeating and growing patterns (Figure 5.1).

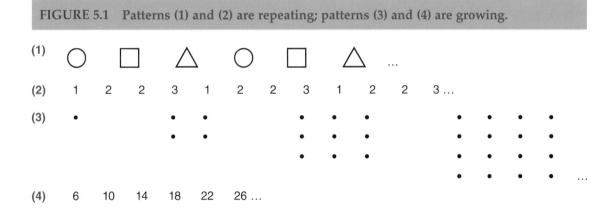

FIGURE 5.1   Patterns (1) and (2) are repeating; patterns (3) and (4) are growing.

As children mature, students learn that the concept of pattern encompasses more than just visual, auditory, movement, number, or shape patterns. It connotes *regularity, order, structure,* and *relationship,* basic notions of mathematics and science (Devlin, 2000). That is why patterning activities are pervasive in elementary school curricula around the world. In grades 3 through 5 especially, "patterns offer a powerful vehicle for understanding the dependent relations among quantities that underlie mathematical functions . . . as well as a concrete and transparent way for young students to begin to grapple with the ideas of abstraction and generalization" (Moss, Beatty, Barkin, & Shillolo, 2008, p. 156).

Patterns and the Human Mind. The second reason we study patterns is that it comes naturally to us. "The ability to see patterns and similarities is one of the greatest strengths of the human mind," explains Keith Devlin, the "math guy" on National Public Radio and author of the second foreword of this book. He goes on to explain that our minds have a predisposition toward "recognizing patterns, seeing connections, and making rapid judgments and inferences" (2000, p. 62). This talent is present at birth. Studies have shown that the regularity of a poem's rhyme or the repetition of song's rhythm appeals to children's visceral pattern-recognition ability. The purpose of having children explore patterns in mathematics is to help them move gradually beyond the physical actions of the body and into the realm of the mind, which is capable of generalizing, abstracting, and symbolizing. As students move inward, they tap into their power of imagination and learn to see beyond what is known and predict what might come next (for repeating patterns) or what might occur at some future stage (for growing or shrinking patterns).

Mathematics, the Science of Patterns. The third reason for studying patterns, especially in the context of mathematics, is that the field itself has been described as the science of patterns. Mathematicians are intrigued by patterns, phenomena, and objects of all sorts, in all domains, that move or change over time or space, whether originating from our outer world of observation or from our inner world of contemplation. The detection and analysis of patterns by men and women have moved the field forward. The various branches of mathematics were born over time from the study of different categories of patterns: The study of number patterns led to number theory, shape patterns gave geometry, motion patterns inspired calculus, chance patterns grew into probability theory, and so forth. Consequently, since the late 1980s, patterns have become a major pathway into algebraic thinking for elementary school students.

Algebra Connection

• **Inductive Reasoning.** Deductive reasoning is the process of reasoning logically from generalized statements and concluding something about particular cases. Inductive reasoning is the reverse: reasoning from particular cases and drawing conclusions about the general case. Both are cornerstones of all of mathematics. Typical of problems requiring inductive reasoning are those in which students are given a sequence of numbers or shapes and asked to determine the next few terms. Students used induction when reasoning about the first few fences and their perimeter values: They (1) noticed a pattern, (2) made a conjecture, and (3) verified it by building a few more fences and checking the perimeter values. Most students applied inductive reasoning through perimeter #10. These three steps constitute the inductive process. In more formal mathematics, students are expected to *prove* their conjecture rather than simply verify it. Raven and Donnell were the more formal thinkers of the lot.

• **Generalization.** Generalizing is a close cousin of inductive reasoning. The latter leads to the former. Algebraic reasoning and the study of mathematics share the common defining feature of seeking *generalization*. Without this feature there is no algebra; without this feature, there is no mathematics. "To see what is general in what is particular and what is permanent in what is transitory is the aim of scientific thought" (Whitehead, 1948, p. 4). Generalization is addressed further in Section 4 of this chapter, "Class Sharing."

Growing Patterns I

Looking back, students in grades 3–5 have had experience with repeating patterns in grades preK–2; looking ahead, they begin to plant the seeds for proportional reasoning that grow and mature in middle school. (For repeating patterns, see *Planting the Seeds of Algebra, PreK–2*; for proportional reasoning, see further down). Growing patterns are a quintessential topic of the upper elementary grades. They constitute a perfect pathway into the study of functions. A function is a special type of relationship between varying quantities. Specifically, it is a relationship between a set of input values and a set of output values,[1] subject to one condition: each input must correspond to *exactly one* output. Creating quadrilaterals with craft sticks is an example of a function. The input is the number of quadrilaterals desired, and the output is the number of craft sticks needed to make them. In this case, both inputs and outputs are whole numbers. The functional relationship can be expressed algebraically by the equation $Q \times 4 = C$, where Q for quadrilaterals is the input or *independent* variable, and C for craft sticks is the output or the *dependent* variable, since it *depends* on the chosen input Q. Letters x and y are commonly used for the input and output variables in the upper grades, but any sensible symbols children propose are acceptable. The equation, $Q \times 4 = C$, called the *function rule* in elementary school, is known as the *correspondence rule* in secondary school. A function table, an outgrowth of "in-out tables" familiar to many primary students, is a child-friendly representation that unambiguously reveals the uniqueness of the output ("exactly *one*") for every input (Table 5.1).

TABLE 5.1   Function table for the "times 4" relationship between quadrilaterals and craft sticks

Q (Input)	C (Output)
1	4
2	8
3	12
4	16
5	20
.	.
.	.
.	.
Q	$Q \times 4 = C$

Algebra Connection

- **Function.**

It can be argued [that function] is the single most important concept from kindergarten to graduate school and is critical throughout the full range of education. Arithmetic in the early grades, algebra in middle and high school, and transformational geometry in high school are all coming to be based on the idea of function. (Harel & Dubinsky, 1992, p. vii)

Many mathematicians and mathematics educators consider function as the fundamental object of algebra and recommend that it be explored in a variety of representations in the teaching and learning of algebra from the outset (Yerushalmy & Schwartz, 1993). Consequently, a fundamental component of algebraic thinking in the elementary grades is working with functions (NCTM, 1989, 2000; NGA/CCSSO, 2010). (*Note*: NCTM uses the term *function* for all grades, whereas the Common Core State Standards for Mathematics—CCSSM—use *relationship* through grade 7 and function in grades 8–12.) Functions arise in all sorts of places, starting with numbers and operations. In grades 3–5, multiplication can be treated as a function (Schliemann, Carraher, & Brizuela, 2007). For example, the 3-times table can be regarded as the simple function rule, $3 \times n$, which assigns a unique output to every input selected from the set $\{0, 1, 2, 3, 4 \ldots \}$.[2] Table 5.2 displays this relationship, where n denotes any whole *number* and m its corresponding *multiple of 3*.

TABLE 5.2   Conceptualizing the 3-times table as a functional relationship

n (Input)	m (Output)
1	3
2	6
3	9
4	12
5	15
.	.
.	.
.	.
n	$n \times 3 = m$

---

1. In later years, students come to know the set of input values as the function's *domain* and the set of output values as its *range*.

2. Braces,{}, are used to denote sets.

"This reconceptualization of arithmetical operations shifts the emphasis away from the number crunching to the relations among sets of numbers" (Carraher & Schliemann, 2010, p. 26). Students who think functionally about multiplication will later be able to conceptualize linear function $n \times 3 + 2 = m$ as a variation on the 3-times table, $n \times 3$.

- **A Note on Algebraic Notation of Function Rules.** Consider this last example, $n \times 3 + 2 = m$. The common textbook way, or adult way, of writing this function rule would be $m = 3n + 2$ (analogous to the standard form, $y = mx + b$, which readers may remember from their middle school years). Although concise and algebraic, it does not mimic the actions performed by the child in the *process* of computing an output. Suppose the input, n, equals 5. "I multiply my input 5 by 3, and I get 15; I then add 2, and I finally get 17 for my output," describes the sequence of actions most students follow. Therefore, the equation $5 \times 3 + 2 = 17$, or better yet, $5 \times 3 + 2 \rightarrow 17$, where the arrow conveys, "I compute and I get," speaks to the child. Once they accept the use of letters for inputs and outputs, $n \times 3 + 2 \rightarrow m$ or $n \times 3 + 2 = m$ will make more sense than $m = 3n + 2$. Moreover, the progression from $n \times 3 + 2 = m$ to $3 \times n + 2 = m$, then to $3n + 2 = m$, and finally to $m = 3n + 2$, takes time and shouldn't be rushed. The equivalence among these equations, while obvious to us, is challenging for students in grades 3–5 to see, understand, accept, and adopt (see discussion on expressions in Chapter 8, Section 3, "Unpacking the Distributive Property of Multiplication"). The bottom line is this: In the elementary grades, students can express generalizations *without* necessarily using purely symbolic notation.

Growing Patterns II

In the second set of growing patterns, the four functional relationships associated the number of students (S) with the total number of certain body parts (T). While the two sets of Growing Patterns I and II—*Polygon Craft Sticks* and *Student Body Parts*—differed in the *nature of the quantities* involved, they shared the same mathematical structure:

1. $S \times 3 = T$ (Total eyes and noses combined per S students)
2. $S \times 4 = T$ (Total eyes and ears combined per S students)
3. $S \times 5 = T$ (Total eyes, ears, and noses combined per S students)
4. $S \times 6 = T$ (Total eyes, ears, and hands combined per S students)

But students were not rushed into finding or expressing these function rules, because interesting discoveries (not reported in Chapter 4) occurred while they were observing the parallel patterns in their function tables. For instance, in response to, "How might we find the number of eyes and ears on nine students using the first few lines of the table?" Ja'Nae exclaimed, "We can *add* line 4 and line 5" (Table 5.3, in blue). Later in the lesson, when predicting the 20th output (while still looking *down* the columns), students applying Ja'Nae's finding were adding either five 4s, or four 5s, to get 20. But David proposed *multiplying by a constant*: "If you multiply 2 by 10, it's 20, and if you multiply 8 by 10, that's 80, and that works!" he said proudly (Table 5.3, in orange). Ja'Nae and David, unknowingly, had discovered the additive and multiplicative properties of proportional relationships.

TABLE 5.3	Additive and multiplicative properties of proportional relationships

S Students (Input)	T Total (Output)
1	4
2	8
3	12
4	16
5	20
⋮	⋮
9	?
⋮	⋮
20	?

2×10 $4 + 5$ $16 + 20$ 8×10

Ratios.

> Proportionality has been called both the capstone of elementary school arithmetic and the cornerstone of higher mathematics. . . . Yet proportionality is also tied to a long-standing nemesis of teachers of mathematics in the middle grades—the teaching and learning of rational number concept and skills. (Smith, Silver, & Stein, 2005b, p. xiv)

In an attempt to remedy this situation, and to facilitate the transition from fractions to ratios, NCTM published *Developing Essential Understandings of Rational Numbers for Teaching Mathematics in Grades 3–5* (Barnett-Clarke, Fisher, Marks, & Ross, 2010). With a simple money example, let's examine how the seeds of ratio and proportional thinking can be planted early. Table 5.4 shows the dollar-to-quarter relationship, a different problem situation for the same function, $D \times 4 = Q$. The common interpretation of symbol $\frac{a}{b}$ in the elementary grades is, "*a* parts *out of b* equal parts." This basic interpretation implies (1) that the part $\frac{a}{b}$ is included in the whole (or unit) $\frac{b}{b}$, and (2) that therefore part and whole share the same nature—pizza, cake, students, et cetera. But this is only one of many interpretations.

Another is a *ratio*. In Exploration I, we discovered the diameter-to-circumference ratio in *all* circles. Here, the fraction $\frac{1}{4}$ can be used to express the 1-to-4 dollar-to-quarter ratio. The fraction in this case is not an amount. It is a *relationship*. It is a *multiplicative comparison* between two *different* entities, dollars and quarters. If 1 dollar equates 4 quarters in value, then 2 dollars equate 8 quarters, 20 dollars equate 80 quarters, 40 dollars equate 160 quarters, and so forth. The equivalent fractions $\frac{1}{4} = \frac{2}{8} = \frac{20}{80} = \frac{40}{160}$ symbolize these ratios, unchanging in *value*. Adding any number of input-output rows (as Ja'Nae discovered) or multiplying an input-output row by a constant (as David proposed) yields another input-output pair of the relationship. A function table that has these two properties represents a *proportional relationship*. Such a function table that can be used to generate equivalent fractions, or equivalent ratios, is often called a *ratio table*.

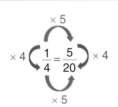

Algebra Connection

• **Proportional Reasoning.**

When work in elementary school allows students to develop deep and flexible meanings for numbers and operations (especially for fractions and multiplication), they have important foundations on which to build an understanding of ratios, proportions, and proportional reasoning in the middle grades. (Lobato, Ellis, Charles, & Zbiek, 2010, p. 57)

Proportional reasoning has both *quantitative* and *qualitative* features (Post, Behr, & Lesh, 1988). Quantitatively, we say in mathematics that a relationship is proportional if its function rule is of the general form $x \times m = y$. Examples include $x \times 4 = y$, $x \times \frac{1}{2} = y$, and $x \times 11.7 = y$. The proportional relationship is the first type of function students encounter in their algebra journey. It is a subset of the *linear* function family. Qualitatively, proportional reasoning involves a sense of reasonableness, as in asking oneself, "If there are four quarters to a dollar, does it *make sense* that there would be 20 quarters to five dollars? Should it be more? Should it be less?" Comparing two ratios is complex: Since *one* ratio is already a multiplicative comparison, comparing *two* ratios, such as $\frac{1}{4}$ and $\frac{5}{20}$, actually means comparing two comparisons. Students in grades 4 and 5 can learn to appreciate these two multiplicative comparisons: *downward, within* each ratio ($\times 4$), and *across, between* the two ratios ($\times 5$). If there is consistency downward *and* across, then $\frac{1}{4} = \frac{5}{20}$ is assured (Figure 5.2). Students will soon learn that such an equation—between two equivalent ratios—is called a *proportion*. Ratios, proportions, and proportional thinking are useful in solving a wide variety of problems that affect our daily lives—speed, scaling, conversion, pricing, and consumption, to name a few. They are the gateway into middle school math and the heart of prealgebra math.

TABLE 5.4 The function table of a proportional relationship is a ratio table.

D (Dollars)	Q (Quarters)
1	4
2	8
3	12
4	16
5	20
.	.
.	.
.	.
D	D × 4 = Q

FIGURE 5.2 Two multiplicative comparisons are involved when comparing two ratios.

$$\times 4 \left(\frac{1}{4} = \frac{5}{20} \right) \times 4$$
$$\times 5 \qquad \times 5$$

RATIONALIZE . . .

When two quantities are related proportionally, the ratio of one quantity to the other is invariant as the numerical values of both quantities change by the same factor.

—Joanne Lobato, Amy Ellis, Randall Charles, and Rose Mary Zbiek (2010, p. 11)

Day 1 Wrap-Up

By the end of Day 1, students had engaged in six different representations of their growing patterns, what I call the "worlds of algebra" (Figure 5.3):

- **Verbal.** Two real-world problem situations were described in natural language.
- **Concrete.** Craft sticks were used to construct polygons, and students' own eyes, ears, noses, and hands were used for verification when necessary.
- **Pictorial/Iconic.** The craft-stick polygons were drawn on the worksheets provided.
- **Tabular/Numeric.** The input-output pairs of values were recorded in function tables.
- **Symbolic.** All function rules had the form $x \times m = y$, where m equaled 3, 4, 5, or 6.
- **Graphical.** A series of points were plotted in the Cartesian plane, corresponding to the ordered pairs of input-output values from the respective function tables.

FIGURE 5.3   The worlds of algebra

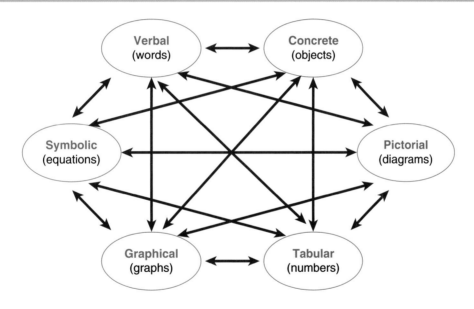

Algebra Connection

- **Multiple Representations.** In 1757, when Euler summarized all work on algebra to that time in his book, *Introduction to Algebra*, which was principally on equation solving, he made not one diagram. The advent of graphing technologies has changed the face of algebra by opening the door to a new language in which to speak about algebra: the *language of representations*. Algebra, especially early algebra, is a way of thinking about and representing all situations—and functional relationships are no exception. The algebraic aspect of functional thinking occurs precisely when children invent—or appropriate—representations to express a generalization of a particular situation or relationship. Traveling back and forth among and within different modes of representation helps learners comprehend new ideas. No representation alone suffices to fully convey the concept of function to a child; what one representation blurs, another often clarifies. It is the totality of representational systems that enriches and deepens the meaning of a concept. With the advent of tablets and other computer technologies in the elementary grades, children are becoming facile with multiple forms of representation at younger ages than they did in the past. Finally, parallel to the outer representations listed above, we mustn't forget the internal representations students develop to interact with new concepts and ideas, resolve ambiguities as they arise, and make sense of connections over time.

• **Graphical Representation.** As teachers, we can't expect students to invent all forms of useful representations spontaneously. Their awareness of, and ability to use, various representations must therefore be systematically encouraged. At the start of the lesson, students revisited function tables. They noticed *numerically*—say in the *quadrilaterals* pattern—that each increment of 1 in the number of quadrilaterals corresponds to an increment of 4 in the number of craft sticks needed. At the end of the lesson, students were exposed for the first time to a new representation: a graph of points in a two-dimensional Cartesian plane, where the horizontal axis represents the number of quadrilaterals, and the vertical axis the number of craft sticks (Figure 5.4).

FIGURE 5.4   Graph of the quadrilaterals (Q) to craft sticks (C) relationship. It depicts *linear* growth.

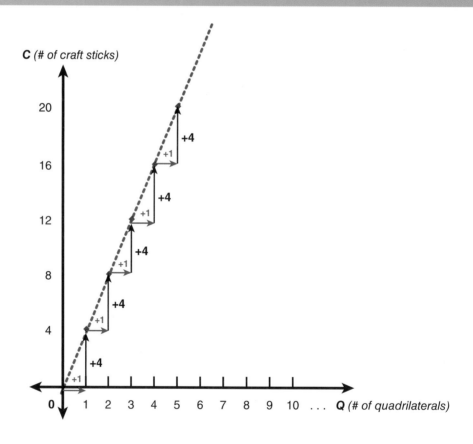

Each point (in red) represents an input-output pair of numbers (Q, C) from Table 5.1. The dotted line through all points confirms they live on the same line, hence the *geometric* meaning of a *linear* function. It makes sense that point (0, 0), the origin, is on the line, since creating zero quadrilaterals requires zero craft sticks.

A closing word on the notion of *slope*: Visualize the profile of a mountain slope as a straight line. There are steep slopes and gentler slopes. *Geometrically,* a slope can be thought of in terms of the amount of slant, measured by the angle the line makes with the horizontal. But *numerically*, it can be thought of as the embodiment of a ratio, like a regular staircase in which each stair has a run of 1 and a rise of 4. (Readers may recall the phrase "rise over run," which is this case is $\frac{4}{1} = 4$.) The higher the rise, the steeper the slope. That explains why a graph of the 10-times table would generate points on a steeper line than a graph of the 4-times table. Finally, for *all* proportional functions $m \times x = y$, the slope is the embodiment of the ratio $\frac{m}{1} = m$.

REFLECT . . .

On the same coordinate system (Figure 5.4), imagine two other lines: Both begin at (0, 0). In one, each stair has a run of 2 and a rise of 8; in the other, each stair has a run of 3 and a rise of 12. Visualize the regular "staircases." What do you observe? What is the slope of each line? What does this mean about the ratios embodied by the slopes?

---

2. Day 2: Pattern Block Fences

Growing Patterns III

We will not revisit here the concept of perimeter, as it was discussed in depth in Exploration I, *Circling Circles*. Rather, we will address the challenge in using manipulatives such as pattern blocks when exploring the perimeter concept.

Imperfect Manipulatives. As with any technology (used here in the broad sense), manipulatives are helpful but often conceal mathematical truths. Consider geometric shapes—flat, tile-like triangles, squares, rhombi, hexagons, and so on—frequently used to study perimeter and area in grades 3–5. Clearly, the physical manipulative must contain the polygon (the outline) *and* its interior region; otherwise it would be too fragile to hold up. But, if teachers don't explicitly distinguish the shape *outlines* (the actual polygons) from their enclosed interior regions, students move on to more abstract mathematics carrying with them the tacit, erroneous definition that a polygon is *the entire shape, outline plus interior*. Fence and garden are not the same!

The second limitation of these practical tools is their thickness. When square tiles are used to model the *area* of a rectangle for example, the joined tiles in the shape of a rectangle (Figure 5.5) actually model *volume*, as students often realize. The point here is not to discourage the use of manipulatives but to encourage their perspicacious use. Model the notion of area by pointing to the *top surface* of the rectangular tiling, preempting the comment, "But that's volume!" which typically arises. The key to guiding students from concrete tool to abstract concept lies in how we use these tools and orchestrate discourse around them.

FIGURE 5.5 The top surface of the tile arrangement models *area*; its outline models *perimeter*.

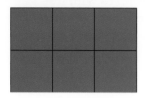

FIGURE 5.6 What is the surface area of each tower of cubes (include the bottom)? As the towers get taller, how does the surface area change?

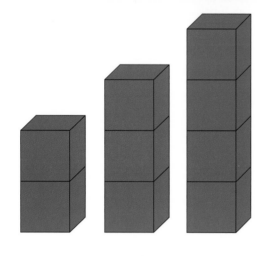

Guiding Questions

In the algebra content standard for grade band 3–5, *Principles and Standards for School Mathematics* (NCTM, 2000) states that students should "have opportunities to make generalizations based on [geometric] patterns" (p. 160). Figure 5.6 is the example provided. This problem concerning surface area, like *Fancy Fences* concerning perimeter, addresses the four fundamental components of algebraic thinking, as stated in the algebra standard (abbreviated here):

- Understanding patterns, relations, and functions
- Representing and analyzing situations using algebraic symbols
- Using mathematical models to represent and understand quantitative relationships
- Analyzing change in various contexts

It is important to realize that such problems represent a huge shift from the types of problems found in 20th century elementary math books, which favored computational skills and memorized procedures as a preparation for higher mathematics. At best, one may have found a single-numerical-answer question addressing the surface area of a particular cube tower. "Understanding the increasingly complex mathematics of the 21st century will require children to have a type of elementary school experience that goes beyond arithmetic and computational fluency to attend to the deeper underlying structure of mathematics" (Blanton & Kaput, 2011, p. 8). Cube-tower and fancy-fence type problems, once the domain of secondary mathematics, are becoming commonplace in grades 3–5.

Algebra Connection

- **The Interplay Between Stasis and Change.** Of the four pillars of algebraic thinking listed above, the fourth has been the least addressed so far in this book.

There are two perspectives from which we can examine patterns:

1. We can study a pattern by describing what *is*. In this case we are focusing on *stasis* (or *state*). Stasis refers to *the static features* of an object or a phenomenon, to *what does not change* or *what remains constant.*

2. We can also study a pattern by describing the way(s) in which it can be continued or extended. In this case, we are focusing on *change*. Change refers to the *dynamic features* of an object or phenomenon; it is addressed by questions such as "How does the perimeter change with the addition of one more hexagon?" or "Predict the perimeter of the 25th hexagon fence."

Stasis and change are distinct yet related in the flow of experience; distinguishing one from the other helps us make sense of our experience. Instinctively, students move back and forth between the two as they examine the patterns in their lives. "The relationship between stasis and change provides a conceptual underpinning for much of the work students do with patterns and functions in grades K–12" (Smith, 2003, p. 137). In the next section, we will see how covariational thinking is analyzing change and correspondence thinking is analyzing stasis.

3. Functional Thinking

Functional thinking—or reasoning and working with relationships in quantitative situations—is well established in the mathematics education community as a pathway into early algebra (Cai & Knuth, 2011; NCTM, 2000; NGA/CCSSO, 2010). The emphasis on functions in the elementary grades can be explained in part by a growing emphasis, in our technological world, on a *functions-based approach* to algebra in secondary schools, prominent in North America (Chazan & Yerushalmy, 2003). The two types of functional thinking, covariational and correspondence, were observed as students examined function tables in *Growing Patterns I–III.* Recursive thinking is subsumed under covariational thinking.

Algebra Connection

- **Covariational Thinking (the Change Perspective).** The prefix *co* means together or simultaneously. *Variation* means change. Young students instinctively explore function tables from a *covariation* viewpoint. In all the patterns discussed, the 4th–5th grade combo class students were drawn by the sequential, row-to-row changes of +1 in the input column and of + *c* in the output column. (In this discussion, *c* stands for *constant* change or synonymously *constant* difference.) They had an informal taste of functions with a *constant rate of change* (a phrase they will ultimately adopt), all of which are *linear*. The covariational perspective embraces the *actions of change*, occurring simultaneously (vertically in the function table) in both columns. This approach of observing the change from one stage to the next, and expressing each stage *in terms of the previous stage* (e.g., the 6th hexagon-fence perimeter equals the 5th perimeter *plus 4*), involves *recursive thinking.* Recursive thinking comes naturally to children. Counting is a recursive *mental* process: "Add 1" to any number to get the following one. Walking is a recursive *physical* action: Take *one* step at a time to move forward. "Recursive thinking is a vital part of algebraic thinking and reasoning at all levels . . . Simply put, recursive thinking is a habit of mind that embraces step-by-step sequential change" (Bezuszka & Kenney, 2008, p. 81). A note about sequences: While examining the growth of a sequence such as 2, 4, 6, 8, 10, and so on, statements such as "they're growing by 2" are indications of a child thinking recursively. In the absence of a second quantity, no covariation analysis is possible. With a small change however—namely, by introducing the counting numbers to denote the term positions (in red on the right)—any sequence can be transformed into a function, thus offering children opportunities for covariational thinking:

1	2	3	4	5	6	7...
↓	↓	↓	↓	↓	↓	↓
2	4	6	8	10	12	14...

- **Correspondence Thinking (the Stasis Perspective).** While the covariational perspective in analyzing a function focuses on the change in variables, the *correspondence* perspective focuses on what remains unchanged (stasis). From this viewpoint, students move beyond the step-by-step changes toward an invariable, *generalized rule* that produces the output for *any* input. This perspective requires looking at the function globally (horizontally in the function table) and noticing that a *same correspondence rule* pairs each input with its corresponding output. Next, it requires describing this consistent rule in English, and/or expressing it algebraically in the form of an equation if students are ready and able to. In the elementary grades, the equation is called the *function rule* or simply the *rule*. Raven and Donnell, along with a few others, found functions rules for their fence's perimeter pattern. The leap from seeing the recursive patterns in the input and output variables to expressing the generalization was challenging for most students. Why? Because looking *down* their function tables required *additive* thinking; looking *across*, however, required *multiplicative* thinking—another reason for the introduction of more multiplicative thinking in grades 3–5!

Instructional strategies can help students along the path to generalization. *Circling Circles* and *Fancy Fences* illustrate some of these strategies:

- Use concrete models to help with visualization; this helps students connect the concrete with the symbolic; in our case, shape with number.
- Don't always list consecutive numbers in both columns; this dissuades students from looking covariationally at the patterns.
- Move students away from computing the specific and toward reasoning about the general by asking for finite yet large function values that are impossible to compute.
- Guide students to connect the different features of the concrete model with the different symbols (numbers or letters) in function tables and/or with function rules.
- Practice with different patterns of change. Students come to see patterns of patterns, such as the two constant-change patterns, $x \times m = y$ or $x \times m + c = y$.

REMEMBER . . .

Covariational patterns of change in input and output variables attract children. As a result of algebra training, adults often rush students to formulate a function correspondence rule. Covariation is concrete; correspondence is abstract. A good grasp of the former leads to a deeper understanding of the latter. Thus, students need time to explore *all patterns* inside functions before rushing to answer "What's the function rule?"

—Monica Neagoy (2012, p. 138)

Delving Deeper

4. Class Sharing

This section mainly addresses the difficulty behind Question 3. It also includes a comment on generalization, the object of Question 4, already discussed at length.

Question 3: The 62-Inch-Long Perimeter

In the discussion below on how to find the number of unit blocks that correspond to a fence with a 62-inch perimeter, U denotes the input variable (# of unit polygons) and P denotes the output variable (perimeter in inches), as used in the lesson.

Algebra Connection

• **Using Recursive Thinking.** Research experts on recursion state that recursive thinking is a vital part of algebra. It is possible, but tedious, to answer Question 3 using recursion. In the house-fence example, by repeatedly adding +3 in the P column, we eventually arrive at the value 62 in row 20: So the 20-unit fence is the answer (Table 5.5, orange row).

• **Using the Function Rule.** Some students found the function rule. But most fell into the same trap, which we will call here the incorrect use of *reversibility* (NCTM, 2000; NGA/CCSSO, 2010). Reversibility of all actions is an important mathematical habit of mind exemplified by the following: "If *multiplying U by 3* gives me P, then *dividing P by 3* gives me U." In arithmetic and in algebra, we say that multiplication and division are *inverse* operations. But in *Growing Patterns III*, all four function rules contained a "+2" following the multiplication of U by 1, 2, 3, or 4 (Figure 5.7): Reversing the action is more difficult in this case.

Taking the house-fence example again, reversing the actions requires *first* subtracting 2, and *second* dividing by 3:

If $(U \times 3) + 2 \to P$, then $(P - 2) \div 3 \to U$

(The parentheses in each case indicate the *first* action.)

Some students *first* divided by 3, and *second* subtracted 2. This was incorrect but not surprising, as they were only beginning to appreciate the importance of the order of operations. Done correctly, $(62 - 2) \div 3 \to 60 \div 3 \to 20$, corroborating that fence #20 (a 20-unit fence) is the answer to the question (Table 5.5).

Question 4: Strategies Toward a Generalization

We have already stated that generalization is an algebraic habit of mind par excellence. Moreover, it is at the core of all of mathematics. Studies of early childhood show that children are adept at generalizations from a very young age. They learn by ascending from *concrete observations* to generalizations and by descending from generalizations back to concrete examples. As they mature, students learn to generalize from *logical necessity* as well. For example, a child who states, "The sum of two odd numbers is always even, because the two 'lonely people' in the odd numbers get together, and so everyone has a partner," generalizes out of logical necessity that combining any two odds *must yield an even* (Tierney & Monk, 2008). Both forms of generalization can be cultivated. Teachers who are observant of what students do, and attentive to what they say, can help foster the habit of looking for the general in the particular.

TABLE 5.5　House fence function table

House-Fence Group	
U	P
1	5
2	8
3	11
4	14
5	17
.	
.	
.	
20	62

$\times 3 + 2$
$U \longrightarrow P$

FIGURE 5.7　Function rules of *Fancy Fences* growing patterns

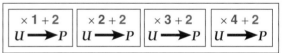

Whenever a teacher becomes aware of an implicit generality in some particular instances, there is an opportunity to make a choice: to pause for a moment and prompt learners to try to express that generality before continuing, or keep going. (Mason, 2008, p. 80)

Algebra Connection

• **A Common Opportunity.** Suppose a third-grade student remarks, offhandedly, "3 × 5 is the same as 5 × 3." A teacher should pause and ask questions such as, "How do you know?" or "Can you show us why?" or "Does it work with other numbers?" or "Do you think it works with *any two numbers*?" and finally, "How might you convince the class that your conjecture (about multiplication) is always true?" This last question prods students forward onto the path of mathematical *proof*, the one feature that distinguishes mathematics from other disciplines. Mathematically proficient students "make conjectures and build a logical progression of statements to explore the truth of their conjectures" (CCSS.Math.Practice.MP3). Generalization is intimately connected to proof, since the statements we seek to prove in mathematics involve *all* cases, be they numbers, operations, shapes, functions, or something else. Figure 5.8 illustrates an acceptable proof of the conjecture, "3 × 5 = 5 × 3" for use at the third- to fifth-grade level.

FIGURE 5.8   An acceptable "proof" of the conjecture "3 × 5 = 5 × 3" for grades 3–5

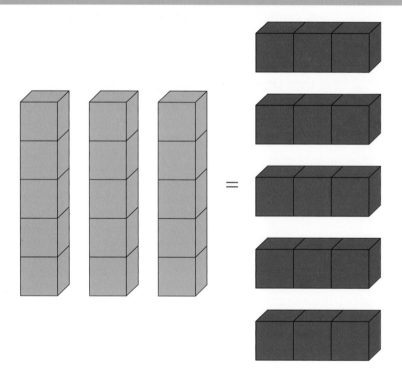

The commutative property of multiplication ($a \times b = b \times a$, for all numbers a and b) is central to algebra, as are other operation properties. Too often, these properties are passed down *to* students as givens without discussion. If students don't engage with these ideas, they don't make sense of them. Further, when these same properties come up in the context of variables, they seem devoid of meaning. "Teachers should look for opportunities for students to revise, expand, and update generalizations they have made" (NCTM, 2000, p. 192).

5. Reflecting on the Work

Embryonic Symbolic Thinking

Symbolic thinking, like functional thinking and representational thinking, is a component of early algebraic thinking. In symbolic thinking, "the focus is on the symbols themselves, without regard for what they might refer to" (Smith, 2008, p. 133). Students in the combo class were not at that level yet, but some were closer than others. While we have already noted that in early algebra one need not use symbols to express a generalization,

> mathematically proficient students . . . bring . . . to bear on problems involving quantitative relationships: the ability to *decontextualize*—to abstract a given situation and represent it symbolically and manipulate the representing symbols as if they have a life of their own, without necessarily attending to their referents. (CCSS.Math.Practice.MP2)

In the *Fancy Fences* lesson, most students needed to refer to the concrete manipulatives and the derived measures in order to give meaning to the symbolic equations. However, there were exceptions like Donnell, who could reason abstractly without referring to any *particular* fence number. As students move from concrete to abstract, the embodied meanings of symbols don't completely disappear. Rather, they morph into more abstract ones. Symbolic thinking occurs gradually. In becomes formalized by high school. We must therefore be patient with and realistic about students in grades 3–5: Their journey has only just begun.

A Pattern of Patterns

Fancy Fences ended with four fancy functions:

1. $(U \times 1) + 2 \rightarrow P$ (triangle fence)

2. $(U \times 2) + 2 \rightarrow P$ (square fence)

3. $(U \times 3) + 2 \rightarrow P$ (pentagon or house fence)

4. $(U \times 4) + 2 \rightarrow P$ (hexagon fence)

In this chapter, we have seen how patterns can be transformed into functions, and we have explained that functional relationships constitute a pillar of 21st century early algebraic thinking. For teachers to appreciate how the algebraic landscape has shifted from equations at center stage to functions at center stage, we use the fourth function, $(U \times 4) + 2 \rightarrow P$, in equation form, $(U \times 4) + 2 = P$, as our example.

Algebra Connection

• **Set Perspective: Equation $(U \times 4) + 2 = 14$.** For most of the 20th century, solving equations such as $(U \times 4) + 2 = 14$ was central to first-year algebra curricula in the United States. Here the letter U is called the *unknown*. Even though this equation can be solved mentally, the algebraic manipulations that take us from "unknown to known" are worth a closer look:

$$
\begin{aligned}
(U \times 4) + 2 &= 14 \\
- 2 \quad &\quad -2 \\
\hline
(U \times 4) + 0 &= 12 \\
(U \times 4) &= 12 \\
\frac{(U \times 4)}{4} &= \frac{\mathbf{12}}{4} \\
U &= 3
\end{aligned}
$$

The symbolic manipulations involve one fundamental property of equality, two fundamental properties of addition, and one fundamental property of multiplication, all of which students should be sensitized to early on:

a. **Additive Property (of equality).** Adding or subtracting any number to both sides of an equation yields an equivalent equation. Here, we subtracted 2 from both sides.

b. **Additive Inverse (a property of addition).** Every number x has an additive inverse (or an "opposite"), labeled $-x$, such that $x + (-x) = (-x) + x = 0$. To isolate $(U \times 4)$ on the left side, we chose to subtract 2 from both sides, since $+ 2 - 2 = 0$.

c. **Additive Identity (a property of addition).** Zero is the additive identity element for addition, because adding it to any number leaves the number unchanged (*identical* to itself). In algebra we write, $x + 0 = 0 + x = x$, for all x. Here $(U \times 4) + 0 = U \times 4$.

Photo by Wendy Glasser

d. **Multiplicative Inverse (a property of multiplication).** Every number x, except 0, has a multiplicative inverse (or a "reciprocal"), labeled $\frac{1}{x}$, such that $x \times \frac{1}{x} = \frac{1}{x} \times x = 1$. To isolate U on the left side, we chose to multiply by $\frac{1}{4}$ on both sides (penultimate line), since $4 \times \frac{1}{4} = 1$; thus $(U \times 4) \times \frac{1}{4}$ or $\frac{(U \times 4)}{4} = U$.

From this classic perspective, solving an algebraic equation yields a "solution *set*." Our equation yields the solution set {3} with *one* element. Substituting 3 for U, we get $(3 \times 4) + 2 = 14$, thus verifying that 3 is the correct solution. So, $(U \times 4) + 2 = 14$ is an *algebraic equation* with *a particular solution*. For the hexagon fence, it means that a fence with a perimeter of 14 units requires 3 hexagon units. The solution is represented *graphically* by *one point* on a line (see Chapter 6, Figure 1, point (3, 14) on the hexagon-fence graph).

• **Function Perspective: Equation $(U \times 4) + 2 = P$.** Broadening our perspective, the mathematical model $(U \times 4) + 2 = P$ expresses an *infinite set of whole-number pairs*, U and P, whose relationship is defined by the function rule. In the context of our hexagon-fence problem, it yields *all possible solutions* of the hexagon-fence problem in the form of ordered pairs of numbers, where the first is the fence number (number of hexagonal units in the fence), and the second its perimeter: (1, 6), (2, 10), (3, 14) . . . The equation $(U \times 4) + 2 = P$ represents a functional *relationship* between quantities U and P that vary together. Quantities that take on a range of values are called *variables. Graphically,* the ordered pairs are *points* on a line (see Chapter 6, Figure 1, entire hexagon-fence graph).

Closing Thoughts

I hope I have stimulated my readers to use new ways of fostering functional thinking, representational thinking, and symbolic thinking in our young. To this end, we must examine carefully the instructional tasks and sequences we design for our students. We must seek to surpass single-answer questions and broaden narrow computational tasks into opportunities for students to build and analyze patterns, make conjectures, explore relationships, and generalize with these relationships. I end with a screenshot (Figure 5.9) of handheld graphing technology that has become commonplace in many middle schools today. It displays simultaneously three representations of the simple linear function "input $\times$ 2 = output": symbolic, graphical, and tabular. Knowing that this awaits our students around the corner makes it imperative that we explore these notions with them *now* so that their experiences with functions and algebra *later* will be richer, deeper, and more meaningful. Guide your students' first steps on the path to a functions-based approach to algebra.

FIGURE 5.9   **Simultaneous display of the symbolic, tabular, and graphic representations of the "double function" on a handheld computer**

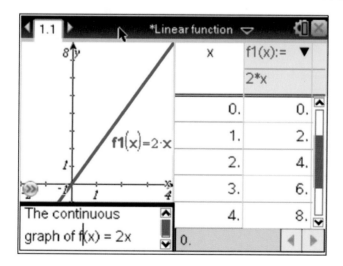

6

Beyond *Fancy Fences*

More Problems to Explore

Answers and explanations to the nontrivial questions in this chapter can be found in the Appendix, page 195.

I. Next Steps

1. Answering Student Questions

On Day 3 of *Fancy Fences*, Mr. Ramsey addressed student questions that arose from observation of the *pattern of patterns* that emerged at the end of the *Fancy Fences* lesson. (Refer back to Chapter 4, Table 4.4.)

- "If the red numbers (the constant changes) are all "+", why is it "×" in the rule?" (For example, the house-fence perimeters change by + 3, but the rule is × 3 + 2.)
- "How come all rules have a + 2?"
- "Would the pattern keep on going if we used octagons or even bigger shapes?"

He also revisited Guiding Question #3 from the lesson: "How many unit polygons are in a fence of perimeter 62?"

2. Graphing Patterns With Technology

The technology-curious students revisited the graphing software used Day 1. This time, they entered the four sets of (U, P) ordered number

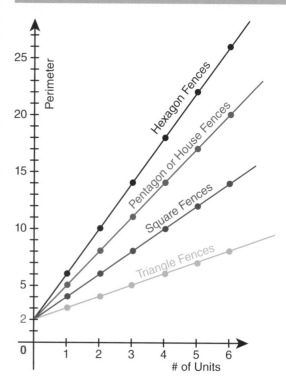

FIGURE 6.1   Four polygon-fence functions graphed as sets of colinear points in the Cartesian plane

pairs from the function tables, and the technology plotted before them four sets of points, all on the same graph (Figure 6.1). They were amazed. As before, Mr. Ramsey added four lines to confirm that each set of points live on a same line (the root of *linear*). Students observed that the graphs of function rules—$\times 1 + 2, \times 2 + 2, \times 3 + 2,$ and $\times 4 + 2$—all converge at the point (0, 2), whereas the graphs of the times tables, $\times 1, \times 2, \times 3, \times 4, \times 5 \ldots$ had converged at (0, 0), the origin. These surprising images, engraved in their memories, will serve them in middle school when they will study *linear* functions of this same form: U will be x, y will be P, and the perimeter fence functions will be written as $x \times m + b \to y$, better known as $y = mx + b$. Seeds of proportionality, linearity, and the function-graph connections had been planted. Did students understand everything? Of course not! Were they intrigued by novel technology and filled with wonder and curiosity? Absolutely!

READ . . .

Whenever the first encounter with an object surprises us, and we judge it to be new or very different from what we knew before . . . we are caused to wonder at it. . . . [Wonder] makes us learn and retain in our memory things that until then we were ignorant of.

—Philip Fisher (1998, pp. 45–46), translating René Descartes' definition of *wonder*

---

3. Growing Patterns IV

I also left Mr. Ramsey with a final exploration, Growing Patterns IV: The same-shaped polygonal fences but this time made with unit logs, modeled by craft sticks. (See the worksheet in the Appendix, page 198.)

II. For Your Own Learning

1. Function Misconceptions

The concept of function is complex. Research studies highlight misconceptions students accumulate over the school years. As with all misconceptions, the longer they are held, the harder it is for students to unlearn them. Early experiences with functions can help prevent two particular misconceptions.

Misconception 1: Constant Functions Are Not Functions

A function is called *constant* if all inputs are assigned *the same output.* Thus, the outputs remain *constant* as the inputs vary (Figure 6.2). Students who think a constant relation is not a function misinterpret the function definition. Recall that a function is a special kind of relation between two sets of variables—inputs and outputs—that pair each input with *exactly one output. Exactly one* output per input is interpreted as a *different* output per input. The function definition makes no mention of difference: It does not exclude the case where *all inputs* are paired with *one and the same output.* Constant

FIGURE 6.2   Arrow mapping and function table of the constant function $n \to 2$

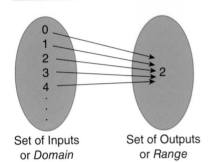

Set of Inputs
or *Domain*

Set of Outputs
or *Range*

Input	Output
0	2
1	2
2	2
3	2
4	2
...	...

relations, such as a constant temperature (output) over an extended number of hours in a day (inputs) are therefore functions, albeit boring ones, to study.

Misconception 2: All Functions Can Be Represented by Algebraic Rules

Since primary students essentially work with numerical functions and middle and high school students essentially work with algebraic functions, students leave high school with the misconception that every function can be represented by a numerical, and later an algebraic, *rule*. Figure 6.3 displays the algebraic rules of two simple functions of natural variables n (f and g) and two advanced functions of real variables x (h and k). Moreover, students think that inputs and outputs must be *numbers*. To dispel this misconception, students must engage with functions that

1. *Do not have* numerical or algebraic correspondence rules, and

2. *Do not have* numerical inputs or outputs.

FIGURE 6.3   Algebraic function rules: n is used for natural numbers and x for real numbers

$$f: n \to n + 4 \qquad g: n \to 3n - 2 \qquad h: x \to 10x^2 - 7x + \tfrac{1}{2} \qquad k: x \to \frac{\sqrt{-5x + 8}}{\frac{1}{x}}$$

"Polygon $\to$ # of sides" is a function, because every polygon has a unique number of sides (Table 6.1a). The function rule is *verbal*: "Count the polygon's sides." "Child $\to$ Mother" also has a verbal rule: "has a mother," assumed to be the *biological* mother (Table 6.1b). In this case, neither inputs nor outputs are numbers. Such examples help broaden the function concept beyond a mere *formula between input and output numbers*.

2. Expressions, Equations, and Functions

Middle school students tend to confuse *expressions* and *equations*, on one hand, and *equations* and *functions* on the other. Aware of these common confusions, elementary teachers can get students off to a good start.

Expression Versus Equation

Rush to Solve. Expressions are the building blocks of equations and functions. For this reason, students rush to solve them. But there is nothing to *solve*. An expression *describes* a quantity under study. In *Fancy Fences*, $5 \times 3 + 2$ was a *numerical* expression describing the

TABLE 6.1 Examples of functions that *are not* relationships between sets of numbers and *cannot* be expressed numerically or algebraically by a formula or rule

Input: Polygon	Triangle	Square	Rectangle	Trapezoid	Rhombus	Pentagon	Hexagon …
Output # of sides	3	4	4	4	4	5	6 …

(a)

Input: Child's Name	Edu	Olivia	Tyron	Ana-Maria	Felipe	Jared	Tasha …
Output: Child's Mother's Name	Mrs. Smith	Mrs. Smith	Mrs. Tyrone	Mrs. Garcia	Mrs. Garcia	Mrs. Abeje	Mrs. Brown …

(b)

perimeter of a 5-unit house fence, and $U \times 3 + 2$ an *algebraic* expression for a U-unit house fence, where U is *any number* of units. If students spent more time working with expressions as objects of study—writing, comparing, and finding *equivalent* expressions, they would realize they're not about *solving*. Table 6.2 shows two parallel sets of expressions; explaining their equivalence doesn't require solving but rather knowing properties of operations. Recognizing that $(3a)(3b)$ and $9ab$ are equivalent but that $\frac{x+y}{x+5}$ and $\frac{y}{5}$ are *not* will be a vital skill in middle school.

TABLE 6.2 Two sets of parallel equivalent expressions

Numerical Expressions	Algebraic Expressions
$5 \times (3 + 4)$	$a \times (b + c)$
$(5 \times 3) + (5 \times 4)$	$(a \times b) + (a + c)$
$5 \times 3 + 5 \times 4$	$ab + ac$

Rush to Compute. The rush to solve comes from the rush to compute, ingrained in the early years, when students first encounter the equals sign. Well-intended parents flash cards at children with equations such as $4 + 5 = \Box$ or $8 - 5 = \Box$. The equals sign triggers the implicit command to *act*. The action required is *to compute* and the goal is *to produce a numerical answer*. A famous study confirmed children's narrow interpretation of equality. Given the equation $8 + 4 = \Box + 5$, surprisingly 49% of third- and fourth-graders and 76% of fifth- and sixth-graders gave the answer 12 (Falkner, Levi, & Carpenter, 1999). To foster the meaning of equality as *equivalence*, time would be well spent in grades 3–5 verifying equivalences such as the ones below, *without computing*. After all, in algebra, $a + b$ or $2x + 1$ *cannot* be computed!

- **Grade 3.** $14 + 35 = 16 + 33$, because one number increases by 2 ($14 \rightarrow 16$) while the other decreases by 2 ($35 \rightarrow 33$). The total change is $+2 - 2 = 0$.
- **Grade 4.** $58 - 56 + 83 = 85$, because $58 - 56 = 2$, and 85 is 2 more than 83.
- **Grade 5.** $102 \times 43 = 51 \times 86$, because one number is divided by 2 ($102 \rightarrow 51$), while the other is multiplied by 2 ($43 \rightarrow 86$). The total change is $\times \frac{2}{2}$ or $\times 1$.

Equation Versus Function

Chapter 5, Section 5, discussed the difference between equation and function.

3. Function Notation

Historically, in the evolution of mathematics, notation is introduced last, after the concepts are well developed and people need to encode new concepts. The same is true in the elementary classroom. If we introduce symbols prematurely, students memorize them, but they are devoid of meaning. Teachers must work with students to gradually introduce symbols. Students naturally propose or accept shortcut notations, such as **U** for *number* of **unit polygons,** or **P** for the **perimeter** of the fence. In grades 3–5, students see a function as an *action*, going from input to output, so the arrow precedes the equals sign in function notation. Below is an evolution of function notation for the simple doubling function.

Input times 2 gives output (early elementary)

$\Downarrow$

Input $\times$ 2 $\rightarrow$ Output; $I \times 2 \rightarrow O$; and $I \times 2 = O$ (upper elementary)

$\Downarrow$

$x \times 2 = y$; $2 \cdot x = y$; $2x = y$; and $y = 2x$ (middle school)

$\Downarrow$

$f: x \rightarrow 2x$ and $f(x) = 2x$ (late middle and high school)

(*Note*: I and O stand for input and output, but any letters students pick are good.)

4. Multiple Uses of Variables

Variables denoted by letters—found in expressions, equations, and functions—are central to algebra. Equations and functions both contain equals signs. Depending on the context, the equals sign has different meanings, and consequently so do the variables (Table 6.3). Teachers must be aware of the different kinds of equations and the

TABLE 6.3 Meanings of equations and letters they contain

Meaning of Equations	Interpretation of letters in equations
1. Formulas *Example (area of a rectangle):* $A = l \times w$	Letters are **labels** for formula components. Formulas provide useful information.
2. Properties of operations *Example (commutativity):* $n \times m = m \times n$	Young students learn operation properties. Letters are **generalized natural numbers**.
3. Special Algebraic Identities *Example:* $(x - y) \times (x + y) = x^2 - y^2$	Algebra students must know special identities. Letters stand for **real numbers**.
4. Function rules *Example:* $I \times 4 \rightarrow O$ (ES); $y = 4x$ (MS)	Letters are **variables;** they actually *vary* over a range of values.
5. Equations (to solve) *Example:* $2n + 4 = 8$ (*Solution:* $n = 2$)	Letters stand for **unknowns** to solve for.

corresponding interpretations of variables (Usiskin, 1988) if they are to cultivate in future algebra students a deeper understanding of algebra's staple. People who took algebra decades ago think of "variable" as synonymous with "unknown." In fact *only one category of equations* contains letters that are unknowns *to be solved for.* (*Note*: The use of letters as *parameters* is beyond the scope of this book.)

5. Families of Functions

Studying functions from a covariational perspective is not only natural to children but also useful. The change in the output value as the input value increases by 1 will become a function's *rate of change* or *growth rate* in middle school. By high school, students

---

FIGURE 6.4 (a) A *linear* pattern of L-shaped figures made with unit tiles; (b) an *exponential* pattern of rectangles obtained by repeatedly folding a piece of paper; and (c) a *quadratic* pattern of areas of consecutive perfect squares

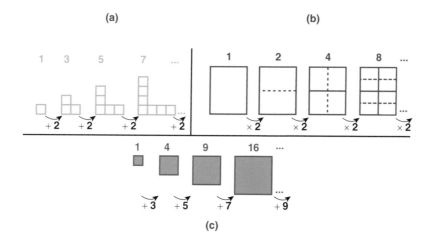

---

differentiate between *average* and *instantaneous* rates of change, the latter being the *derivative*. Three main function families studied in middle school are the *linear*, *exponential*, and *quadratic*. Younger children experience all three in the form of patterns. A key criterion for differentiating them is their pattern of growth (or decay).

Adding or subtracting a constant characterizes the growth pattern of a *linear* pattern (Figure 6.4a). Multiplying or dividing by a constant characterizes the growth pattern of an *exponential* pattern (Figure 6.4b). Increases (decreases) that are *not* constant, but change themselves at a constant rate characterize the growth pattern of a *quadratic* pattern (Figure 6.4c; the increments themselves change by + 2). Recall that any pattern can be turned into a function by making the counting numbers the input values and the pattern terms the output values. Table 6.4 shows the function table of pattern 6.5a turned into a function. (*Note*: Suggested explorations 3, 4, and 5, in Section III of this chapter, offer one of each type of pattern.)

TABLE 6.4 Pattern of L-shaped figures, made of unit tiles (Figure 6.4a), turned into a function

Input Figure Number	Output Number of unit tiles
1	1
2	3
3	5
4	7
. . .	. . .

III. For Your Students' Learning

1. Function Table Puzzles

Function tables with missing values help students see inverse relationships between operations (Figure 6.5). Tables can have either inputs or outputs missing (c and d) or some of each (a and b). Notice that rows are not consecutive. Tables may be simplified to include a set of *consecutive* rows. Use different letters for *I* (input) and *O* (output).

FIGURE 6.5 Function-table puzzles

Function Rule: $I + 5 \rightarrow O$	
Input	Output
0	
	6
3	
	9
7	
	15
. . .	. . .

(a)

Function Rule: $I - 2 \rightarrow O$	
Input	Output
2	
	1
5	
	5
	6
13	
. . .	. . .

(b)

Function Rule: $I \times 3 \rightarrow O$	
Input	Output
	3
	9
	12
	18
	33
	60
. . .	. . .

(c)

Function Rule: $I \times 5 - 2 \rightarrow O$	
Input	Output
0	
1	
5	
7	
10	
50	
. . .	. . .

(d)

2. Multiple Representations

Select a function with a simple rule like "input + 5 → output." Over time, explore *different* representations of this *same* function. Ensure that students understand the *unvarying* mathematical structure of the relationships represented in *varying* forms and are able to go back and forth between representations. Introduce students to at least three representations (Figure 6.6). Post student-created examples of different representations and label them accordingly. This is a nice way for students to learn!

3. Hexagon and Square Sandwiches: Proportional Relationships

With simple geometric shapes, have students construct relationships between larger shapes and smaller "unit" shapes that can be combined and arranged to create the larger shapes, and record them in function tables. Figure 6.7 illustrates two examples.

Proportional thinking is difficult, even for middle school students, but exposure begins in elementary mathematics. Hold up a yellow hexagon with six green triangles on top and ask, "What is the *relationship* between the yellow hexagon and the green triangles?" Settle on the language, "a one-to-six relationship." Next, hold up two hexagon sandwiches and ask the same question. Students will answer, "two-to-twelve." (You can share that later on they will use the notation 1:6 and 2:12). Probe further: "Is two hexagons to twelve triangles the same *relationship* as one hexagon to six triangles?" Many students

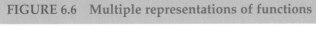

FIGURE 6.6 Multiple representations of functions

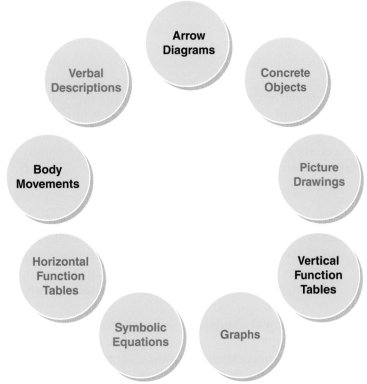

FIGURE 6.7 Planting seeds of proportional thinking: (a) 1-to-6 ratio, (b) 1-to-4 ratio

(a)

Input: # of hexagons	1	2	3	4	5	6 ...	*I*
Output: # of unit triangles	6	12	18	24	30	36. . .	*I* × **6** = **O**

(b)

Input: # of gray squares	1	2	3	4	5	6 ...	*I*
Output: # of blue squares	4	8	12	16	20	24. . .	*I* × **4** = **O**

will say no, because they see the parts of a ratio as separate numbers. Insisting on the word *relationship* will foster gradual understanding of ratio. Students will come to see any combination, say 4:24, as an iteration of the basic ratio 1:6. We will see in Chapter 10 that when fractions represent ratios, addition written as $\frac{1}{6}+\frac{1}{6}+\frac{1}{6}+\frac{1}{6}+=\frac{1+1+1+1}{6+6+6+6}=\frac{4}{24}$ makes sense. Understanding equivalent fractions such as $\frac{1}{6}=\frac{4}{24}$ is the basis for understanding proportionality. The hexagon sandwich rule is *linear* (the (I, O) points live on a line).

4. Folding to the Sky

Hold up a regular sheet of paper and fold it in half once, twice, three times, four times, and so on, asking with each fold, "How many rectangular regions am I creating (Figure 6.4 b)? Students record the answers in a function table (Table 6.5). The two first folds engender correct answers, but on the third fold, students often say "six." They're thinking, "Consecutive even numbers: 2, 4, 6, . . . " After modeling five folds, pause to analyze.

TABLE 6.5 Function table showing the number of rectangular regions created by repeatedly folding a sheet of paper in half

Input ize # of folds	Output # of rectangles
0	1
1	2
2	4
3	8
4	16
5	32
. . .	. . .

Growth Pattern. Some students will see the numbers doubling; others will see each number being added to itself in order to produce the next. Seeing the equivalence between the two processes is an important experience in reasoning about numbers. With grade 5 students who are ready, practice exponential notation with powers of 2.

Mathematical Modeling. After six folds, it will be hard to continue. Have a conversation about modeling and the difference between the real world and the mathematical world: Folding becomes impossible, yet continuing the pattern, introduced by the modeling, *is* possible (see Chapter 2 for discussion on modeling). Encourage students to think of other situations, modeled by the same number pattern, that *can continue* in the real world. (*Note*: Have them look up Britney Gallivan, who, while a junior in high school, proved that paper could be folded 12 times!)

Mindboggling. Finally, imagine a huge sheet of paper of consistent thickness, and imagine invisible elves helping you *cut it in half* repeatedly and *stack* the pieces (instead of *folding it in half*). Suppose you wanted to create a million rectangles, one for each person in a large city. How many *virtual cuts* would it take? [*Answer*: Only 20!] Use calculators and multiply by two until six digits appear. *Challenge*: Equipped with a powerful calculator, ask, "How high will the stack be after 50 cuts?" [*Answer*: A whopping 149,000,000 kilometers high!] A standard sheet of paper is about 0.1 mm thick. The virtual stack, after only 50 cut-and-stacks, will be about ¾ the distance from the earth to the sun. That's mindboggling!

5. Connecting Patterns of Numbers to Patterns of Shapes

Begin with a unit tile. Observe its shape (*square*), and record the number 1. Ask students if 1 is odd or even. Once they are clear on odd or even (see Exploration IV in Neagoy, 2012, *Planting the Seeds of Algebra, PreK–2*), have students wrap *consecutive odd numbers* around two sides of the square, using a different color each time. They will observe something beautiful—that the sums of consecutive odd numbers form consecutive squares

(Figure 6.8). Explore the equivalent sum and product expressions. Adventure into exponents with grade 5 students.

Follow-Up. Do the same with *consecutive even numbers*. Instead of wraparound squares, create wraparound rectangles. What is particular about all the rectangles? Can they predict the dimensions of the 5th, 10th, 100th rectangle? Can they generalize?

FIGURE 6.8   Visualizing that "the sum of n consecutive odd numbers equals n^2"

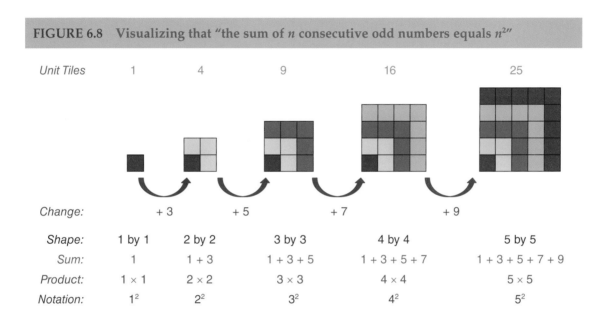

Unit Tiles	1	4	9	16	25
Change:		$+3$	$+5$	$+7$	$+9$
Shape:	1 by 1	2 by 2	3 by 3	4 by 4	5 by 5
Sum:	1	$1+3$	$1+3+5$	$1+3+5+7$	$1+3+5+7+9$
Product:	1×1	2×2	3×3	4×4	5×5
Notation:	1^2	2^2	3^2	4^2	5^2

---

6. Operation Patterns

Operation patterns help children (1) cultivate friendliness with operations, (2) differentiate operation behaviors, and (3) build understanding of operations' properties.

Investigating. In the two patterns below, investigate what happens as one number increases while the other decreases—*by one each time*. Continue until the second sequence reaches 0. What do you notice? Explore other numbers such as $5+5$ and 5×5, or $8+8$ and 8×8. Make two observations about *any* starting values $n+n$ and $n\times n$.

- $10+10 \rightarrow 11+9 \rightarrow 12+8 \rightarrow 13+7 \rightarrow 14+6 \rightarrow 15+5\ldots$
- $10\times10 \rightarrow 11\times9 \rightarrow 12\times8 \rightarrow 13\times7 \rightarrow 14\times6 \rightarrow 15\times5\ldots$

Applying. Apply the patterns discovered above to predict—*without computing*—the answers to the large-number problems below. Then verify with your calculator.

- $100+100=200$. What is $97+103$? What about $85+115$ or $74+126$?

- $500+500=1{,}000$. What is $493+507$? What about $450+550$ or $399+601$?

- $100\times100=10{,}000$. What is 99×101? What about 98×102 or 97×103?

- $500\times500=250{,}000$. What is 499×501? What about 498×502 or 497×503?

Reflection. State two different things you learned from these operation patterns.

7. Thinking Functionally About Operations

Some researchers have shown (Schliemann, Carraher, & Brizuela, 2007) that presenting time-honored elementary mathematics topics such as operations in their *algebrafied personalities* called functions "helps students learn mathematics better and more deeply" (p. 66). Figures 6.9a and 6.9b represent the actions of adding 5 and multiplying by 5 in function-table form, and Figures 6.9c and 6.9d show the plotting of the first six numbers pairs, or points, from the function tables. This exploration casts differences between the effects of addition and multiplication on numbers in yet another light.

FIGURE 6.9   The actions of "adding 5" and "multiplying by 5" conceived and represented as function tables (a) and (b) and as plotted points in the plane (c) and (d)

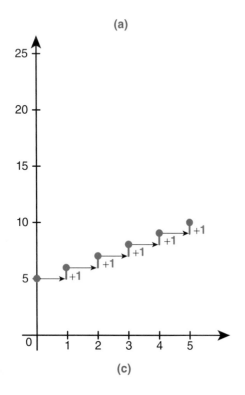

(a)

(c)

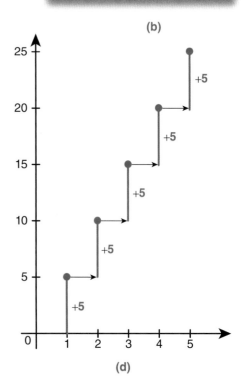

(b)

(d)

8. More Fence or Train Patterns/Functions

Students can build geometric patterns with commercial manipulatives such as pattern blocks (Figure 6.10a) or colored tiles, or with common objects such as craft sticks, toothpicks, or shapes they make (Figure 6.10b). For more challenge, the patterns in Figure 6.10a can be shown with repeating units *touching* rather than apart. Outputs sought can be (1) total number of pieces, (2) perimeter, as in *Fancy Fences*, or (3) area, as a multiple of a specified unit of measure such as the green triangle.

FIGURE 6.10 Lovely patterns made with commercial manipulatives (a) and student cutouts (b)

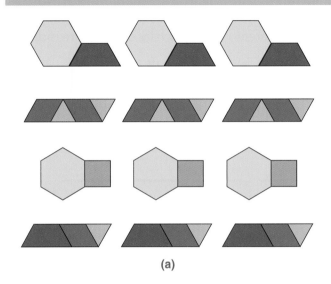

(a)

Photo by Sarah Coste

(b)

9. Practicing With Equivalent Expressions

Example

Take the fifth hexagon fence. The perimeter is the sum of the unit lengths along the figure's outline (assuming each side length is 1). Write at least two different expressions for the perimeter. Compute the *numerical answer* once the class has discussed equivalence among expressions. Such practice prepares students for *algebraic* symbol manipulation.

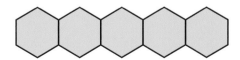

- One student, like Martín, might think: "I add all five individual perimeters (5 x 6) and subtract the side lengths where blocks touch," giving $5 \times 6 - 4 \times 2 = 22$.
- Another student, like Donnell, might count 10 sides *on top*, 10 sides *on the bottom*, and two more for the *left* and *right* ends: $10 + 10 + 2 = 22$.

Photo by Jim Conner and Kathleen Watt

- If given the chance to be creative, students will think of other approaches, such as, "Blocks 1 and 5 have five sides each, yet blocks 2, 3, and 4 have only four": $2 \times 5 + 3 \times 4 = 22$.
- Depending on student readiness, some will be able to write equivalent expressions for 10 or 100 hexagons, or even attempt to generalize (verbally?) for any number of hexagons.

Practice

1. Write an expression for the number of tiles in the border of a 5-by-5 square (Figure 6.11a) and the number of toothpicks to make a 5-square row (Figure 6.11b).

2. Can you approach the problems in a different way, and write other expressions?

3. Repeat for a 10-by-10 square of tiles, and a 10-square row of toothpicks.

4. Can you describe a general expression with words or symbols or both combined?

FIGURE 6.11   (a) 5-by-5 square of unit tiles; (b) 5-square-row made with toothpicks

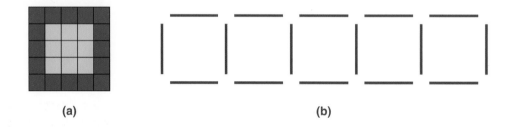

(a)   (b)

10. A Magical Pattern of Numbers (Calculator Exploration)

- *Multiply* 142,857 by 1, 2, 3, 4, 5, and 6 respectively, and record your answers.
- *Divide* 1, 2, 3, 4, 5, and 6 by 7 to compute fraction values $\frac{1}{7}$ through $\frac{6}{7}$.

What do you notice? Adventure beyond 6 and try 7, 8, and 9 in both cases. Surprise? Magicians use this famous cyclical number. I use it in my *MathMagic* show as well!

EXPLORATION III

Making Sense of Multiplication

The Importance of the Distributive Property

The distributive property is possibly the most central idea in elementary school arithmetic, key to understanding the algorithms, at the core of fluent mental calculations, and the logical basis for many rules of algebra that might otherwise seem arbitrary. This property relates multiplication and addition, but children know it long before they even meet multiplication.

—E. Paul Goldenberg, June Mark, and Al Cuoco (2010, p. 548)

RATIONALE FOR EXPLORATION III

- Today we have tools that compute more rapidly and efficiently than we do—and accurately, to boot! Thus, our technological world has raised the bar on our purpose for teaching arithmetic: Algebraic thinking is the new and higher goal.

- The concept of multiplication holds a position of prominence in the mathematics of grades 3–8.

- Students come to grade 3 with multiple images of multiplication upon which we must help them build new ones. They learn in grades 3–5 that multiplication, like division, can model different types of situations.

- Learning multiplication "facts" is much more than committing them to memory. It's knowing, for example, how to find harder facts such as 8×6 using easier facts such as 4×6: One way is by *doubling* 4×6 to get 8×6 $[2 \times (4 \times 6) = 2 \times 24 = 48]$.

- Students must make sense of the multiplication algorithms they use. Properties of operations are fundamental to a conceptual understanding of arithmetic and algebra.

- The distributive property is particularly important, as it bridges grade 3 multiplication to college abstract algebra. Teaching this property can be a challenge for teachers.

- It's vital to lay a solid foundation for multiplication, because the strategies for computing quotients rely on the same understanding of multiplication but cast in terms of division. After all, division is the inverse operation of multiplication!

7

Multiplication Musings

The Lesson (Grades 3–4)

For centuries, many students have learned mathematics, from simple number facts in arithmetic to complex derivatives in calculus, without much understanding. Arithmetic computation is an example of where our classroom practice has not always capitalized on mathematical thinking. Children have been forced to memorize their basic facts and have learned computational algorithms by rote, without making sense of the successive steps that constitute them. Since computation was the heart of elementary mathematics for most of our nation's history, those children became the adults who believed, and perpetuated the belief, that mathematics is mostly about memorizing rules, performing procedures, and solving single-answer problems. The era of national standards has thankfully brought about change. But change takes time.

A big idea central to early childhood mathematics is the concept of addition—and its inverse operation subtraction (see Neagoy, 2012, *Planting the Seeds of Algebra, PreK–2*). The new big idea in grade 3 regarding number and operations, which develops through grades 3, 4, and 5, is the concept of multiplication.

> Not only is the operation of multiplication inextricably connected with the operation of division, but multiplication also plays an integral role in many other significant mathematical topics. These include prime and composite numbers, factorization and prime factorization, factor and greater common factor, multiple and least common multiple, area and volume, proportional reasoning, mean, algebraic expression, linear function, and place value. (Otto, Caldwell, Hancock, & Zbiek, 2011, p. 8)

In Exploration I, we discussed the importance of multiplicative thinking, and in Exploration II, we analyzed multiplicative functions. Exploration III investigates multiplication further, first by attending to third-graders' mental images of multiplication, then by focusing on single-digit multiplication facts, and finally by making sense of multidigit multiplication algorithms. The connecting thread throughout the chapter is the *distributive property of multiplication over addition*, a central concept that weaves through school mathematics curricula, from simple computation to abstract algebra and advanced college mathematics, where operations are no longer the four common ones and the objects operated on are no longer numbers. Even though multiplication has been a focus of grade 3 mathematics for some time, the additional focus on the distributive law of multiplication, its interpretation and representation through the geometric concept of area, and its intimate connection to multidigit algorithms is relatively recent (NCTM, 2000; NGA/CCSSO, 2010). This chapter addresses all three issues.

> ### READ . . .
>
> As students learn about the meaning of multiplication and develop strategies to solve multiplication problems, they will begin to use properties such as distributivity naturally (Schifter, 1999). However, discussion about the properties themselves, as well as how they serve as tools for solving a range of problems, is important if students are to add strength to their intuitive notions and advance their understanding of multiplicative structures.
>
> —National Council of Teachers of Mathematics (2000, p. 161)

Setup

The grade 3 lesson centered on the distributive law of multiplication over addition was inspired by Ms. Clark's question during professional development work. Ms. Clark, a dedicated third-grade teacher in a U.S. urban public school system, was serious about mathematics and volunteered to be on the Common Core math standards committee of her school. She was charged with fleshing out the recent standards, identifying the sections from their current math textbook that were aligned with the Common Core State Standards for Mathematics, and supplementing where the textbook was lacking. When it came to the operations and algebraic thinking standard, she was surprised that the distributive property was emphasized in grade 3, as it was a concept she had learned much later in her high school algebra course. She thought students might react to examples such as $5 \times (3 + 6) = (5 \times 3) + (5 \times 6)$, with, "What's the point?" or, "Why do *three* operations when I can do *two*?" She didn't see the purpose of teaching properties and admitted lacking the farsightedness to see that learning the properties of operations in third grade would prepare students for learning algebra later. Hence, Ms. Clark's request for suggestions gave birth to *Multiplication Musings*. The manipulatives needed for this lesson are shown in Figure 7.1.

FIGURE 7.1 Manipulatives needed for the lesson

Lesson Tool Box

- *"MULTIPLICATION" slide or transparency to project*
- *Colored one-inch tiles*
- *100s chart*
- *White slates and markers*
- *Base-10 blocks*

Discussion

1. Third-Graders' Images of Multiplication (Grade 3)

"Today we're going to explore a new idea and learn a new word that rhymes with *activity* but has *six* syllables!" was my lesson opener. "But before we begin, take out your journals, turn to a new page, and write today's date at the top of the page," I added. Ms. Clark ran a tight ship; her students executed requests in quite an orderly fashion. Third grade journals always remained in the classroom and were stacked in two piles ordered by last names—A to M and N to Z—on a specified shelf. Ayo, the gofer of the day, picked Ruthe to help hand out the journals. I interrupted at that moment to ask for verbs describing the girls' action: Answers "to hand out," "to give out," "to deliver," or "to distribute"—*to every student in the class*—were recorded on the board, a prelude to the new word of the day. Students knew where to get pencils if they had forgotten theirs. Ms. Clark was a pro at organization for less procrastination. Students had a maximum of three minutes to follow a housekeeping instruction, and they were timed by a large sandglass on her desk. Once journals were open, dates inscribed, and students ready, I proceeded: "On the board, I will flash a word you *know*. It will stay up for five *seconds*. After it disappears, you'll have five *minutes* to write down any idea, symbol, problem, drawing, or whatever went through your mind while looking at my word, okay?" The children were intrigued, but they knew by then they were in for a new twist whenever Dr. Monica visited. So they politely obliged. I then projected the word *multiplication* on the white board for five seconds.

Group Share Time

Ms. Clark's lessons commonly included a group-share time, either toward the beginning or at the end, and sometimes both, so these students were accustomed to sharing. They were getting better at listening to one another, since the teacher had instituted an incentive for this courtesy as a new year resolution: A *good-listener* sticker was rewarded whenever a student's comment evidenced attending to, or building upon, another student's statement. The characteristics of a good listener were listed on a poster titled, "Third Grade Behavior Goals." Twenty stickers ensured a "special" reward.

Skip Counting. The first category of shared ideas was mental images, or metaphors, students had of the fairly new operation called multiplication. Some were the products of their second grade experiences, others from earlier that same school year. "Skip counting by 2s or 5s or 10s on a hundred chart," offered Boris. Before he could elaborate, Mia added, "Yeah, like when you color them they make patterns, like straight lines or diagonal lines" (Figure 7.2). By *straight* lines she obviously meant *vertical* lines, a slip Ms. Clark immediately picked up on. While drawing a vertical, horizontal, and diagonal line on the board, she asked, "Which ones are *straight* lines, Mia?" "*All* of them!" Mia quickly replied. "Well then, why did you say, 'straight lines *or* diagonal lines'?" "I meant vertical lines," the clever young girl retorted—a nice aside and good review for the class! Returning to Mia's patterns on the 100 chart, I inquired further, "Does anyone know which skip-counting numbers give *vertical* line[1] patterns?"

"Twos and fives," was Kayin's reply, to which Cesar assented, adding, "Counting by 10 is straight down too!" Impressed by the students' images of patterns on the 100 chart, I inquired after class and found out that these patterns had been the third grade's contribution to a schoolwide art-and-math project a month earlier. Capitalizing on the class's familiarity with these patterns, I asked them to complete my sentences in unison, as I randomly selected multiples: "To get 10, I multiply 2 by . . . " or "To get 20, I multiply 2 by . . . " or "To get 100 I multiply 2 by . . . ." The purpose was to introduce a new word: "All those numbers, 6, 10, 20, 100, and so on are called *multiples of 2*, because I can make that number by multiplying 2 by a whole number." Ms. Clark wrote the vocabulary word on the board, along with an arrow to symbolize the *action of multiplying*, so as to establish the verb–noun connection (Figure 7.3).

---

1. It was obviously a column, not a line, but since Mia used the word, and Ms. Clark clarified her misstatement using the same word, I used *line,* as everyone knew we were speaking of *numbers in a line.*

FIGURE 7.2 Patterns of multiples on the 100 chart

Multiples of 2

1	2	3	4	5	6	7	8	9	10
11	12	13	14	15	16	17	18	19	20
21	22	23	24	25	26	27	28	29	30
31	32	33	34	35	36	37	38	39	40
41	42	43	44	45	46	47	48	49	50
51	52	53	54	55	56	57	58	59	60
61	62	63	64	65	66	67	68	69	70
71	72	73	74	75	76	77	78	79	80
81	82	83	84	85	86	87	88	89	90
91	92	93	94	95	96	97	98	99	100

(a)

Multiples of 3

1	2	3	4	5	6	7	8	9	10
11	12	13	14	15	16	17	18	19	20
21	22	23	24	25	26	27	28	29	30
31	32	33	34	35	36	37	38	39	40
41	42	43	44	45	46	47	48	49	50
51	52	53	54	55	56	57	58	59	60
61	62	63	64	65	66	67	68	69	70
71	72	73	74	75	76	77	78	79	80
81	82	83	84	85	86	87	88	89	90
91	92	93	94	95	96	97	98	99	100

(b)

FIGURE 7.3 Connecting the action of multiplying with the resulting noun, the multiple

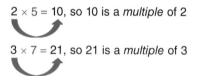

$2 \times 5 = 10$, so 10 is a *multiple* of 2

$3 \times 7 = 21$, so 21 is a *multiple* of 3

Equal Groups. The second category of volunteered ideas consisted of multiplicative problem situations. In all examples given, such as Ruthe's example, multiplication modeled *equal-group* situations: "At snack time, every student gets 3 cookies. How many cookies in all?" After a peer's remark, "You can't do the problem," Ruthe realized a factor was missing. She corrected herself: "Let's pretend there're 10 students in the class, so there's 30 cookies, because 10 times 3 is 30." she explained, delightfully. Referred to as *equal groups* (*equal* or *fair shares* for division) in most elementary textbooks, this class of multiplicative situations is the first students encounter and the easiest to understand, as it appeals to their innate sense of fairness: *Every student has the same share,* and the combined equal shares make up the answer. In this model, the two numbers play different roles: The first number, called the *multiplier*—in this case 10 (students), acts upon the second number, called the *multiplicand*—in this case 3 (cookies) to generate the product. Because teachers and books often mention *repeated addition,*[2] this concept is most students' internal representation of equal-groups situations (Figure 7.4).

FIGURE 7.4 Most students have this mental image for Ruthe's equal-groups problem.

$3 + 3 + 3 + 3 + 3 + 3 + 3 + 3 + 3 + 3 = 30$

Arrays. There was yet a third category of ideas. I had noticed earlier, while students were writing in their journals and Ms. Clark and I were walking among them, that Noah drew a picture of an array. I used that observation to help me get them onto another track of thinking: "Noah, what did *you* write in your journal," pretending I hadn't seen. "I *drew* something, is that OK?" "Absolutely! Human beings express their

---

2. A growing school of thought, based on research evidence, suggests *not* introducing repeated addition from the start. It is, regrettably, the only model most students know.

ideas with words, or pictures, or symbols, or gestures—in so many ways—isn't that what artists do?" They hadn't thought about that, that dancers or painters talk to us through their art. "Did anyone else draw a picture rather than write sentences?" Several students had drawn arrays—of dots, crosses, stars, or daisies. We reviewed the *naming* system for arrays (Figure 7.5), which I insisted was a "choice" mathematicians made: "It could have been the other way around, just like, in traffic lights, we *could* have decided long ago that orange means stop and blue means go. We make choices, then they become rules."

After allotting some think time, I carried on: "So what are some real-life examples of arrays?" At first, there was silence. Obviously, the journal drawings were abstract . . . no real-world referents in mind. Then, a little girl from the back of the class raised her hand: "An egg carton?" she asked timidly. "Excellent! Can you name that array?" I probed. "Two by six?" she answered, with the same hesitation (Figure 7.6). Anthony begged to differ, "It depends how you hold it." "Correct. You are both correct," I settled. "Since the 12 eggs inside the carton are neither on the book page, nor on your journal page, nor on a computer screen, it really *depends* on how you look at them. A 12-egg array has two names, '2-by-6' and '6-by-2,'" I resolved. Of course, if one considers the label *on* the carton, one could argue it's 2-by-6, but the children where discussing the eggs *inside*.

Ms. Clark and I gave other examples like fruit trees in orchards, chairs in an auditorium, students' lockers, teachers' mail cubbies against a wall, and cells in calendars and spreadsheets.

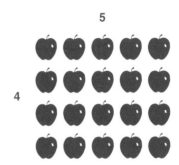

FIGURE 7.5 An array with 4 rows and 5 columns, called a "4-by-5 array," represents 4×5.

FIGURE 7.6 An array of 12 eggs in a carton has two names: "2-by-6" and "6-by-2."

2. Stuck on the Distributive Property of Multiplication (Grade 3 Continued)

As explained in the section "Setup" earlier in this chapter, third-grade teacher Ms. Clark was having trouble finding good problems for Common Core Math Standard 3.OA.B.5 (Table 7.1). The commutative and associative properties were passable, but she was at a loss when it came to the distributive property of multiplication. My task was therefore to present an engaging lesson to help her students visualize the distributive law and find a purpose to it.

TABLE 7.1   Description of Common Core Math Content Standard 3.OA.B.5, for Grade 3

Understand properties of multiplication and the relationship between multiplication and division. CCSS.Math.Content.3.OA.B.5

Apply properties of operations as strategies to multiply and divide. Examples: If $6 \times 4 = 24$ is known, then $4 \times 6 = 24$ is also known. (Commutative property of multiplication.) $3 \times 5 \times 2$ can be found by $3 \times 5 = 15$, then $15 \times 2 = 30$, or by $5 \times 2 = 10$, then $3 \times 10 = 30$. (Associative property of multiplication.) Knowing that $8 \times 5 = 40$ and $8 \times 2 = 16$, one can find 8×7 as $8 \times (5 + 2) = (8 \times 5) + (8 \times 2) = 40 + 16 = 56$. (Distributive property.)

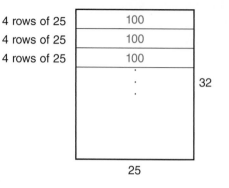

FIGURE 7.7 Sketch of the classroom floor in number of tiles

Building Up to the Distributive Property

Area Model. No student had drawn an area model in his or her journal. Yet relating area to multiplication and division is a third grade content standard (CCSS.Math.Content.3.MD.C.7), so I brought it up by asking two students to count the number of floor tiles along the respective dimensions of the rectangular classroom. Some students were counting along with one or the other, quietly, as if to double-check their counts. Their findings: Twenty-five tiles and about thirty-two tiles, recorded on the board by Ms. Clark. "Who has an idea how we can now calculate the total number of square tiles on this floor?" "We could count by fours," proposed Felix. "Do you mean four *rows* at a time?" "Yeah! Four rows make a 100." Who likes that idea?" Several hands went up, so we carried out Felix's strategy. I began sketching the floor on the board (Figure 7.7), and then I stopped after a few chunks of 100 tiles: "Anyone know how many fours in 32?"

Sun, one of the class mathletes, called out, "4 times 8 equals 32!" "Do I need to go on?" I inquired. "No, it's 800!" replied Sun. Asked to elaborate, he said, "There're eight groups of four rows, so eight times 100 is 800." "Very nice," commented Ms. Clark, adding, "And since every tile is one square *foot*, what do we call '800 square feet'?" "The area," answered Sun, again. "You *all* know that!" reacted Ms. Clark, "Remember when we did area?" Yes, they remembered. But textbook lessons often examine small, gridded rectangles living in journals or textbooks. Not all students make the connection between rectangular pictorial *representations* of area and real-life *applications* of area. Thus, this was a nice connection. Transliterating Sun's words into number sentences gave:

"8 groups of 4 rows   so 8 times 100 = 800"

$$8 \times (4 \text{ rows of } 25 \text{ tiles}) = 8 \times 100 = 800$$

$$8 \times (4 \times 25) = 8 \times 100 = 800$$

Later we added

$$(8 \times 4) \times 25 = 32 \times 25 = 800$$

The Associative Property of Multiplication. This review was unplanned but welcome, as it was important to honor Felix's number sense. Besides, chunking tiles in groups of 100 appealed to his peers. We reviewed the name of the property—the *associative property*—that allows multiplication of the three numbers in two ways: $8 \times (4 \times 25)$, and $(8 \times 4) \times 25$. The first way, $8 \times (4 \times 25)$, directly derived from Felix's thinking and Sun's talking, seemed clear. The second way, $(8 \times 4) \times 25$ or 32×25, surprised some students at first. But after connecting back to that lesson on areas of rectangles, they recalled that indeed *length × width = area (of rectangle)*. Ms. Clark reiterated that the area of a rectangle is another helpful model for visualizing the multiplication of two numbers, with length and width representing the two factors. Each factor can be broken down further. In the case of the classroom floor area, the factor 32 was broken down as the product 8×4. All students had experience with numerical instances of the associative property, and one or two had even seen its algebraic form, $a \times (b \times c) = (a \times b) \times c$. However, it takes years and various embodiments of this abstraction before students own its significance. I closed this short digression for a quick reassessment by pointing out that the associative property of multiplication is about *grouping* three or more factors in a multiplication problem, as in $8 \times (4 \times 25) = (8 \times 4) \times 25$. Also important was noticing that such equivalent expressions contained *only one operation: multiplication.*

Using Easy Combinations to Find Harder Ones. We segued from one-foot-square tiles on the classroom floor to one-inch colored tiles on student desks. In small groups, students were asked to build the rectangles for the first five multiples of 6, specifically modeling the products 1×6, 2×6, and so forth through 5×6, each one in a solid color—a straightforward, simple task accomplished without difficulty. Students remarked, as with the egg carton, that depending on one's perspective, each rectangle had two names. Correct. Next, I showed a slide of the 100 basic multiplication combinations, with the six hardest ones—according to neuroscientists and educators—highlighted in red (Dehaene, 1997). Even adults take split seconds longer to recall these multiplication facts (Figure 7.8).

"Suppose you didn't know, or forgot, 8 times 6," I suggested, pointing to the question marks in cells 8×6 and 6×8 of the table. "Show geometrically how you could use the smaller combinations of the 6 times table to find 8×6." The classroom floor diagram still on the board helped some students catch on. "Oh, by putting *chunks* together to make a bigger rectangle?" asked Daniel with a smile, adopting the new word that had amused him in our earlier discussion. "Why not!" I answered. Each group proceeded to create at least two of the five configurations in Figure 7.9.

FIGURE 7.8 Multiplication table highlighting in red the six hardest multiplication combinations

×	1	2	3	4	5	6	7	8	9	10
1	1	2	3	4	5	6	7	8	9	10
2	2	4	6	8	10	12	14	16	18	20
3	3	6	9	12	15	18	21	24	27	30
4	4	8	12	16	20	24	28	32	36	40
5	5	10	15	20	25	30	35	40	45	50
6	6	12	18	24	30	36	42	?	54	60
7	7	14	21	28	35	42	49	56	63	70
8	8	16	24	32	40	?	56	64	72	80
9	9	18	27	36	45	54	63	72	81	90
10	10	20	30	40	50	60	70	80	90	100

REFLECT . . .

The distributive law of multiplication over addition—knowing that factors can be broken up and distributed to make partial products, which can then be added together to produce the product of the original factors—is one of the most important ideas about multiplication. It is the reason that the standard pencil-and-paper algorithms for multiplication and division work, and its use for mental arithmetic is powerful as well.

—Antonia Cameron and Catherine Twomey Fosnot (2008, p. 6)

3. Unpacking the Distributive Property (Grade 3 Continued)

Students, with assistance from the teachers when needed, practiced describing the rectangles in the form of *unexecuted* numerical expressions. Figure 7.9 reflects many of them. An unexecuted number sentence is an expression containing numbers, operations, and perhaps other symbols that is *not* computed. (The phrase "*not* computed" was used

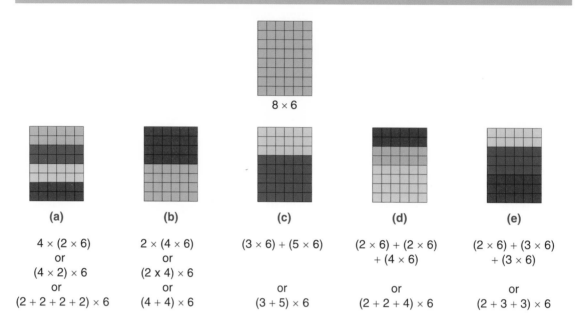

FIGURE 7.9 Using combinations 2 × 6, 3 × 6, 4 × 6, and/or 5 × 6 to find the harder 8 × 6

with the students.) Such expressions allow students to see the connection between the colored parts of the rectangle and the corresponding parts of the number string. In algebraic language, we say that the *structure* of the geometric shape and the structure of the numerical expression are transparent. Once the numerical expression is computed down to a single numerical answer (48 for *all five* configurations), this structure is lost.

Decomposing Left or Right Factor

Rectangles (b) and (c) (Figure 7.9) were the preferred combinations: students thought that doubling 24 (4 × 6), or adding 18 (3 × 6) and 30 (5 × 6), were the easiest and quickest ways to get 48, if one didn't know 8 × 6. We therefore used these two examples to unpack important aspects of the distributive property and distinguish it from the associative property. Focusing first on rectangle (c), I drew the same rectangle in *both* positions to illustrate that the single factor 6 could be on *either* side of the multiplication symbol (Figure 7.10). When introducing the distributive property in grade 3 by breaking apart one of two factors as in this example, it's essential that students practice with the decomposed factor (3 + 5) on *either* side. If students work only with 6 × (3 + 5), of the form $a \times (b+c)$, the expression $(3 + 5) \times 6$, of the form $(b+c) \times a$, confuses them.

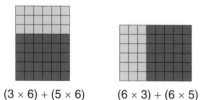

FIGURE 7.10 Depending on how one orients the rectangle, each factor can be on the right or left.

(3 × 6) + (5 × 6)
= (3 + 5) × 6

(6 × 3) + (6 × 5)
= 6 × (3 + 5)

Distributivity: The Meaning of the Name

The long word that rhymes with *activity* and has six syllables was finally revealed: it was *dis-tri-bu-ti-vi-ty*. A mouthful for most, but it amused the students. In U.S. math textbooks, the word *distributivity* is rarely used. The adjectival form is preferred, namely, the *distributive property* or the *distributive law*, which when used alone implicitly means the *distributive property of multiplication over addition*. To help students make sense of the new terminology, an analogy was drawn between the factor 6 *handing out* or *distributing* multiplication to each addend of the sum *inside* the parentheses (Figure 7.11), and Ayo *handing out* or *distributing* journals to each student of Ms. Clark's grade 3 *inside* the classroom. The synonyms of "to hand out," were still on the board from earlier in the lesson. Bottom line: the concept is primary; the terminology is secondary and can be learned later on.

FIGURE 7.11 Factor 6 multiplies (3 + 5), so it must multiply *both* terms of this sum, from left or right.

$6 \times (3 + 5) = (6 \times 3) + (6 \times 5)$ $\quad$ $(3 + 5) \times 6 = (3 \times 6) + (5 \times 6)$

Distinguishing Distributivity From Associativity

It was time to bring awareness to a significant distinction between the concepts of associativity and distributivity. To this end, I illustrated the two properties—in the form of *numerical equations*—using expressions[3] for each of rectangles (b) and (c) in Figure 7.8 that students had devised. Once these expressions were aligned vertically on the board to make similarities and differences evident (Figure 7.12), students were asked to study the numeric-algebraic structure of both pairs of equations and write two observations on their dry-erase slates. The objective here was to look at the numerical equations through algebraic lenses, detaching them momentarily from the geometric structures that had generated them. The enlightening exchange confirmed to Ms. Clark that much more practice was needed before students would understand deeply the differences between the distributive and associative properties. This was to be expected from a third grade class. Discerning observations nonetheless emerged during the final group share time. Table 7.2 paraphrases the main student comments; teacher comments are in bold.

FIGURE 7.12 Computing 6 × 8 using the distributive property (a) and 8 × 6 using the associative property (b)

(a) $6 \times (3 + 5) = (6 \times 3) + (6 \times 5)$ or $(6 \times 3) + (6 \times 5) = 6 \times (3 + 5)$ (Distributive)

(b) $(2 \times 4) \times 6 = 2 \times (4 \times 6)$ or $2 \times (4 \times 6) = (2 \times 4) \times 6$ (Associative)

Decomposing a Two-Digit Factor

Students seemed to understand that the area of a rectangle, albeit a small one in this case (Figure 7.9), equals the sum of the areas of the smaller rectangles that compose it. Some students for instance $(2\times6)+(2\times6)+(2\times6)+(2\times6)=12+12+12+12=48$ for the decomposition of rectangle (a), even though they were less comfortable with the equivalent form, $(2+2+2+2)\times6$. This evidence of area conservation, a *geometric* illustration of the distributive law, allowed me to press on.

Individual Practice. I assigned products of single-digit by double-digit numbers for individual practice, such as 7×24 or 18×8, and asked students to make rectangles with corresponding areas. Reviewing what had just transpired, I said, "Just as you did with 8×6,

3. Expressions are the building blocks of equations. In equation 6 × (3 + 5) = (6 × 3) + (6 × 5), 6 × (3 + 5) is an expression. So is (6 × 3) + (6 × 5). See Chapter 8 for further explanation.

TABLE 7.2 Distributive and associative properties of multiplication: Similarities and differences. Statements refer to equations (a) and (b) in Figure 7.12.

Distributive Property of Multiplication *over* Addition	Associative Property of Multiplication
Similarities	
1. When computed, all expressions give the same answer, 48.	
2. Both expressions on the left, $6 \times (3 + 5)$ and $2 \times (4 \times 6)$, contain three numbers.	
3. **Both properties tell us something about how multiplication works.**	
Differences	
1. Expressions and equations have two operations: × and +.	1. Expressions and equations have one operation: ×.
2. In both equations (a), there are three numbers on one side and four on the other.	2. In both equations (b), there are three numbers on each side.
3. **A product becomes a sum [(a) left side] or a sum becomes a product [(a) right side].**	3. **There are only products [(b) both sides].**

you'll break apart your rectangle into smaller rectangles; the areas of these smaller rectangles should be easy to compute mentally. Then, by adding up the smaller areas, you'll find the larger area, or product." The options were to draw rectangles or build them with colored tiles. The area of each part of the decomposed rectangle, as well as the large rectangle itself, had to be labeled in the form of an unexecuted expression (we called it a "not computed" expression).

Figure 7.13 shows Miguel and Sadiki's respective decompositions of 7×24 and 18×8.

FIGURE 7.13 Application of the distributive law to 7×24 (Miguel) and 18×6 (Sadiki)

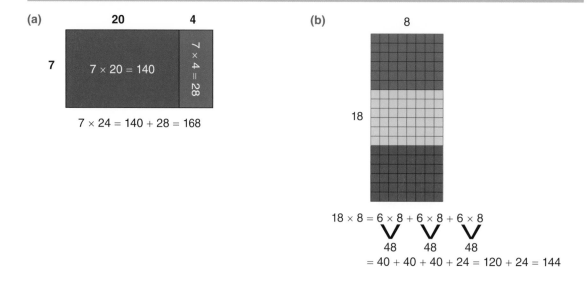

(a)

	20	4
7	$7 \times 20 = 140$	$7 \times 4 = 28$

$7 \times 24 = 140 + 28 = 168$

(b)

$18 \times 8 = 6 \times 8 + 6 \times 8 + 6 \times 8$

48   48   48

$= 40 + 40 + 40 + 24 = 120 + 24 = 144$

Miguel drew and colored in his rectangles. Sadiki used tiles, as buckets of them were available. Both students heeded the direction to write noncomputed expressions for parts *and* whole. Many students focused on *single-number answers* out of habit and didn't see the value in writing out the intermediary stages. As was my intention behind 18×8, Sadiki applied three copies of the recently reviewed "6×8" to create her decomposition. Neither Miguel nor Sadiki, like many others in the class, used parentheses to express the distributive law, as in $7 \times (20+4) = (7 \times 20) + (7 \times 4)$ or in $(6+6+6) \times 8 = (6 \times 8) + (6 \times 8) + (6 \times 8)$. Use of parentheses in grade 3 is new and, moreover, students haven't yet developed an *order-of-operation* sense. But, we teachers used them to facilitate conversation about the building blocks of various expressions. Students seemed to understand the concept of breaking apart one factor into a clever sum—a first step toward understanding multiplication algorithms in grade 4 (Figure 7.14).

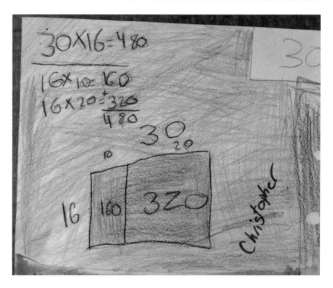

FIGURE 7.14 Christopher, a fourth-grader, applies the distributive property to compute 16 × 30. He brakes down the product into the sum of simpler products he knows, 16 × 10 and 16 × 20.

Photo by Katherine Weeden

Final Group Task: Real-World Application. I ended the class with group work on a real-world problem in which the distributive law can facilitate finding the total number of seats in a theatre (Figure 7.15). Given the short math period, Ms. Clark spent much of the following day discussing students' thinking about the problem. The theatre diagram was purposely placed at a 45° angle so as not to influence the application of the distributive law. A vertical layout, with the stage at bottom, may have led students to write 18×11 and to decompose the *left factor* into $(5+6+7)$; a horizontal layout, with the stage at left, may have led to 11×18, and the decomposition of the *right factor* in the same way. All ways of thinking were welcome.

REVEALS . . .

I had a revelation: Because of the Common Core, this year we had to teach the distributive law. I realized that the simple multiplication algorithm, for a problem like 82 × 4, is an instance of it. The algorithm breaks 82 apart into 80 and 2, and then 4 multiplies each part: $(4 \times 80) + (4 \times 2) = 320 + 8 = 328$. But here the distributive law is hidden. It's camouflaged.

—Lisa, a veteran third-grade teacher

Delving Deeper

A fitting continuation of the third grade lesson in Ms. Clark's classroom, the second episode related in Section 4 below occurred during a professional development session with fourth-grade teachers at an international school in Europe. More precisely, it is a sequence

FIGURE 7.15 Before opening, the staff of a new theatre has still to create seat labels, first for five rows in orange, next for six rows in turquoise, and last for seven rows in yellow. With eleven seats per row, how many seat labels must they create?

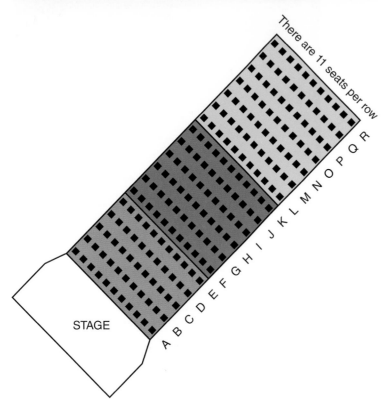

of instructional tasks I proposed to a group of fourth-grade teachers *in response to* Ms. Shena's perspicacious question: "How do I get my students to see the connection between arrays, which opened our unit on multiplication, and the partial products algorithm, which we're working on now?" Always reflective about her math teaching and her students' learning, Ms. Shena felt her textbook had not connected the dots between the different parts of the chapter in a meaningful way. The succession of ideas presented here has been implemented many times with students and teachers since that day, and I always credit Ms. Shena for my inspiration. Teachers may use the sequence of tasks as suggested, or modify it as they see fit. (The limited space in this book does not allow for the recounting of a particular lesson on the bridge from multiplication array to multiplication algorithm.)

4. From Array to Area (Grade 4)

Both arrays and areas are powerful representations of multiplication, but there is a fundamental mathematical difference between the two. The distinction can be attended to in grades 3–5, as students are able to grasp the nuance between array and area.

Discrete Versus Continuous

How Many? It is important for teachers and students to become sensitive to the difference between *discrete* and *continuous* quantities. While these vocabulary words are introduced later on, elementary students can understand their meanings. One way to explain a discrete quantity to students is to say that it's a quantity whose magnitude can be determined by the act of *counting*. Another way of putting it is this: Its magnitude—or "amount"—is the answer to the question, "How many?" Numbers of houses, students, pets, bicycles, chairs, tablets, and connecting cubes are all discrete quantities. In problems, there are always whole-number amounts of them; no halves, no quarters, no three-point-twos. In short, the amounts of such quantities can be represented by the whole-number tick marks on a number line and *not* by points anywhere *in between*.

How Much? How Long? How Heavy? Et Cetera. In contrast, the magnitude of a *continuous* quantity can be determined by the act of *measuring*. Or, we can say, its magnitude—or "amount"—is the answer to questions such as, "How much? How long? How heavy?"

and so forth. Continuous quantities that students work with in elementary school include but are not limited to time, money, length, and area.

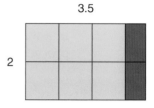

FIGURE 7.16   Area representation of product 2 × 3.5 = 7 square units

Use Arrays and Areas Mindfully. Arrays are appropriate for pictorial representations of discrete quantities such as rows of chairs in an auditorium or rows of trees in an orchard (Figure 7.5). As students come to know decimals in grades 3–5, they will appreciate the fact that areas—first rectangular, and then other polygonal forms—can have *non*integer dimensions. The rectangle in Figure 7.16, for example, has dimensions 3.5 and 2 *linear* units, and represents an area of *7 square* units, as the two half square units (in green) add up to the *7th* whole square unit. So areas are suitable representations of multiplication, whether of two whole numbers, decimals, fractions, or any combination thereof.

5. From Area to Algorithm (Grade 4 Continued)

Mathematical algorithms are formidable inventions of the minds of men and women. Directly relevant to the overarching goal of this book, the word *algorithm* is derived from the name Algoritmi, a transliteration into Latin of *al-Khwarizmi*, the name of the famous ninth-century Persian mathematician known in the history of mathematics as the father of algebra. Algorithms can be helpful or harmful to students' development of number sense depending on when, how, and in what context they are introduced. Many math educators say they are harmful if they "encourage children to give up their own thinking, and 'unteach' place value, thereby preventing children from developing number sense" (Kamii & Dominick, 1998, p. 135). Algorithms for multidigit multiplication incorporate the distributive property of multiplication over addition, some more explicitly than others. We shall examine two such algorithms closely.

Common Algorithms for Multidigit Multiplication

The U.S. Standard Algorithm. The U.S. standard algorithm for multidigit multiplication[4] (USSAM) sacrifices sense making for the purpose of efficiency. Consequently, students frequently see it as an arbitrary sequence of steps to follow. Consider the simple example in Figure 7.17. The common procedure, usually memorized rather then understood, perplexes children in at least four ways:

1. It starts on the right and moves *from right to left*, going against the grain of children's natural reasoning: They read, write, and build number models *from left to right*.

2. It betrays their *place-value sense*, emphasized and reinforced throughout grades preK–2, when teachers or students say, "three times two" or "one times two" instead of "three times twenty" or "ten times twenty."

---

4. This is often called the Standard U.S. Algorithm for Multidigit Multiplication. I refer to the algorithm many adults were taught in school, the one described in *Adding It Up* (Kilpatrick, Swafford, & Findell, 2001, p. 207).

3. It mystifies them with its *move to the left* on line 2 (and moving another place on line 3 for three digits, and so on). "The mystery is usually unresolved; students are simply instructed to put a zero or a smiley face and move to the left one place," an experienced teacher once told me.

4. It does not reveal the inherent distributive property of multiplication over addition in a way that is transparent to students. In fact, the focus on procedural step after procedural step obfuscates this fundamental connection even for experienced teachers like Lisa, the teacher whose words about her revelation are stated in the box on page 123.

FIGURE 7.17   The U.S. standard algorithm for multidigit multiplication

```
   2 1
 × 1 3
 ─────
   6 3
   2 1
 ─────
 2 7 3
```

When the standard multiplication algorithm is introduced too early and the meanings behind the procedural steps either are not explained by the teacher or, if they are, are not understood by the student, logical sense making succumbs to memorization, and number sense cultivation surrenders to digit sense concentration. Thus, the beauty of the forest is lost because of the careful focus on the individual trees. (*Note*: Chapter 8 addresses the fifth challenge posed by this algorithm, related to carrying.)

The Partial Products Algorithm. Consider the same simple product, 21 × 13. Expanding the factors gives 20 + 1 and 10 + 3. Thus, multiplying 21 by 13 means multiplying each "place-value part" of 21 by each "place-value part" of 13. The four double arrows in Figure 7.18a symbolize the four subproducts, called *partial products*. The partial products algorithm for multiplication (PPAM) is somewhat similar to the USSAM, but it explicitly reveals *all* partial products, requiring no "carrying" (Figure 7.18b).

The beauty of this algorithm lies in its logic and transparency. All four perplexities listed above vanish: (1) Students may proceed from left to right, as the order of the four partial products is irrelevant. (2) Place value is honored throughout. (3) The smiley face, zero, or placeholder is a nonissue. (4) The distributive property is apparent, as the four partial products derive directly from it. Following the four arrows in Figure 7.18c, one obtains: $(20+1) \times (10+3) = 20 \times (10+3) + 1 \times (10+3) = 20 \times 10 + 20 \times 3 + 1 \times 10 + 1 \times 3.$ Further below, we revisit these partial products in a geometric representation (Figure 7.20).

FIGURE 7.18   (a) A product of two 2-digit numbers yields four partial products; (b) vertical layout of partial products algorithm showing all partial products; (c) horizontal layout students will use in algebra to multiply binomials applying the distributive property of multiplication over addition

Connecting Area to Algorithm

Now that we've analyzed the PPAM, let's revisit Ms. Shena's question: "How can I help my students see the connection between arrays and the PPAM?" We've already seen that both arrays and area are powerful visual representations of multiplication, and we have specified the type of quantities suitable for each. Now let's look at the PPAM *geometrically*, namely, *as an area*.

Multiplying Whole Numbers. Students can make sense of the area formed by the product 21 × 13 by constructing the corresponding rectangle with

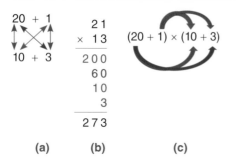

(a)   (b)   (c)

base-10 blocks. These blocks are specifically designed to embody place value. Students or teachers are given a sheet of paper (Figure 7.19; see Appendix, page 214, for student worksheet) and instructed to place the dimensions of the rectangle (or factors of the product) in one color, say yellow, along two perpendicular edges, (Figure 7.20). These base-10 blocks are *not* part of the resulting area, or final product; they simply represent the magnitude of each factor, or *length* and *width* of the rectangle. Then, using flats (100s), rods (10s) and unit cubes (1s) of a different color or colors, the "product-rectangle" is constructed with the appropriate length and width. (Figure 7.20). This resulting rectangle clearly reveals the four components, corresponding to the four partial products in Figure 7.18b: the two flats for 200 (red), the six rods on the right for 60 (purple), the one rod at the bottom for 10 (blue), and the three units in the bottom right corner for 3 (green). Many a teacher I have worked with has been awed by the perfect correspondence between partial products and subrectangles.

Multiplying Decimals. Base-10-block rectangles can also model products of decimals. If each flat counts for 1, then each rod stands for $\frac{1}{10}$, and each unit for $\frac{1}{100}$. In this case, the rectangle in Figure 7.20 could equally represent the product $2.1 \times 1.3 = 2.73$. Figure 7.21 shows teachers learning to use base-10 blocks.

From Building to Drawing

After sufficient experience with base-10 blocks, and once students understand the connection between concept and representation, the next stage is an abstraction of the blocks in the form of a hand drawing. Ms. Shena and her students called it the *rectangle method.* Figure 7.22 illustrates a simplified rectangle showing the four partial products of 34×57, not necessarily drawn to scale. This visual helps students remember that the product of a 2-digit number by another 2-digit number always yields four partial products, since the rectangle is divided into 2×2 or four sections. Similarly, multiplying a 2-digit number by a 3-digit number yields 2×3 or six partial products. And so on. As will be explained in Chapter 8, this will provide an indispensible foundation for applying the distributive law to binomials and trinomials, which students begin to learn about in middle school.

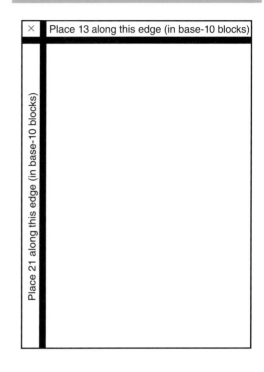

FIGURE 7.19   Handout for area model of partial products algorithm

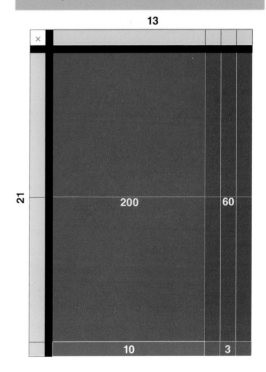

FIGURE 7.20   Area model corresponding to the multiplication 21×13, constructed with base-10 blocks

FIGURE 7.21 Fourth- and fifth-grade teachers discover the connection between rectangle area materialized by base-10 blocks and the partial products algorithm, for multiplication problem 21 × 13.

Source: Planting the Seeds of Algebra 2013 Summer Institute, Alexandria, VA

FIGURE 7.22 The rectangle method for representing 34 × 57 shows all four partial products.

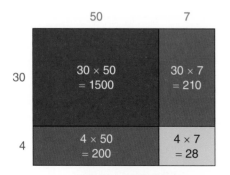

Closure

This chapter makes clear that knowing multiplication in depth—for teaching multiplication in grades 3–5 with meaning—requires more than knowing vocabulary words such as *product*, *factor*, and *multiple*; more than mastering the 100 single-digit multiplication combinations; and more than correctly carrying out algorithms for multidigit multiplication. I recall working with a fifth-grade student who proudly told me, "I know all about division." When asked to describe what it means to *know all about division*, she replied, "I know how to do long division with big numbers," which for her was the ultimate challenge. She then proceeded to choose two large numbers and diligently displayed her skill. After congratulating her, I selected smaller numbers and asked if she could tell me, *without computing*, whether the division $98 \div 7$ would yield the same answer as the sum, $(98 \div 3) + (98 \div 4)$, of two smaller divisions by 3 and 4, called partners of 7. The question puzzled her, but opened the door to a new world of questions and explorations into multiplication and division. She ultimately revised the meaning of, "I know all about division."

Hopefully *Multiplication Musings* has clarified deeper issues, such as

- The difference between the associative and distributive properties of multiplication;
- The distinction between discrete and continuous quantitates, and the consequent distinction between array and area representations;
- The connection between the distributive property and single-digit multiplication combinations; and
- The connection between the distributive property and multidigit multiplication algorithms.

8

Behind *Multiplication Musings*

Algebra Connections

A rithmetic and algebra are intertwined. A profound understanding of the former supports a profound understanding of the latter. Memorization of multiplication "facts" and rote learning of multiplication algorithms *without* understanding can have a negative influence on the construction of algebraic knowledge. Studies have shown that the nature of elementary school arithmetic is too often procedural and concentrated on computational results (Carpenter, Franke, & Levi, 2003; Kieran, 1989; Linchevski, 1995). While every teacher's wish is for students to know their basic "math facts," focusing on procedural fluency and privileging right answers, *at the expense of* understanding the processes that lead to them, serves neither arithmetic *nor* algebra. It is pretty much established that cognitive obstacles arising from early arithmetic experiences that focus on recall, procedure, and right answers can create future conceptual blocks that hinder the development of algebraic thinking (Malara & Navarra, 2003).

Mathematics researchers and educators in the past decade have argued for more coherence, depth, and understanding in early mathematics explorations (Kaput, Carraher, & Blanton, 2008; Lins & Kaput, 2004) because they have shown that children are more capable than previously believed of "mathematizing," which is a form of mathematical modeling of real problems or of organizing and synthesizing mathematical ideas (Bass, 2005). More specifically, they have called for teachers to "algebrafy" mathematics in general, and arithmetic in particular. The verb *algebrafy,* coined by Maria Blanton and James Kaput, means to cultivate opportunities for thinking about, and doing, elementary mathematics in algebraic ways.

Unpacking the distributive property of multiplication over addition—a property often hidden inside mental math strategies, algorithmic procedures, quantitative comparisons, and problem situations—is a perfect arena for cultivating algebraic ways of thinking for ourselves and our students. The distributive law is powerful because it connects the two fundamental operations, addition and multiplication. Working with distributivity requires understanding of the properties of *both* operations, their connections, and their effects on numbers.

In prealgebra and algebra, understanding the distributive law profoundly and being able to use it fluently are indispensable because this law shows its head everywhere: in simplifying fractions, identifying equivalent expressions, solving equations, factoring polynomials, and much more. Dr. Math, from The Math Forum website (http://mathforum.org/dr.math), once made this analogy: "Trying to learn algebra without having a real understanding of the distributive property is like trying to learn to cook without pots and pans." He further advised, "Do not think that you can keep going in math without being able to apply the distributive property in your sleep." All the more reason to lay the groundwork early!

Following the pattern of the first and second chapters of previous Explorations, Chapter 8 revisits Chapter 7, unpacking the not-so-obvious connections between *Multiplication Musings* and the worlds of algebra. The focus is on the most important mathematics in Chapter 7, but also on pedagogical suggestions for meaningful engagement with the mathematics. After reading this chapter, readers will realize the rich potential of planting algebraic seeds of distributivity in the early grades, seeds that foster an appreciation for the concept now and promise a robust algebraic proficiency later—for *all* students.

CHAPTER 8

THE BIG IDEAS OF

- The *equal-groups* interpretation of multiplication is the simplest for students to grasp. Teachers must be aware of the two very different interpretations of the inverse operation in this case: *partitive* division versus *quotative* division.
- *Multiplicative comparison* problems are among the most difficult for students to comprehend. That's because, prior to grade 3, students have always thought additively. Students must be exposed to multiple uses of *multiplicative thinking*.
- The *distributive property* of multiplication over addition is an important property, for it involves a special relationship between these two fundamental operations.
- Applying the distributive property involves breaking apart one or both factors of a product to create a simpler problem. For example, $9 \times 6 = (5 + 4) \times 6 = 5 \times 6 + 4 \times 6 = 30 + 24 = 54$. The distributive property is indispensible in expanding and factoring algebraic expressions: $5x + 4x = (5 + 4)x = 9x$.
- All properties of multiplication are important. Students need to distinguish one from the other. For example, the distributive property involves *two* operations $[a \times (b + c) = a \times b + a \times c]$, whereas the associative property involves only *one* operation $[a \times (b \times c) = (a \times b) \times c]$.
- The distributive property of multiplication over addition is the foundation for the partial products algorithm for multiplication (PPAM), which makes sense to children. Moreover, the PPAM has a direct relationship with the quadratic polynomial identities students will learn about in the second year of algebra.
- Teachers must cultivate an algebraic approach to arithmetic, which involves pausing to notice structure before rushing to compute. A thoughtful student knows that $5 \times 96 = 10 \times 48$ *without computing*, because she notices that 5 is doubled ($\rightarrow$ 10) while 96 is halved ($\rightarrow$ 48). Analogously, the equality would hold if 5 were tripled ($\rightarrow$ 15) and 96 were "thirded" ($\rightarrow$ 32).

Discussion

1. Third-Graders' Images of Multiplication (Grade 3)

Skip counting, equal groups, and array models are among the common contexts and visualizations of multiplication students encounter in grade 3, so it was normal that Ms. Clark's students expressed all three. First a word on each, then a word on all the multiplicative situations students should experience in grades 3–5.

Skip Counting

Patterns of multiples on the 100 chart are fun and aesthetically pleasing to students. But we must capitalize on the mathematics learned. For one, students must sense the meaning of *multiple.* When simply coloring in the columns or diagonals of multiples, they don't always take away from the experience the fact that a multiple of 3, for instance, means a number that can be arrived at by repeating counts of 3 a certain number of times. For students who do not grasp this notion, I propose an exploration that connects *concept* with *body sound and movement.* Place four geoboards together (Figure 8.1a) to make a large, square—a 100 chart of *pegs.* Give the student or group a set of same-colored multilink cubes, and a "magic number," say 3. Starting from one corner of the square board, which they will select, have them count the pegs by touching them one by one, and place a cube on every *third* peg (Figure 8.1b). This repetition of "one, two, three, one two three, one two three . . . " to obtain all multiples of 3 remains in the body memory and later formalizes first into verbal expressions, "three once," "three twice," "three thrice," et cetera, and ultimately into the generalized algebraic expression $3 \times n$, or just $3n$, for *any multiple of* 3.

FIGURE 8.1 (a) A 100 chart of *pegs* created by joining together four 5-by-5 geoboards. (b) By placing a red cube on every third peg, students find 33 multiples of 3.

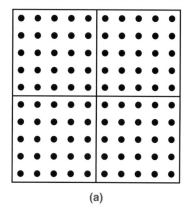
(a)

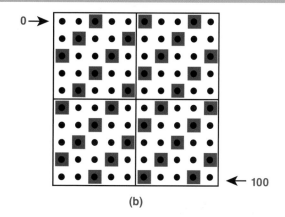
(b)

REFLECT . . .

Figure 8.1(b) is a semiabstraction, as it symbolizes the first 100 whole numbers and the first 33 multiples of 3 without explicitly revealing their numerical values. Thinking algebraically, try to prove that *the sum of any three consecutive whole numbers* is always a multiple of 3.* (For proofs, see Section II, "For Your Own Learning," of Chapter 9.)

---

*This fact actually holds for any three consecutive *integers.* The set of integers, denoted by the symbol $\mathbb{Z}$, is the set of all positive and negative whole numbers, plus zero. Thus, $\mathbb{Z} = \{...-3, -2, -1, 0, 1, 2, 3...\}$.

Algebra Connection

• **Inverse Proportion.** Students can also begin to develop the concept of inverse proportion from comparing different patterns of multiples. Two *directly proportional* quantities vary together, at the same rate: As one increases, so does the other, and, similarly, as one decreases, so does the other. The number of melons bought (*m*) and the number of dollars spent (*d*) is an example. Using algebraic notation, *m* and *d* are directly proportional if and only if their *ratio* is constant, namely, if $\frac{m}{d} = k$, where *k* is called the *constant of proportionality*. This concept is the basis for understanding equivalent fractions (see Chapter 10). On the other hand, two quantities are *inversely proportional* if one increases as the other decreases, at the same rate. For example, a car's average speed over some distance (*s*) is inversely proportional to the time it takes to travel that distance (*t*); the greater the speed, the less time to one's destination. As students are guided to explore patterns of multiples on the 100 chart through inquiry, they observe that the smaller the number, the greater the number of its multiples; and the greater the number, the smaller the number of its multiples. Hence 2 has fifty multiples between 1 and 100 (Figure 8.2a) whereas 5, a larger number, only has twenty multiples between 1 and 100 (Figure 8.2b). Students will learn in middle school that two quantities *x* and *y* are inversely proportional if and only if their *product* remains constant as they vary inversely: $x \times y = k$, where *k* is a constant. In our example, *x* is a chosen number (2, and then 5) and *y* is the number's number of multiples between 1 and 100 (50, and then 20): $2 \times 50 = 5 \times 20 = 100$. Another way of thinking about this relationship is this: 5 is *2.5 times greater* than 2, whereas 20 is *2.5 times smaller* than 50.

FIGURE 8.2 Inverse proportion between numbers 2 (a) and 5 (b) and their respective numbers of multiples 50 (a) and 20 (b)

1	2	3	4	5	6	7	8	9	10
11	12	13	14	15	16	17	18	19	20
21	22	23	24	25	26	27	28	29	30
31	32	33	34	35	36	37	38	39	40
41	42	43	44	45	46	47	48	49	50
51	52	53	54	55	56	57	58	59	60
61	62	63	64	65	66	67	68	69	70
71	72	73	74	75	76	77	78	79	80
81	82	83	84	85	86	87	88	89	90
91	92	93	94	95	96	97	98	99	100

(a)

1	2	3	4	5	6	7	8	9	10
11	12	13	14	15	16	17	18	19	20
21	22	23	24	25	26	27	28	29	30
31	32	33	34	35	36	37	38	39	40
41	42	43	44	45	46	47	48	49	50
51	52	53	54	55	56	57	58	59	60
61	62	63	64	65	66	67	68	69	70
71	72	73	74	75	76	77	78	79	80
81	82	83	84	85	86	87	88	89	90
91	92	93	94	95	96	97	98	99	100

(b)

Equal-Groups Multiplication

Four bags containing five apples each, four rivers with five tributaries each, and four jumps of five units each on the number line can all be modeled mathematically by the same multiplication, $4 \times 5 = 20$. As noted in Chapter 7, the number 4 in this case is the *multiplier*, meaning the agent that carries out the action of multiplying, and the number 5 is the *multiplicand*, meaning the entity that incurs the action. In the case of equal groups, it is clear that the two numbers or quantities play asymmetric roles.

Algebra Connection

The concepts of function and rate are central to algebra. While both conceptualizations of equal-groups multiplication below involve the notion of invariance, an algebraic concept, be mindful of the difference between the two.

• **Multiplier as Function.** As we saw in Exploration II, the action "times 4" can be thought of as the function applied to the *particular* input number 5, for which the output is 20 (Figure 8.3). Changing the input value would change the output value, but the *function rule*, "× 4," remains invariant.

> **FIGURE 8.3** The expression $4 \times 5 = 20$ implies that the multiplier 4 acts upon the entity 5 to produce the product 20.

• **The Notion of Rate.** "An alternative way of conceptualizing the equal-groups situation is in terms of a rate" (Greer, 1992, p. 277). From this perspective, the first example with bags of apples may be expressed as follows:

If there are five apples per bag, how many apples do four bags contain?

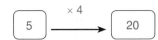

Implicit in this interpretation is the *invariance of the rate.* In other words, the rate of *five apples per bag* is understood to be a constant, and the total number of apples is found by multiplying the rate by the *particular* number of bags, which in this case is 4: $(5 \text{ apples per bag}) \times (4 \text{ bags}) = 20 \text{ apples}$. Change the number of bags, and the total number of apples will change, but the rate per bag remains invariant.

Division as the Inverse of Equal-Groups Multiplication

Since division is the *inverse* of multiplication, the asymmetric roles of the two factors generate two different interpretations of division worthy of mention: division by multiplier and division by multiplicand. Consider the example $20 \div 4$; what situations might this numerical expression model? "If I have 20 apples and I wish to put them into four bags, how many go in each bag?" is an example of the type of problem adults and children are most comfortable with. The action required here is to partition equally or distribute equal (or "fair") shares in each bag. For this reason, this type of division problem is called *partitive division*. In such situations, we use division to describe *equal* or *fair sharing*. Metaphorically, I like to say the number of "containers" is *known* but the number contained in each is *unknown* (Figure 8.4). Containers can be all sorts of things, such as bags holding apples, students getting cookies, or cars carrying people.

> **FIGURE 8.4** In partitive division, the number of containers is known, but the amount/number contained is unknown.

I could also pose another type of question modeled by the same expression, $20 \div 4$: "I have 20 apples and wish to ship them in bags of four apples each; how many bags would

FIGURE 8.5   In quotative division, the number of containers is unknown, but the amount/number contained in each is known.

I need?" The action required here is to count out groups of four apples until all twenty are used up. This type of division problem is called *quotative division* (also known as *measurement division*). *Repeated subtraction* is the terminology children understand. In such situations, we still use division to describe *equal grouping,* but the unknown is different. Metaphorically, I like to say the number of "containers" is *unknown* but the number contained in each is *known* (Figure 8.5).

(*Note:* To make sense of the word *quotative,* think of this type of problem as providing the *rate per unit,* in this case, *4 apples per bag.* But a rate, such as 4 : 1, can also be written as a quotient: $\frac{4}{1}$.)

Algebra Connection

Why is division important from an algebraic perspective? Because "formally, fractions are constructed as a reaction to the lack of closure of the integers under division (Greer, 1992, p. 277). Furthermore, "Historically, the development of algebra grew from a consideration of the arithmetic of rational numbers"[1] (Saul, 1998, p. 137). What does "lack of closure of the integers under division" mean?

• **Lack of Closure Under Division.** Have you ever thought of how fractions and decimals were born? The following are answers students in grades 3–5 can understand. Fractions first arose by applying division to whole numbers that do not yield a zero remainder, such as 3 divided by 4 or 17 divided by 5. Thus, numbers denoted by $\frac{3}{4}$ and $\frac{17}{5}$ were conceived. Decimals came about when measuring procedures were applied to continuous quantities, such as measuring the length of a rope or the weight of a person. Chances are, we don't obtain whole-number measurements. The phrase *lack of closure of the integers under division* simply means that when applying division to integers, we are not guaranteed to obtain another integer. Said differently, the answer may fall *outside of* the set of integers. The same holds for whole numbers (the positive integers), which students are familiar with: Unlike multiplication of two whole numbers, which *always yields another whole number,* division of two whole numbers does not. Chapter 10 addresses the introduction of rational numbers in grades 3–5.

Other Multiplicative Contexts

There are many other multiplicative situations, especially when differentiating multiplication of discrete quantities from multiplication of continuous quantities. But even in the realm of discrete quantities (meaning countable wholes), there are at least two other types of problems students should be exposed to in grades 3–5: multiplicative comparison and Cartesian product. Let's take a quick look at each.

Multiplicative Comparison Problems. In Exploration I, *Circling Circles,* we addressed the importance of assigning problems with the goal of comparing quantities additively *as well as multiplicatively.* Here is one example, expressed in two ways:

---

1. The set of rational numbers, denoted by the symbol $\mathbb{Q}$, is the set of all fractions $\frac{a}{b}$, such that a and b are integers, and $b \neq 0$.

1. Erin has 4 times as many Moshi Monster cards as Ty. If Ty has 6, how many does Erin have?

2. Erin has 4 times as many Moshi Monster cards as Ty. If Erin has 28, how many does Ty have?

The first invites a multiplication, the second a division, even though the second can also be solved using multiplication: "How many *times* 4 will give me 28?" Students cleverly bypass division by using multiplication, just as younger students avoid subtraction by using addition, namely, by counting up. As students become sophisticated with numbers and techniques, multiplicative comparison evolves into multiplicative change:

1. A piece of shock cord 30.5 cm long can stretch to a maximum length of 72.3 cm. By what factor is the original piece lengthened when stretched to its maximum?

Cartesian Product. The Cartesian product, a very different conceptualization of multiplication, is relatively recent in the history of mathematics. We learned in Exploration I that the word *Cartesian* comes from René Descartes, the 17th-century inventor of analytical geometry, the confluence of numbers, algebra, and geometry. Cartesian-product multiplication arises in problems such as this one:

1. Jamie has three shirts and two pairs of pants. If an outfit consists of a shirt and a pair of pants, how many different outfits can Jamie come up with?

Common representations are tree diagrams and two-dimensional tables (Figures 8.6 a and b). The first lends itself well to additional variables, such as a pair of shoes added to the problem definition of an "outfit." If Jamie had two pairs of shoes, two additional branches would extend each of the six terminal nodes of the tree, for a total of $3 \times 2 \times 2 = 12$ outfits. The 2-dimensional matrix, however, would have to turn into a 3-dimensional one, which is difficult to represent in a clear and child-friendly way.

FIGURE 8.6 Jamie's six outfits represented by a tree diagram (a) and by a two-dimensional table (b). The same five colors are used in both representations: blue, red, and green for the 3 choices of shirts, and purple and orange for the 2 choices of pants.

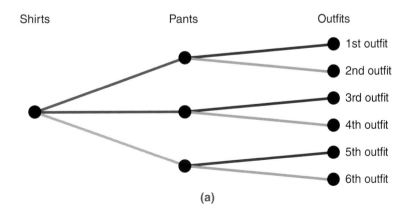

(a)

(Continued)

FIGURE 8.6 (Continued)

	Blue Shirt	Red Shirt	Green Shirt
Purple Pants	BS & PP	RS & PP	GS & PP
Orange Pants	BS & OP	RS & OP	GS & OP

(b)

Algebra Connection

• **Abstraction.** Just as in the case of additive situations, multiplicative situations are numerous and varied. Nevertheless, they can all be represented by a simple equation of the type $4 \times 5 = 20$, or in general, $f_1 \times f_2 = p$, where f_1 and f_2 are the factors, $\times$ the operation acting upon them, and p their product. Whether numerical ($4 \times 5 = 20$) or algebraic ($f_1 \times f_2 = p$), such an equation is a mathematical abstraction that shows the relatedness among *all* multiplicative situations, some of which are very dissimilar. Abstraction for the purpose of generalization is the main characteristic of algebra.

2. Stuck on the Distributive Property (Grade 3 Continued)

Building Up to the Distributive Property

Decomposing and Recomposing: A Big Idea in Mathematics. First encounters with the distributive property of multiplication (DPM) over addition in grade 3 consist of cleverly breaking down one of two factors into a sum, to render the multiplication easier. This ability to see smaller numbers embedded inside larger ones begins to develop in the early grades, when students first learn addition. The notion that a whole consists of parts and can be broken down into these parts, and that parts can be combined back together to form the whole, is considered a "big idea" (Baroody, 2004), an "essential understanding" (NCTM, 2010) in early mathematics. Moreover, "decomposing and composing are used throughout mathematics at every level and in all topics." (National Research Council, 2009). Jean Piaget coined the term *additive composition* for this part-whole (P-W) relationship that is at play in the distributive law. The knowledge illustrated below is prerequisite to the construction of algebraic knowledge. Teachers would do well to foster this algebraic habit of mind in their students early on.

Algebra Connection

• **Number.** P-W is fundamental to understanding place value. It is at work when breaking down a number in different ways, depending on what is needed: For example, 135 may be broken down into 1 hundred, 3 tens, and 5 ones; or 1 hundred and 35 ones; or 13 tens and 5 ones, and so on. P-W is also indispensible in understanding common fractions: seeing $\frac{3}{4}$ as three "one-fourths" is a prerequisite for developing proportional thinking. It requires breaking down a whole into four fourths, taking three of them, and realizing that $\frac{3}{4}$ is *3 times* greater than $\frac{1}{4}$.

• **Mental Math or Computation Algorithms.** Recognizing the value of each digit marks the difference between parroting a computation algorithm and making sense of it.

Adding tens and ones in the problem 35 + 27 is an example of a child-friendly strategy: $35 + 27 = (30 + 5) + (20 + 7) = (30 + 20) + (5 + 7) = 50 + 12 = 62$. "For multiplication, the ability to break numbers apart in flexible ways is even more important than in addition or subtraction" (Van de Walle & Lovin, 2006, p. 113), especially for the purpose of the distributive law. Here are two examples:

$$8 \times 27 = 8 \times (25 + 2) = (8 \times 25) + (8 \times 2) = 200 + 16 = 216$$

$$7 \times 29 = 7 \times (30 - 1) = (7 \times 30) - (7 \times 1) = 210 - 7 = 203$$

- **Geometry.** Consider a 3-by-4 rectangular grid (Figure 8.7). It can be seen as composed of three longer 1-by-4 rectangles (a), four shorter 3-by-1 rectangles (b), two 3-by-2 rectangles (c), or 12 unit squares (d). Other decompositions are possible. The unit-square decomposition facilitates understanding of the *area* concept: The area of the large rectangle equals 12 square units.

FIGURE 8.7   Four choices of units (a through d) in the decomposition of a 3-by-4-rectangle

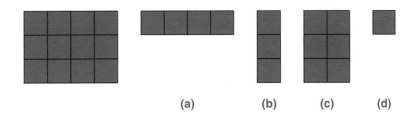

(a)   (b)   (c)   (d)

- **Patterns.** As a final elementary example, consider a pattern of cubes. The ability to break down the pattern in Figure 8.8 in one's mind is precisely what enables students to discern its repeating unit, its building block. The P-W relationship helps them decompose the repeating pattern of cubes and conceive of it as the juxtaposition of "blue-red-green" units placed end to end. Understanding a pattern's structure therefore requires conceptualizing the whole as composed of multiple repetitions of its basic unit.

FIGURE 8.8   Decomposing a repeating pattern to discern its elemental repeating unit, blue-red-green

The Associative Property of Multiplication

The commutative property allows us to multiply factors in any *order*: $4 \times 3 = 3 \times 4$. (Mnemonic: The factors can *commute* from one side to the other of the symbol × without affecting the product). The associative property allows us to multiply more than two factors in either *grouping* arrangement: $4 \times (3 \times 2) = (4 \times 3) \times 2$. (Mnemonic: People who associate with each other work or play in groups).

Knowing these properties and how to use them in calculations is part of having a strong understanding of multiplication. An understanding of them is also critical to establishing an understanding of algebra, since they are used extensively in symbolic situations. (Otto, Caldwell, Hancock, & Zbiek, 2011, p. 33)

But this property of multiplication, expressed algebraically as "$a \times (b \times c) = (a \times b) \times c$, for any three numbers $a, b,$ and c," is neither meaningful nor accessible to upper elementary students, since they rarely engage in multiplying many factors. Following are suggestions for engaging them with the associative property of multiplication (APM).

Visualizing the APM. If area models products of two factors, then volume models products of three factors. Encourage students to pick three single-digit numbers and multiply them. They can't multiply them all at once, so have them compute the product of all three factors by grouping them in different ways. Then, using multilink or connecting cubes, ask them to build a 3-D model for each product and *see* what an equivalence such as $4 \times (3 \times 2) = (4 \times 3) \times 2$ actually *means* (Figure 8.9).

FIGURE 8.9 (a) $4 \times (3 \times 2)$. (b) $(4 \times 3) \times 2$. Joining the four copies in (a) and the two copies in (b), respectively, creates the same rectangular solid of dimensions 4 by 3 by 2, with the same volume $4 \times 3 \times 2$, but seen from different perspectives.

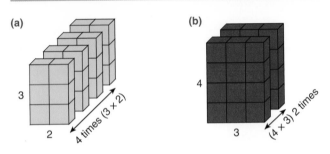

Doubling and Halving. In *Planting the Seeds of Algebra, PreK–2* (Neagoy, 2012), Exploration I discussed the equals sign *relationally*—rather than as a silent instruction to compute and produce a numerical answer. In equations between two sums, we discovered what I called the *n up, n down* rule for addition. To illustrate with a simple example, one way of explaining why the sum 38 + 27 equals the sum 40 + 25, *without computing,* is to realize that 38 increases by 2 while 27 decreases by 2, hence 2 up, 2 down. Generalizing for the sum of *any two numbers,* we have the *plus n, minus n* rule for equivalent sums, as shown in Figure 8.10. This phrase renders *n up, n down* more explicit.

FIGURE 8.10 The *plus n, minus n* rule for equivalent sums

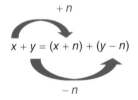

Often, students apply this rule to multiplication and don't understand why it doesn't work. In the process of guiding them to discover the analogue rule for multiplication, students will interact with the APM in a sense-making way. Begin with a simple product like 8 × 6, from Chapter 7. Ask students to compute 4 × 12, 8 × 6, and 16 × 3, and then to draw a rectangle for each. Have them articulate *why* the areas of these three rectangles are equal. The area models are helpful here (Figure 8.11). Students will notice that as one side length of the rectangle *doubles,* the other is *halved.* To visualize the process, slice the red rectangle in half (vertically), stack the halves, to create the yellow rectangle; similarly, slice the yellow rectangle in half (vertically), stack the halves, to create the blue rectangle.

FIGURE 8.11   Rectangular area remains constant as one side is doubled and the other is halved.

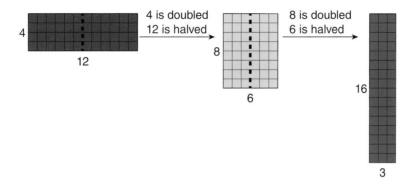

The same is true for any other factor, not just 2. For instance, the product 8 × 15 equals the product 2 × 60, because 2 is *one fourth of* 8 whereas 60 is *four times* 15. Students may find 2 × 60 easier to compute than 8 × 15. Generalizing, as we did with addition, gives us the *times n, divided by n* rule for equivalent products, as shown in Figure 8.12.

FIGURE 8.12   The *times n, divided by n* rule for equivalent products

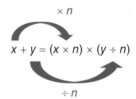

$$x + y = (x \times n) \times (y \div n)$$

STUDENT WORK SAMPLE 1   Lauren, a fourth-grader, applies doubling and halving to transform 30 × 16 into 60 × 8 (or 8 × 60) and obtains 480. She used 8 × 6 = 48.

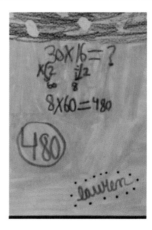

Photo by Katherine Weeden

REPORT . . .

Monica, I wanted to share how my fourth-grade student George multiplied 12 × 35. (He was in the group you worked with yesterday on the division story.) He said, "I know 12 × 5 = 60 and 35 ÷ 5 = 7, so I can use 60 × 7 to find 12 × 35." It's pretty neat how students understand the doubling-and-halving relationship and extend the concept to tripling and "third-ing," quadrupling and "fourth-ing," and, like in this case, quintupling and "fifth-ing!"

—E-mail from Katherine, fourth-grade teacher

Algebra Connection

• **Unpacking the APM.** One can explain the equivalence between 8×6 and 4×12, or between 8×6 and 16×3 (Figure 8.11), by invoking the hidden APM:

$$8 \times 6 = (4 \times 2) \times 6 = 4 \times (2 \times 6) = 4 \times 12$$

$$8 \times 6 = 8 \times (2 \times 3) = (8 \times 2) \times 3 = 16 \times 3$$

• **The Identity Elements.** There is another explanation for why the two general rules—*plus n, minus n*; and *times n, divided by n*—always work. It lies in *another* property of algebra. In addition to the commutative, associative, and distributive properties of multiplication, students need to know *two other properties* by the end of fifth grade. The pertinent one here is the *identity element*. In figure 8.10, the total change from one side to the other side of the equals sign is $+ n - n$, or $+ (n - n)$, which equals 0 for *any number n.* The number 0 is called the *identity element of addition,* because, for any number x, $x + 0 = x$. In other words, adding (or subtracting) 0 leaves a number unchanged, that is, *identical* to itself. Similarly, in figure 8.12, the total change from one side to the other side of the equals sign is $\times n \div n$, or $\times (n \div n)$, which equals $\times 1$ for *any number n* (except 0, as $\frac{0}{0}$ is undefined). The number 1 is the *identity element of multiplication,* because, for any number x, $x \times 1 = x$. In other words, multiplying (or dividing) by 1 leaves any number or quantity unchanged, that is, *identical* to itself.

3. Unpacking the Distributive Property of Multiplication, or DPM (Grade 3 Continued)

A Word on Unexecuted Expressions

In exploring the DPM over addition, students expressed 8×6 by using combinations of simpler multiplications of the form $n \times 6$. To this end, they broke apart the rectangular area of 8×6 into several smaller rectangular areas of 2×6, 3×6, 4×6, or 5×6. Figure 8.13 recalls eight numerical expressions students worked with. Why did we insist on students writing "unexecuted," "unclosed," or "not-computed" numerical expressions, despite their entrenched tendency to carry them out to a final, single, numerical answer? Because

> most arithmetic statements are read [by students] as instructions to compute and are indeed executed as such, typically leading to a numerical result. Because in algebra they need to be thought about in a fundamentally different way . . . students have particular difficulty making the transition unless their work with arithmetic treats arithmetic statements in a more algebraic way. (Kaput, Blanton, & Moreno, 2008, p. 45)

For this reason, it is indispensable that students learn to work with unexecuted expressions as mathematical *objects* in their own right, to be studied, discussed, and compared. We know this from studies showing that many middle school students cannot accept expressions such as $6a + 12$ or $x - 3$ as valid answers. They feel compelled to carry out the computational *process* but cannot, in either expression, because the terms are not "like terms."

An important study (Falkner, Levi, & Carpenter, 1999) alerting educators to students' *process* versus *object* interpretation of expressions and equations, asked students in grades 1–6 to complete the equation $8 + 4 = \underline{\quad} + 5$. Less than 10% of students in *any* grade gave

4 × (2 × 6)   2 × (4 × 6)   (3 × 6) + (5 × 6)   (2 × 6) + (2 × 6) + (4 × 6)
(4 × 2) × 6   (4 + 4) × 6   (3 + 5) × 6   (2 + 2 + 4) × 6

the correct answer of 7! Forty-nine percent of third- and fourth-graders and 76% of fifth- and sixth-graders answered 12. Why? Because they could not think of "8 + 4" as an object, analyze it, and compare it with "___ + 5." They carelessly computed the sum and wrote 12.

Algebra Connection

Expressions are foundational for algebra, as they are the building blocks of equations and functions. A main purpose of early algebra is to develop expressions—first with numbers and operations, and later with numbers, variables, and operations—that describe situations, be they geometric structures or problem stories. Figure 8.14 depicts a situation in which students can either be given one or more expressions for the area of the yellow picture frame and asked to explain why they are equivalent, or given neither

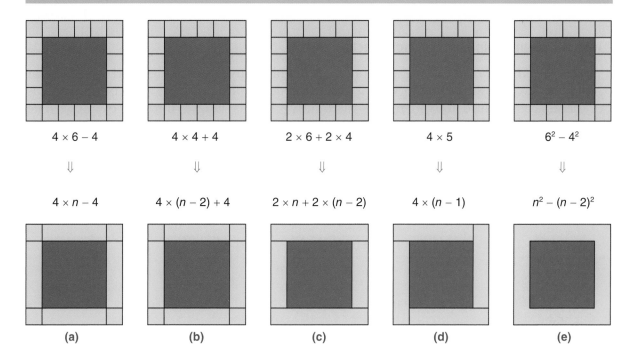

$4 \times 6 - 4$ $4 \times 4 + 4$ $2 \times 6 + 2 \times 4$ 4×5 $6^2 - 4^2$

⇓   ⇓   ⇓   ⇓   ⇓

$4 \times n - 4$ $4 \times (n-2) + 4$ $2 \times n + 2 \times (n-2)$ $4 \times (n-1)$ $n^2 - (n-2)^2$

(a)   (b)   (c)   (d)   (e)

expression but asked to come up with as many as they can. The unit of measure for the area of the picture frame is in square units (yellow squares).

Showing the equivalence between the numerical expressions (b) and (d), without computing, requires the DPM *over addition* (in bold): **4 × 4 + 4 = 4 × (4 + 1)** = 4 × 5. Using the DPM *over subtraction* (in bold), we can show that (a) and (d) are equivalent: **4 × 6 − 4 = 4 × (6 − 1)** = 4 × 5. Showing the equivalence between expressions (c) and (e), both equal to the simpler expression 2 × 10, is a secondary school challenge:

Expression (c): $\mathbf{2 \times 6 + 2 \times 4 = 2 \times (6 + 4)} = 2 \times 10$

Expression (e): $6^2 - 4^2 = (6 - 4) \times (6 + 4) = 2 \times 10$

The equations for (c) again involve the DPM (in bold); however, to understand the equations for (e), students would need to know the special identity called *the difference of two squares*,[2] which they don't yet know in the upper elementary grades. But their teachers may recall it from their own algebra experience. Finally, the expressions in the second row of Figure 8.14 are the algebraic generalizations of the numerical expressions for *any* square of side length n. (*Note*: The side length of the interior square is $n - 2$.)

RESEARCH . . .

For most Americans, the identifying feature of algebra is the formal equation consisting of variables and signs for the operations and equality. However, beneath the high abstraction of equations like $a(b + c) = ab + ac$ lie ways of reasoning about how quantities can be decomposed and recombined under different operations—ways of reasoning, unlike the conventions of the notation itself, fully accessible to elementary-school aged students.

—Deborah Schifter, Virginia Bastable, Susan Jo Russell,
Lisa Seyferth, & Margaret Riddle (2008, p. 263)

Decomposing Left or Right Factor

The *Multiplication Musings* lesson starts intentionally by breaking apart the *left* factor of 8 × 6 to get products like $(3 + 5) \times 6$, of the general form $(b + c) \times a$. This beginning was necessary because too often, the distributive law is taught through examples like $6 \times (3 + 5) = (6 \times 3) + (6 \times 5)$, which are quickly generalized to the single equation,

$$a \times (b + c) = (a \times b) + (a \times c) \quad \text{(Equation I)}$$

Students rarely see the reverse equation, namely,

$$(b + c) \times a = (b \times a) + (c \times a) \quad \text{(Equation II)}$$

2. The difference of two squares, $x^2 - y^2$, equals $(x - y) \times (x + y)$, for any two numbers x and y.

They remain with the notion that the single factor *a must* be on the *left* of the multiplication symbol, and the broken-down-into-a-sum factor $b + c$ *must* be on the *right*, as in Equation I above. Then, when they encounter the reverse, Equation II, they find it more difficult to apply the DPM, or they simply don't recognize it at all. Beware of one-way mathematics! The truth is this: Multiplication is distributive over addition only if *both equations I and II are true for all numbers a, b, and c.* This is also true for multiplication over subtraction.

Algebra Connection

In the middle grades, students will call the left sides of both equations I and II the *factored forms*, as the main operation is *multiplication*. The right sides are called the *expanded forms*, as the central operation is *addition*. (*Note*: By fifth or sixth grade, students learn the algebraic notation for multiplication between variables and write *3a* for $3 \times a$, and $a(b + c) = ab + ac$ for $a \times (b + c) = (a \times b) + (a \times c)$.)

What About Division? At the end of Chapter 7, you were left with a question to ponder: "Is the division $98 \div 7$ [or $98 \div (3 + 4)$] equivalent to $(98 \div 3) + (98 \div 4)$?" Computation proves that $98 \div 7 = 98 \div (3 + 4) = 14$, whereas $(98 \div 3) + (98 \div 4) = 32.\overline{6} + 24.5$. So, $98 \div (4 + 3)$ is *not* equal to $(98 \div 4) + (98 \div 3)$. In general,

$$a \div (b + c) \neq (a \div b) + (a \div c) \text{ (Equation III)}$$

But, if we break apart the dividend of the same division problem instead of the divisor, the distributive property of division (DPD) over addition holds: $98 \div 7 = (63 + 35) \div 7 = (63 \div 7) + (35 \div 7) = 9 + 5 = 14$. This is true for *any* two addends of 98. In general,

$$(b + c) \div a = (b \div a) + (c \div a) \text{ (Equation IV)}$$

Algebra Connection

Since equations III and IV are not *both* true, division is *not* distributive over addition (or subtraction). However, when referring to the right-sided DPD (Equation IV), mathematicians say that division is *right distributive* over addition.

Connecting Equation IV to Fraction Addition. It is important that students be aware of the right-distributive property of division (Equation IV) by the time they leave grade 5. What may not be obvious to students (nor to some teachers) is that Equation IV is hidden inside the addition of fractions with like denominators. For example, the sum of fractions $\frac{3}{3} + \frac{9}{3} = \frac{3+9}{3} = \frac{12}{3} = 4$ can be written horizontally as, $(3 \div 3) + (9 \div 3) = (3 + 9) \div 3 = 12 \div 3 = 4$. The bolded part here is an instance of the right-distributive property of division (Equation IV).

Practicing breaking apart expressions such as $\frac{3+9}{3}$ or $\frac{6+12}{3}$ or $\frac{4+20}{4}$ into sums, and computing the answer *both ways* (by direct computation *and* by applying the right-DPD over addition) in grades 4 and 5 is tantamount to practicing with expressions such as $\frac{3x+9}{3}$ or $\frac{6y+12}{3}$ or $\frac{4z+20}{4}$ in middle school. It will help students avoid common algebraic errors such as simplifying $\frac{(3x+9)}{3}$ to give $x+9$. "Cancelling out the 3s" is proof of a lack of understanding of division's *right*-distributive law. Its correct application is as follows: $\frac{(3x+9)}{3} = \frac{3x}{3} + \frac{9}{3} = x+3$. Such practice with numerical fractions will prevent senseless "cancelling" of numbers when students work with algebraic fractions.

Distinguishing Distributivity From Associativity

It's easy to see why students confuse the properties APM and DPM, even in high school! Teachers can help. In the early phases of teaching operation properties, teachers should highlight the main distinction between the APM and the DPM: The APM tells us something about multiplication *itself*, and the DPM tells us how multiplication works *in relation to a second operation* (addition or subtraction). We'll consider only *left* distributivity in this discussion. Aligning the equations vertically gives the following:

$a \times (b \times c) = (a \times b) \times c$ APM

$a \times (b + c) = (a \times b) + (a \times c)$ DPM over addition

$a \times (b - c) = (a \times b) - (a \times c)$ DPM over subtraction

Comparing the left expressions of the three equations reveals different operations inside the parentheses. The difference between multiplication and addition (or subtraction) is significant. To appreciate this difference, students need clear and rich models for what multiplication is and for how it differs from addition.

Algebra Connection

An example of a frequent algebraic error in middle school is $3(ab) = (3a)(3b)$. Rewriting this equation with all multiplication signs explicit gives

$$3 \times (a \times b) = (3 \times a) \times (3 \times b).$$

Analyzing this error, we find that students' understanding of the behavior of multiplication's distributivity over *addition*, namely $3 \times (a + b) = (3 \times a) + (3 \times b)$, is mimicked and transferred erroneously to the assumption that multiplication is distributive over *multiplication*, giving $3 \times (a \times b) = (3 \times a) \times (3 \times b)$. But the singularity of the DPM, as we saw, is its relation between *two* operations. If only *one* operation is present, as in $3(ab)$, or $3 \times (a \times b)$, there is *nothing to distribute*. Only the APM or the cumulative property of multiplication (CPM; see next section) could apply. The first modifies grouping: $3(ab) = (3a)b$. The second modifies order: $3(ab) = 3(ba)$.

Delving Deeper

4. From Array to Area (Grade 4)

A Final Word on Areas

In Chapter 7 we discussed arrays versus areas as models for the multiplication of discrete versus continuous quantities. Just as areas can be used to illustrate multiplication of decimals, we will see in Chapter 10 that they are also suitable for fraction multiplication, as fractions are, by definition, nonintegers (meaning, not whole numbers).

Algebra Connection

- **Commutative Property of Multiplication (CPM).** The CPM is the easiest property for students to grasp, as it is the most obvious one, both for addition ($x + y = y + x$) and multiplication ($x \times y = y \times x$). Whether multiplying whole numbers, decimals, or fractions, areas can be used to demonstrate the CPM. Given any two factors x and y, one can create a rectangle of dimensions x and y. Rotating the rectangle 90 degrees allows students to see that the area $x \times y$ equals the area $y \times x$ (Figure 8.15).

5. From Area to Algorithm (Grade 4 Continued)

Common Algorithms for Multidigit Multiplication

The U.S. Standard Algorithm (USSAM). Chapter 7 laid out four challenges to students in making sense of the USSAM. The fifth challenge regards carrying. Consider the multiplication of 34 by 78. After multiplying 8 by 4, we carry a 3, and after multiplying 7 by 4, we carry a 2. Figure 8.16 shows the way in which students place their carried values, 3 and 2. The layout is correct but confusing: While both are lined up in the "tens column," the 3 denotes *three tens*, yet the 2 denotes *two hundreds*. This is yet another betrayal of the place value concept.

The Partial Product Algorithm (PPAM): Seeing the Connection. As we saw, the PPAM reveals all four partial products of the multiplication of 34 by 78 (Figure 8.17). As students mature in their understanding of the PPAM, it's important that they see the connection among different algorithms, especially between the PPAM and the USSAM, as both algorithms are very popular. In some schools, students are forced to use the USSAM, despite the fact that students enjoy—because they make sense of—the PPAM. Thus, teachers can guide them to notice that by simply collapsing the columns of the PPAM rectangular display, the numbers in the USSAM vertical display appear. In our example (as shown in Figure 8.17),

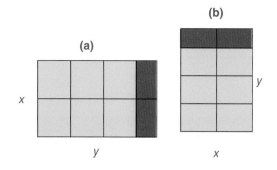

FIGURE 8.15   The product, or area, 2×3.5 (a) equals the product, or area, 3.5×2 (b)

FIGURE 8.16   Example of the USSAM with carrying

$$
\begin{array}{r}
2 \\
3 \\
3\,4 \\
\times\,7\,8 \\
\hline
2\,7\,2 \\
2\,3\,8 \\
\hline
2\,6\,5\,2
\end{array}
$$

- Collapsing the two rows in the first column (blue), we get 2380 (2100 + 280); and
- Collapsing the two rows in the second column (yellow), we get 272 (240 + 32).

On the other hand, in the USSAM (Figure 8.16):

- We get 272 by multiplying 8 by (30 + 4), this can be written $8 \times (30 + 4)$; and
- We get 238 (*in fact*, 2380) by multiplying 7 (*in fact*, 70) by (30 + 4); this can be written $70 \times (30 + 4)$.

Once again, the DPM is the mathematical explanation behind this important connection!

FIGURE 8.17   Collapsing rows in each column of the PPAM diagram reveals its similarity to the USSAM.

	70	8
30	30 × 70 = 2100	30 × 8 = 240
4	4 × 70 = 280	4 × 8 = 32

FIGURE 8.18   (a) Vertical layout of the multiplication 21 × 13 using the PPAM; (b) horizontal layout of the multiplication procedure for (20 + 1) × (10 + 3) using the DPM, which students will apply to the multiplication of binomials later on

$$\begin{array}{r} 2\,1 \\ \times\,1\,3 \\ \hline 2\,0\,0 \\ 6\,0 \\ 1\,0 \\ 3 \\ \hline 2\,7\,3 \end{array}$$

(a)

(20 + 1) × (10 + 3) = 200 + 60 + 10 + 3

(b)

FIGURE 8.19   Progression of expressions of binomials students will encounter as they progress through the grades

(20 + 1) × (10 + 3)

⇓

(x + 5) × (y − 7)

⇓

(x + y) × (z − t)

STUDENT WORK SAMPLE 2   In contrast with her first method (see Student Work Sample 1 on page 139), here Lauren chooses the PPAM to compute the same product, 16 × 30.

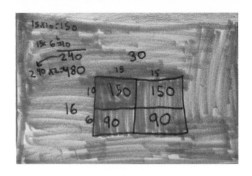

Photo by Katherine Weeden

A Final Connection: PPAM, DPM, and Multiplying Binomials

In Chapter 7, Figure 7.18 b and c, the PPAM for problem 21 × 13 was laid out vertically and horizontally (shown here as Figure 8.18 a and b). Both representations clearly expose the four partial products. Fifth-graders would do well to become familiar and at ease with both representations of the PPAM for double-digit multiplication. The horizontal display contains two instances of the DPM: 20 × (10 + 3) *and* 1 × (10 + 3). The DPM continues to play a key role in prealgebra and algebra courses. Sums (or differences) of *two* terms are called *binomials*. As students progress through the grades, the binomials they encounter evolve from containing all numbers, to numbers and variables, and finally to only variables, as illustrated in the examples of Figure 8.19.

The power of the DPM lies in the invariance of its application: Whether the binomial factors are $(20+1)\times(10+3)$ or $(x+y)\times(z-t)$, the structure is the same, so we proceed with the same logic and obtain four partial products, because "2 terms × 2 terms = 4 partial products."

Algebra Connection

We've kept the best algebra connection for last: a bridge from the fourth grade PPAM to a ninth grade quadratic identity! The product of binomials, $(x+y)\times(x+y)$ is called *the square of a sum*, and for that reason is written more succinctly as, $(x+y)^2$. An unthinking and frequent error high school students make is equating the square of a sum with the sum of the squares, that is, $(x+y)^2 = x^2 + y^2$, an algebra teacher's nightmare. But ninth-grade students who have experienced and made sense of the concepts described in this chapter will know that "2 terms × 2 terms = 4 terms." Moreover, if they remember their practice with Ms. Shena's "rectangle method," they may even have the picture with four different sections still etched in their memory (Figure 8.20). In this particular case, since the two binomial factors are identical, we have a special rectangle called a *square!*

FIGURE 8.20   The PPAM and the DPM extend all the way to high school special identities.

We conclude that $(x+y)^2 \neq x^2 + y^2$ but rather $(x+y)^2 = x^2 + y^2 + yx + xy$. But, by the CPM, we know that $yx = xy$, so the square of a sum is given by the equation: $(x+y)^2 = x^2 + y^2 + 2xy$. Readers may remember this quadratic identity in this order: $(x+y)^2 = x^2 + 2xy + y^2$. This is called a *quadratic identity*: quadratic because it has *squared* terms, and identity because it offers two equivalent expressions for the *square of a sum*. (*Note*: The word *quadratus*, past participle of the verb *quadrare*, meaning to square, gave the adjective *quadratic* in the 17th century.)

Closing Thoughts

This chapter offers something other than the common fare of basic fact memorization, algorithmic rote procedures, and single-answer questions. Rather, it focuses on exploring multiple meanings of multiplication (and the two main meanings of division), understanding properties of the operation, noticing structure in arithmetic, seeing connections between numerical algorithm and geometric area, and, ultimately, appreciating the many bridges from arithmetic to algebra. The distributive property of multiplication is a perfect example of a bridge from early childhood to graduate school mathematics. Whether students are adding

Photo by Susan Hamon

5 fingers $+$ 3 fingers, $50 + 30$, $\frac{5}{7} + \frac{3}{7}$, $5x + 3x$, or even $5a^2b^3 + 3a^2b^3$, the DPM is at work. The answers are clear: 8 fingers, 8 tens or 80, 8 sevenths or $\frac{8}{7}$, $8x$, and $8a^2b^3$, respectively. Less clear to students is the common algebraic structure:

$$5 \times \blacksquare + 3 \times \blacksquare = (5+3) \times \blacksquare = 8 \times \blacksquare,$$

or simply,

$$5\blacksquare + 3\blacksquare = (5+3)\blacksquare = 8\blacksquare.$$

Adding fingers doesn't constitute *knowing* the distributive property but indicates a prerequisite notion. Sophisticated algebraic thinking doesn't develop unaided. The teacher's role is therefore crucial. Hopefully, this chapter will help teachers develop their own deep knowledge of multiplication's many faces so that they in turn may inspire their students to see and appreciate the algebraic character of arithmetic.

RESEARCH . . .

The power of the distributive property is that it connects the two fundamental operations of addition and multiplication and provides explanations for many additional properties of whole numbers. . . . Understanding the distributive property is also critical for competency with and understanding of algebraic manipulations.

— Albert Otto, Janet Caldwell, Sarah Wallus Hancock, & Rose Mary Zbiek (2011, pp. 33–34)

9

Beyond *Multiplication Musings*

More Problems to Explore

Answers and explanations to the nontrivial questions in this chapter can be found in the Appendix, page 201.

I. Next Steps

1. Practicing the Distributive Property on 6 × 8 = 48

Guided by the colored parts in the four unmarked rectangles (Figure 9.1), write at least two equivalent expressions for each, using simpler products of the form $n \times 8$.

FIGURE 9.1   Expressing 6 × 8 as sums of simpler products of the form $n \times 8$

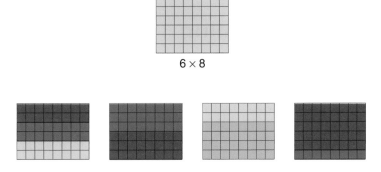

6 × 8

2. Finding the Distributive Property in the Multiplication Table

This exploration connects something old with something new: the multiplication table with the distributive property. One at a time, show tables with three colored cells—two of these are shown in Figure 9.2. Ask students what they notice. (*Answer:* The number in the third colored cell is the sum of the numbers in the first two). Students should explain their observations with words, manipulatives, or drawings, and write at least two equations modeling them. Check for differentiation between + and × symbols, and correct use of parentheses. Invite students to create similar problems.

FIGURE 9.2   Discovering the distributive law in a new context

×	1	2	3	4	5	6	7	8	9	10
1	1	2	3	4	5	6	7	8	9	10
2	2	4	6	8	10	12	14	16	18	20
3	3	6	9	12	15	18	21	24	27	30
4	4	8	12	16	20	24	28	32	36	40
5	5	10	15	20	25	30	35	40	45	50
6	6	12	18	24	30	36	42	48	54	60
7	7	14	21	28	35	42	49	56	63	70
8	8	16	24	32	40	48	56	64	72	80
9	9	18	27	36	45	54	63	72	81	90
10	10	20	30	40	50	60	70	80	90	100

(a)

×	1	2	3	4	5	6	7	8	9	10
1	1	2	3	4	5	6	7	8	9	10
2	2	4	6	8	10	12	14	16	18	20
3	3	6	9	12	15	18	21	24	27	30
4	4	8	12	16	20	24	28	32	36	40
5	5	10	15	20	25	30	35	40	45	50
6	6	12	18	24	30	36	42	48	54	60
7	7	14	21	28	35	42	49	56	63	70
8	8	16	24	32	40	48	56	64	72	80
9	9	18	27	36	45	54	63	72	81	90
10	10	20	30	40	50	60	70	80	90	100

(b)

After practicing with sets of three vertical or horizontal cells, offer this challenge (Figure 9.3): "What is the connection between the numbers in the light blue cells and the number in the dark blue cell? Write different but equivalent expressions describing the connection." Help students with notation.

II. For Your Own Learning

1. Revisiting the Sum of Three Consecutive Numbers

In Chapter 8, page 131, you were asked to prove that *the sum of any three consecutive whole numbers is always a multiple of 3*. To do so, pick three consecutive numbers at random. Call the middle number n, and the first and third $n-1$ and $n+1$, respectively. Adding the three together gives $(n-1)+n+(n+1)=n-1+n+n+1=3n$, since +1 and −1 make zero. We saw that $3n$ is the general expression for a multiple of 3, as in $45=3\times15$. Thus we have proved the claim algebraically.

Noticing that $3n$ is actually *three times the middle* number, which we called n, guide students to discover this fact by observing different sums of three consecutive numbers such as 6 + **7** + 8, 14 + **15** + 16, or 28 + **29** + 30. They will notice that they always obtain the *triple of the middle number*. Solicit algebraic thinking that explains the fact in *all* cases. One fourth-grader put it this way: "It's like three times the middle one 'cause the third number can give 1 to the first number."

FIGURE 9.3   Challenge: Find the connection between the four light blue cells and the dark blue cell.

×	1	2	3	4	5	6	7	8	9	10
1	1	2	3	4	5	6	7	8	9	10
2	2	4	6	8	10	12	14	16	18	20
3	3	6	9	12	15	18	21	24	27	30
4	4	8	12	16	20	24	28	32	36	40
5	5	10	15	20	25	30	35	40	45	50
6	6	12	18	24	30	36	42	48	54	60
7	7	14	21	28	35	42	49	56	63	70
8	8	16	24	32	40	48	56	64	72	80
9	9	18	27	36	45	54	63	72	81	90
10	10	20	30	40	50	60	70	80	90	100

2. Student Multiplication Strategies

Studies show that students develop three main multiplication strategies:

1. Repeated addition strategies, which gradually become more sophisticated. These strategies are based on adding equal groups.

2. Partitioning strategies involving breaking down one factor into a sum of smaller ones, multiplying each of these with the other factor, and then adding the subproducts. These strategies are based on the distributive law, even if it is formally unknown to students.

3. Changing-numbers strategies involve modifying the problem to a simpler problem by changing one or both factors and then compensating afterward if need be.

Students' division strategies correspond to these three multiplication strategies. Drawing on your experience in observing students invent ways of dividing, discuss this topic with colleagues, and describe three common division strategies students use. Allowing students time to develop, make sense of, and share computational strategies moves the study of numbers and operations beyond just counting precisely and calculating exactly.

3. Be Mindful of . . .

Golden Rule Myths

Many students believe in the golden rule, "Addition makes bigger and subtraction makes smaller." Similarly, they believe that "Multiplication makes bigger and division makes smaller." On a diagnostic assessment administered to rising eighth-graders in an international school I consulted for, 45% of the students claimed the latter statement was true. What teachers say and do in classroom discourse, starting in the elementary grades, can help students either dispel or reinforce their beliefs. When such statements are uttered, I suggest a comment of this nature: "In the world of numbers you know *now*, that's true; but as your universe of numbers expands and you get to know numbers called *negative* and *rational*, such rules will no longer be true." Depending on the situation, and your audience age and ability levels, you may pursue the issue further with concrete examples.

Analogies Between Addition and Multiplication

Once students' universe of numbers includes *real* numbers, they realize there are really only two operations: *addition* and *multiplication*. This is because any difference can be written as a sum, using negative numbers [$8-5=8+(-5)$], and any quotient can be written as a product, using rational numbers [$8 \div 5 = \frac{8}{5} = 8 \times \frac{1}{5}$]. By the time students study college mathematics, subtraction and division have essentially dissolved; addition and multiplication emerge as the two prevailing operations of real numbers. It is not too early, in grades 3–5, to foster awareness of fundamental *analogies between addition and multiplication*. Encourage students who discover the analogies below to articulate them, share them, and record them. They are foundational to formal algebra.

TABLE 9.1   Analogies between the addition–subtraction and multiplication–division inverse relationships

Addition vs. Subtraction	Multiplication vs. Division
1. Addition is *commutative,* but subtraction is not.	1. Multiplication is *commutative,* but division is not.
2. Addition is *associative,* but subtraction is not.	2. Multiplication is *associative,* but division is not.
3. Addition of any natural numbers *always* yields a natural number, but subtraction *may* yield a new kind of number: a *negative* number.	3. Multiplication of any two natural numbers *always* yields a natural number, but division *may* yield a new kind of number: a *rational* number.
4. Addition has *identity element* 0: For any number n, $n + 0 = n$.	4. Multiplication has identity element 1: For any number n, $n \times 1 = n$.
5. *Later, students will learn that* every number n has an *opposite* $-n$, called the *additive inverse,* such that $n + (-n) = 0$.	5. Likewise, every number n ($\neq 0$) has a reciprocal $\frac{1}{n}$, called the *multiplicative inverse,* such that $n \times \frac{1}{n} = 1$.

III. For Your Students' Learning

1. The Marvels of the Multiplication Table

If the children's introduction to arithmetic rests *primarily* on the rote memorization of the . . . multiplication tables, . . . then their intuitive understandings of number relationships are undermined and overwhelmed. In effect, they learn to shift from intuitive processing to performing automatic numerical operations without caring much about their meanings. (Sousa, 2008, p. 46)

The following explorations will help students discover new numbers, make new connections, and see properties in a new light.

Getting to Know Perfect Squares

Version 1 (Grades 3–4). Project a multiplication table with a highlighted main diagonal (Figure 9.4). *Ask:* "Why do you suppose these numbers are called *square* numbers?" Without giving away the answer, have students build rectangular arrays for numbers 1, 4, 9, 16, . . . They will see that each of these numbers *can* be configured as a *square array* of tiles (Figure 9.5). *Follow up:* "Can any of the other 90 numbers be represented as squares?"

Version 2 (Grades 4–5). With no multiplication table in sight, assign to each student/group two numbers: one on the main diagonal as shown in Figure 9.4 (call it *n*, for this discussion) and the other elsewhere (call it *m*). *Task:* "Make all possible rectangular arrays, using (*n* or *m*) square tiles or drawing on grid paper. Make one poster per number recording your arrays, and post them on the wall." When all the posters have been posted, have students observe and analyze all of them. Focus their attention on the square arrays. Have them find those numbers in the multiplication table. Why are they *on* the main diagonal? Can numbers *off* this diagonal be represented as squares? Why not? Probe for the name for these special numbers. Does the phrase "square number" make sense?

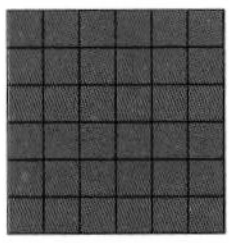

Both versions will set off the debate about whether a square is a rectangle. Rather than *telling* students that *a square is a rectangle*, encourage them to research the definition of the word or observe its etymology: It stems from *rect* (right) and *angle*. These explorations will dispel the mythical *two-long-sides-and-two-short-sides* definition of a rectangle and give students a concrete understanding of square numbers. Mathematicians actually call them *perfect squares* because they are squares of *whole numbers*.

FIGURE 9.4   Exploring the perfect squares

×	1	2	3	4	5	6	7	8	9	10
1	1	2	3	4	5	6	7	8	9	10
2	2	4	6	8	10	12	14	16	18	20
3	3	6	9	12	15	18	21	24	27	30
4	4	8	12	16	20	24	28	32	36	40
5	5	10	15	20	25	30	35	40	45	50
6	6	12	18	24	30	36	42	48	54	60
7	7	14	21	28	35	42	49	56	63	70
8	8	16	24	32	40	48	56	64	72	80
9	9	18	27	36	45	54	63	72	81	90
10	10	20	30	40	50	60	70	80	90	100

FIGURE 9.5   The number 36 as a square array of tiles

Why Are They Equal?

Create puzzles requiring students to identify multiplication properties or characteristics to figure out why two cells, highlighted in a same color, contain equal numbers (see Figure 9.6):

    i. Why are the yellow cells equal $(8 \times 3 = 3 \times 8)$?

    ii. Why are the green cells equal $(8 \times 5 = 4 \times 10)$?

    iii. Why are the blue cells equal $(9 \times 4 = 3 \times 12)$?

Have students create other similar or different why-are-they-equal puzzles.

FIGURE 9.6   Why are numbers in same-color cells equal?

×	1	2	3	4	5	6	7	8	9	10	11	12
1	1	2	3	4	5	6	7	8	9	10	11	12
2	2	4	6	8	10	12	14	16	18	20	22	24
3	3	6	9	12	15	18	21	24	27	30	33	36
4	4	8	12	16	20	24	28	32	36	40	44	48
5	5	10	15	20	25	30	35	40	45	50	55	60
6	6	12	18	24	30	36	42	48	54	60	66	72
7	7	14	21	28	35	42	49	56	63	70	77	84
8	8	16	24	32	40	48	56	64	72	80	88	96
9	9	18	27	36	45	54	63	72	81	90	99	108
10	10	20	30	40	50	60	70	80	90	100	110	120
11	11	22	33	44	55	66	77	88	99	110	121	132
12	12	24	36	48	60	72	84	96	108	120	132	144

FIGURE 9.7   Equivalent fractions in multiplication table

×	1	2	3	4	5	6	7	8	9	10
1	1	2	3	4	5	6	7	8	9	10
2	2	4	6	8	10	12	14	16	18	20
3	3	6	9	12	15	18	21	24	27	30
4	4	8	12	16	20	24	28	32	36	40
5	5	10	15	20	25	30	35	40	45	50
6	6	12	18	24	30	36	42	48	54	60
7	7	14	21	28	35	42	49	56	63	70
8	8	16	24	32	40	48	56	64	72	80
9	9	18	27	36	45	54	63	72	81	90
10	10	20	30	40	50	60	70	80	90	100

Finding Equivalent Fractions

Students, and even teachers, are sometimes surprised when they discover equivalent fractions living inside the multiplication table. The unit fraction $\frac{1}{4}$, for instance, along with nine equivalent fractions, can be formed using corresponding pairs of numbers in the two parallel number rows highlighted in green in Figure 9.7: light green for the numerators, dark green for the denominators. Similarly, the fraction $\frac{3}{7}$, along with nine equivalent fractions, can be formed using the number rows highlighted in light and dark brown. Seeing equivalent fractions in this context connects the concept of equivalence to *multiplication*. Fraction $\frac{3}{7}$ is equivalent to $\frac{12}{28}$ because both numerator *and* denominator of $\frac{3}{7}$ have been multiplied by the same "times table," namely 4, to obtain $\frac{12}{28}$.

My Multiplication Table

The Common Core State Standards for Mathematics (CCSSM) expect third-graders to be able to multiply and divide within 100. While conceptual understanding of multiplication and its properties is essential for thinking algebraically and solving problems, so is procedural fluency with multiplication combinations. But math educators (Sousa, 2008) and cognitive neuroscientists (Dehaene, 1997) explain how challenging and sometimes overwhelming it can be to memorize the 100 products of the multiplication table. My Multiplication Table may help your students (Figure 9.8) with this task. Each student creates his or her personal table, coloring in combinations *the student already knows*. The remaining, uncolored cells indicate the combinations they need to practice. Given the symmetry of the commutative property, students eventually realize they can automatically color in the upper triangle of the table (Figure 9.8, in brown). Moreover, students often master the times-2, times-5, and times-10 products early on, and perhaps parts or all of the times-3 and times-4 products as well. Experience confirms what research shows (Dehaene, p. 127), namely, that the hardest multiplication combinations to memorize—even for adults—are the six products $7\times6, 8\times6, 8\times7, 9\times6, 9\times7$, and 9×8 (see Chapter 7, Figure 7.8, in red).

FIGURE 9.8 An example of a fourth-grader's "My Multiplication Table"

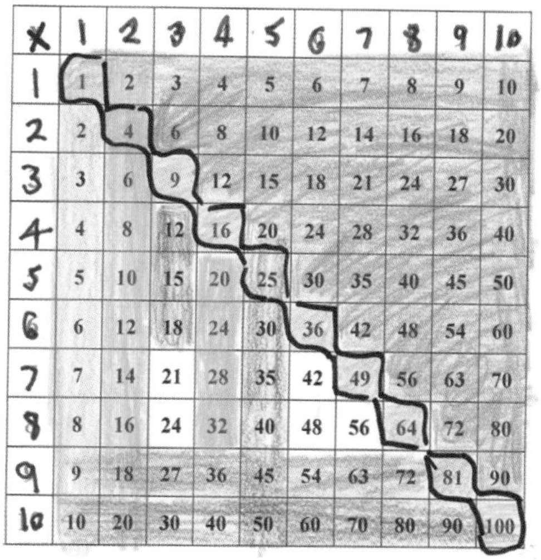

2. Here Is the Model, What Is the Problem?

Assign students a mathematical model such as $4\times5=20$. The task is to come up with different types of multiplication problems modeled by the given equation. In grades 3–5, students should grow their repertoire to include the following contexts:

Multiplication Problem Situation	Example of Problem
Equal Groups	4 bags, 5 apples in each bag, how many apples in all? This is the most basic and easiest problem situation for students to grasp.
Rectangular Array	4 rows of 5 ants marching; how many ants are marching? Arrays stress a geometric configuration, but they still fall under the equal-groups category.
Area	A rectangular carpet is 4 feet by 5 feet; what is the area in square feet? Arrays and areas are often lumped together, but they have significant differences: (1) arrays are discrete, while areas are continuous; (2) in arrays, the same unit measures total number *and* dimensions; in rectangles, different units measure area and dimensions.
Combinations	4 tops, 5 pants, how many outfits? These problems are rare but good.
Multiplicative Comparison	Cable A is 5 m long, cable B is 4 times longer; how long is cable B? This book stresses the import of multiplicative-comparison problems!
Rate	A box of pens costs 5 euros; how much will 4 boxes cost? The rate concept is planted in grades 3–5 but solidifies in middle school. Rate and comparison problems are the most challenging.

These distinct problem situations should not be confused with the drawings or concrete representations students use to model these meanings of multiplication, such as equal sets of objects, hops on a number line, strips of number cubes, rectangular grids, and so on.

Questions to Ponder

- Could you restate the above problems asking for one factor instead of the product?
- In which contexts do the factors 4 and 5 play symmetric roles? What about asymmetric?
- Observe the unit(s) used to measure the first factor, the second, and the product.
- For each context, create a division story. Is there one type or two? How do you know?

3. Multiplying by 10

Do you ever find yourself, or your students, saying, "When multiplying a whole number by 10, you just add a zero." Not only is this rule memorization instead of thinking algebraically about place value, but it is also mathematically incorrect. Adding zero to any number doesn't change it, because 0 is the additive identity. Do students *understand why* they tag on a zero at the end of the numeral when multiplying by 10? Can you *show why* in a visual and convincing way? What about multiplying by 100?

4. Bringing Out the Algebraic Character of Arithmetic

FIGURE 9.9 Each bag contains 3 blue balls and 5 red cubes.

Problem. Six paper bags are on my desk. Each one contains three blue balls and five red cubes. Write a numerical expression for the total number of 3-D shapes on my desk. I'm interested in your thinking about how to find the total number, not the actual numerical answer. Be a thinker, not just a doer! (Figure 9.9)

Strategies will include explanations that can be transcribed symbolically by the following:

1a. $8 + 8 + 8 + 8 + 8 + 8$

1b. $6 \times (3 + 5)$

2a. $3 + 3 + 3 + 3 + 3 + 3 + 5 + 5 + 5 + 5 + 5 + 5$

2b. $(6 \times 3) + (6 \times 5)$

The first method (1a and 1b) consists of first figuring out the total number of shapes in *one* bag (3 + 5 = 8), and then adding 6 iterations of this number—one for each bag, or multiplying it by 6. The expression $6 \times (3 + 5)$ is the factored form of the distributive property. The second method (2a and 2b) consists of counting *all* blue balls, then *all* red cubes, either by addition or by multiplication, and then combining the two sets. The expression $(6 \times 3) + (6 \times 5)$ is the expanded form of the distributive property. Such problems illustrate the distributive property in action and give meaning to its two equivalent forms, $6 \times (3 + 5)$ and $(6 \times 3) + (6 \times 5)$, listed as 1b and 2b above. Later, when numbers are generalized to letters, expressions with similar algebraic structure as $6 \times (x + y) = (6 \times x) + (6 \times y)$ will make sense. Note that in *algebraic* expressions $x + y$ cannot be added (like 3 + 5), so the *only* ways to express "6 times the sum $(x + y)$" are $6 \times (x + y)$ or $(6 \times x) + (6 \times y)$.

5. Differentiating Addition and Multiplication

Analyses of common middle school student errors reveal something fundamental: the difficulty of understanding multiplication as significantly different from addition. Middle school teacher Bill Lancaster laments, "The conclusion I'm coming to is that the students who have the deepest trouble with middle school mathematics are those without a clear and rich set of models for what multiplication is and how it is different from addition" (as quoted in Russell, Schifter, & Bastable, 2011, p. 131). Exercises of the following types will further help students differentiate between behaviors of addition and multiplication.

Examining Structure

Looking at the structure of each of the four expressions below, and without evaluating them, find the ones equivalent to $9 \times (8+7)$.

$$(7 + 8) \times 9 \qquad (9 \times 8) + 7 \qquad (9 \times 8) + (9 \times 7) \qquad (9 + 8) \times (9 + 7)$$

Solving by Thinking

Thinking *relationally* about the equals sign—as a scale with equal weights on both sides—and without computing sums or products, find the value of n that *balances each equation*. Apply the *plus minus n* and the *times n, by n* concepts, as discussed in Chapter 8, Section 2. The diagrams summarizing these concepts are reprinted in Figure 9.10.

Equivalent Sums	*Equivalent Products*
$5 + 100 = 10 + n$	$5 \times 100 = 10 \times n$
$n + 28 = 30 + 14$	$n \times 28 = 30 \times 14$

FIGURE 9.10 (a) $+n, -n$ concept for equivalent sums; (b) $\times n, \div n$ for equivalent products.

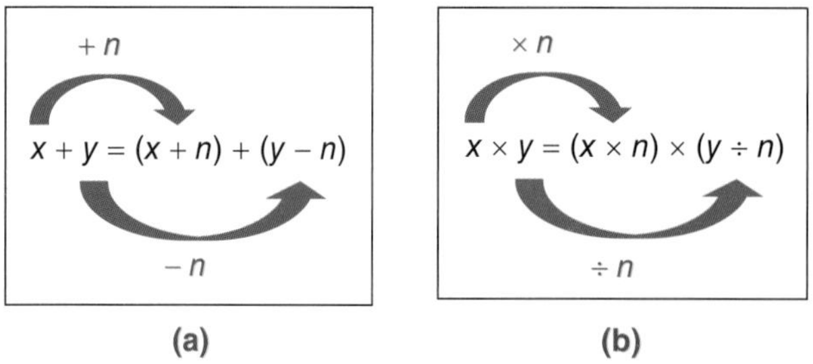

$+n$

$x + y = (x + n) + (y - n)$

$-n$

(a)

$\times n$

$x \times y = (x \times n) \times (y \div n)$

$\div n$

(b)

6. Maximizing Products Without Computing

Pick four different digits at random. Form the two 2-digit numbers that will generate the *largest product*. Suppose digits 9, 7, 4, and 2 are selected. Students will clearly place 9 and 7 in the tens place of their two numbers. The next step is subtler and often eludes students—and sometimes adults as well. Without computing, mentally or with a calculator, but just using your number sense and algebraic thinking, decide which is greater, 94×72 or 92×74. Explain using your understanding of multiplication's effect on numbers.

7. Jennifer's Enigma

Jennifer, a fourth-grade teacher, brought an enigma to a professional development session one day. "Amy claimed that 42×96 should be equal to 52×86 because the -10 and the $+10$ cancel out," she said. Then she added, "Her logic makes sense, but I checked and the numbers aren't equal!" Needless to say, Jennifer's enigma made for an excellent exploration. In the spirit of algebraic thinking about operations, one teacher ordered, "Nobody compute, OK!" Working in pairs, fourth- and fifth-grade teachers found four

FIGURE 9.11   During a parent session, Marjolijn uses the rectangle method to show that 52×86 is greater than 42×96.

Photo by Serena Washburn

different strategies to resolve Jennifer's enigma. I have since used this problem many times in parent math academy sessions (Figure 9.11). How many strategies can your class come up with? Supposing Amy was your student, how would you respond to her convincing argument?

8. Connecting Array and Areas to Addition and Multiplication

Problem 1. A rectangular array of 36 apples is partially hidden by a blotch of paint (Figure 9.12a). Can you figure out the number of columns? How do you know? Write two expressions describing the array, one using *addition* and the other *multiplication*.

Problem 2. A brown rug hides part of a tiled kitchen floor (Figure 9.12b). Can you figure out the floor's total area? How do you know? Write at least two different expressions for the area, using *addition and multiplication*. Starting in grade 3, the CCSSM expect students to relate areas to addition and multiplication.

FIGURE 9.12   A yellow paint spill partially covers part of a rectangular array of apples (a), and a brown rug covers part of a tiled kitchen floor (b).

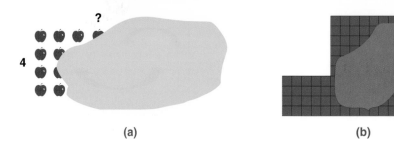

(a)   (b)

9. Magic Tricks and Multiplication

Figuring out magic tricks forces one to think outside the box. Tricks sharpen our problem-solving abilities and foster our creativity. Multiplication and place value, both stressed by the Common Core standards, are required to unravel the following tricks.

Trick 1

- Step 1: Pick any 3-digit number. Enter it in your calculator. Call this number N.
- Step 2: Using a calculator, multiply N first by 7, then by 11, and last by 13.
- Step 3: Record your answer. Try other 3-digit numbers.
- Step 4: What do you always get? Unpack the mathematics to resolve the mystery.

Trick 2

- Step 1: Pick a 3-digit number with *all digits equal*. Call this number N.
- Step 2: Compute the sum of all three digits of N. Call this sum S. Divide N by S.
- Step 3: Record your answer. Try other such 3-digit numbers.
- Step 4: What do you always get? Unpack the mathematics to resolve the mystery.

You or your students are now ready to play these number tricks on the whole class.

10. Folding Into Fraction Multiplication

Visualizing fraction multiplication is important. Take the simple product $\frac{2}{3} \times \frac{1}{4}$. Using a plain piece of paper, have students fold it into thirds and then shade two parts (Figure 9.13a). Multiplying by $\frac{1}{4}$ means taking $\frac{1}{4}$ of the $\frac{2}{3}$, so next have students fold the paper into fourths, making the folds perpendicular to the previous folds. Shading *one* fourth of the paper also shades *one fourth of the two thirds* (Figure 9.13b). The small sections represent the twelfths and the intersection of both colors represents the product, $\frac{2}{12}$ (or $\frac{1}{6}$).

This concrete representation will help students make sense of the fraction multiplication algorithm when they encounter it.

FIGURE 9.13   (a) Folding in thirds, (b) folding in fourths

(a)

(b)

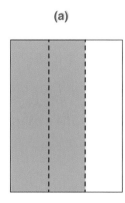
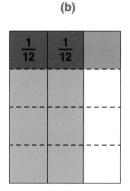

Only after students have an understanding of the meanings of the operations and symbols can the process of memorizing begin.

—Lynn Columba (2013, p. 380)

EXPLORATION IV

Fundamentals of Rational Numbers

Beyond Part–Whole Relationships

Many people have a fear of mathematics. . . . For most of these people, their relationship with mathematics started downhill early in elementary school, right after they were introduced to fractions.

—Susan J. Lamon (2010, p. 15)

RATIONALE FOR EXPLORATION IV

- "Historically, the development of algebra grew from a consideration of the arithmetic of rational numbers"[1] (Saul, 1998, p. 137). Students need to develop a friendliness with these numbers and understand from early on that they are used to model many concepts in our world beyond just a part–whole relationship.

- "Difficulty with fractions (including decimals and percents) is pervasive and is a major obstacle to further progress in mathematics, including algebra" (National Mathematics Advisory Panel , 2008, p. xix).

- One reason students have difficulty with rational numbers is because, in the elementary grades, "fractions are taught in isolation from whole numbers and fraction operations are taught as a collection of procedures" (Empson, Levi, & Carpenter, 2011, p. 410). Also, "A serious instructional error is to rush too quickly to the rule... Intuitive methods are always best at first" (Van de Walle & Lovin, 2006, p. 151).

- Students need to cultivate a deep appreciation for the notion of the whole or unit when working with fractions, because "the concept of the whole underlies the concept of a fraction" (Behr & Post, 1992, p. 213).

- Teachers should "spend whatever time is needed to ensure that students understand what it means for fractions to be equivalent at both the concrete and symbolic levels" (Cramer & Whitney, 2010, p. 21). Teachers are also urged to "delay teaching the formal operations with fractions until students have a sense of the relative size of fractions and an understanding of equivalence" (Cramer & Whitney, 2010, p. 21).

- "One of the greatest errors fifth- and sixth-grade teachers typically make is introducing conversion of fractions to decimals before students have developed mastery with fractions on a conceptual level" (Collins & Dacey, 2010, p.16). Students in grades 3–5 should come to know at least three strategies for comparing fractions (Chval, Lannin, & Jones, 2013).

- "Division of fractions is often considered the most mechanical and least understood topic in elementary school" (Tirosh, 2000, p. 6).

---

1. The set of rational numbers, denoted by the symbol $\mathbb{Q}$, is the set of all fractions $\frac{a}{b}$, such that a and b are integers, and $b \neq 0$.

10
Fractions in Action

From Work With Teachers, Students, and Parents (Grades 3–5)

recent National Council of Teachers of Mathematics (NCTM) publication for teachers reads as follows:

> Rational numbers compose a major area of school mathematics that is crucial for students to learn but challenging for teachers to teach. Students in grades 3–5 need to understand rational numbers well if they are to succeed in these grades and in their subsequent mathematics experiences. (Barnett-Clarke, Fisher, Marks, & Ross, 2010, p. 1)

You may be asking yourself, "What *are* rational numbers anyway?" Well, *rational numbers* are all numbers that can be written in the form $\frac{a}{b}$. But there are two more conditions: a nd b must be *integers,* and b cannot be *zero*. Since we're on definitions, the set of numbers $\{\ldots -3, -2, -1, 0, 1, 2, 3 \ldots\}$ are called *integers*. Integers are themselves special rational numbers with denominators equal to 1. For instance, the integer 7 can be written equivalently as the rational number $\frac{7}{1}$. The phrase *whole number* is used in elementary grades but does not have a universal mathematical definition. Depending on the textbook, *whole numbers* could mean positive integers or nonnegative integers (the latter include zero).

The other question you may have is, "Aren't rational numbers a *middle school* mathematics topic?" Yes, but not exclusively. The higher expectations of the K–12 Common Core State Standards for Mathematics (CCSSM) require a more profound exposure to rational numbers earlier than the middle grades. Rational numbers are the foundation for the most perplexing middle school concepts, which in turn are the foundation for algebra and higher mathematics: ratio, rate, percent, and proportion. Foundational to these topics is *proportional thinking*, a sophisticated way of thinking that develops in late elementary and middle school and evolves and matures in algebra and advanced algebra courses. (*Note*: The difference between *fraction* and *rational number* is the first topic under the heading Discussion below.)

The format of this final chapter differs from that of the previous ones. Eight questions that adults or students have asked me, or I them, open the chapter. They give us pause. Their answers will provide insight into fraction content knowledge. We will refer to them as **Question 1** through **Question 8**, bolded to facilitate locating them in the text. Please refer back to this page to recall each one, as the questions will not be restated. Reflect for a moment on how you might respond to these questions before reading on.

Question 1: Explain why, according to CCSSM, students in grade 3 should interpret $\frac{a}{b}$ as "a parts of size $\frac{1}{b}$" rather than "a parts out of b equal parts?"

Question 2: Can you explain how Figure 10.1 could be a pictorial representation of either $\frac{3}{4}, \frac{1}{4}, \frac{1}{3}$, or $\frac{3}{1}$?

Question 3: Is $\frac{2}{5} + \frac{3}{4}$ ever equal to $\frac{5}{9}$? If so, in what context?

Question 4: Could $\frac{1}{2}$ be more than 1?

Question 5: How might you enlighten a discussion between students disagreeing on the fraction depicted in Figure 10.2? One says it's $\frac{10}{5}$, or 2; the other says $\frac{10}{10}$, or 1?

Question 6: How can we make "equivalent fractions come alive" for students?

Question 7: How would you respond to: "I know how to compare $\frac{7}{9}$ and $\frac{8}{9}$, or $\frac{8}{9}$ and $\frac{8}{10}$, but not $\frac{7}{9}$ and $\frac{8}{10}$. Top and bottom are both *two* apart so they're equal, right?"

FIGURE 10.1 Of what fraction could this be a model?

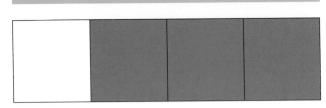

Question 8: How would you guide a student who says, "I understand what it means to divide by a whole number, but I don't *see* what it *means* to divide by $\frac{1}{2}$ or $\frac{5}{6}$?"

If you find these questions challenging, that's because they truly are. Fractions constitute perhaps the most difficult topic students have to learn and teachers have to teach, in elementary school. The topic area is so problematic that a report by The National Mathematics Advisory Panel, titled *Foundations for Success*, warned that proficiency with fractions is severely underdeveloped in the United States. It consequently declared fluency with fractions a major goal for K–8 mathematics education (2008). This report had a significant impact on the writing of the CCSSM. Entering the "new" world of fractions is not just uncomfortable for students; "many elementary school teachers find themselves in unfamiliar territory, skating tentatively on the thin ice of their own limited mathematical understanding" (Barnett, Goldstein, & Jackson, 1994, p. ix). The bright side of this, though, is that discomfort engenders growth!

FIGURE 10.2 Is this $\frac{10}{5}$ or $\frac{10}{10}$?

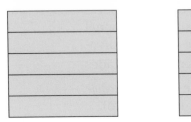

Informed by research and more than 25 years of working with adults and students on this perplexing topic, Chapter 10 addresses foundational ideas about rational numbers:

- Meanings of $\frac{a}{b}$
- Representations of $\frac{a}{b}$
- The whole or the unit
- Equivalence and comparison
- Meanings of division

Discussion

1. What Does the Symbol $\frac{a}{b}$ Conjure Up in Our Minds?

First, What Is a Fraction?

Unlike the phrase *rational number*, the word *fraction* does not have a universal mathematical definition. In elementary math textbooks, *fractions* refer to *positive rational numbers* such as $\frac{3}{5}$ or $\frac{9}{4}$. They are grouped into *proper* and *improper* fractions, depending on whether they are less than or greater than 1. By middle school, though, symbolic expressions such as $\frac{\sqrt{5}}{2}$ and $\frac{\pi}{4}$ are also called "fractions," as they represent quotients of two quantities, albeit noninteger quantities, written in fraction form. Hence, to encompass all cases, a fraction is a symbolic expression of the form $\frac{N}{D}$, where numerator N and denominator D can be any quantities, provided $D \neq 0$. Given this fraction definition, *any rational number can be written as a fraction*, but *not every fraction is a rational number* (Figure 10.3). That said, since this book is written for elementary school mathematics professionals, a *fraction* here will designate a *nonnegative rational number*. Students encounter negative rational numbers in the middle grades.

More Than Just "a Parts Out of b Equal Parts"

Rational numbers have multiple interpretations, but, regrettably, most students have only one image of fraction in their mind: "*a parts out of b equal parts*." While we know this explanation is a helpful introduction to fractions in the early grades, we also know that this *sole* conception can be limiting and even problematic to progressing in mathematics. Following are at least four answers to **Question 1**.

FIGURE 10.3 All rational numbers can be written as fractions, but not all fractions are rational numbers.

F R A C T I O N S	
$\dfrac{\sqrt{2}}{2}\quad \dfrac{\sin x}{\pi}\quad \dfrac{\sqrt[3]{4}}{\sqrt{5}}\quad \dfrac{\pi}{x+2}$	$\dfrac{15}{-4}\ \dfrac{-9}{14}\ \dfrac{2}{3}\ \dfrac{13}{11}\ \dfrac{4}{4}\ \dfrac{5}{1}$
Not rational numbers	*Rational numbers*

Inclusion. If students think of $\frac{a}{b}$ as "*a parts out of b equal parts* ("*ap/bep*"), they gather that *ap* must be a subset of *bep*. From this perspective of *inclusion*, they conclude that *ap* and *bep* are of the same nature. Consequently, they make sense of the question, "What fraction of the children performing in the school play is girls?" because girls *are* children; but they can't make sense of the question, "What fraction of the number of boys [in the play] is the number of girls?" An analogy with continuous variables is, "What fraction of the vinaigrette is oil?" versus "What fraction of the vinegar volume is the oil volume?"

Size. The second limitation of interpreting $\frac{a}{b}$ as *ap/bep* is the inference that *ap* must be *smaller* than *bep*, since you are *taking* the *a* parts *out of* the *b* parts. Thus, fractions $\frac{1}{2}$ or $\frac{2}{5}$ make sense, but $\frac{8}{5}$ or $\frac{10}{7}$ do not. How does one take "8 parts *out of* 5 parts?"

Separate Numbers. The third limitation of the exclusive *ap/bep* interpretation is its delaying effect on the progression toward considering a fraction a *single* number. If a student, when seeing $\frac{3}{4}$, thinks, "Divide the whole into 4 parts and then choose 3 parts," she is mentally manipulating *two* numbers or quantities, each of which has a separate role:

the 4 parts into which she cuts the whole, and the 3 parts she chooses. This delays the more mature understanding of $\frac{3}{4}$ as *one* number, with a unique place on the number line, three fourths of the way from 0 to 1. This number's decimal expression is 0.75.

Additive Thinking. Perhaps the greatest limitation of the sole ap/bep understanding is the obstacle it presents to proportional thinking and to its precursor, multiplicative thinking. Given a fraction $\frac{a}{b}$, thinking of it as the part I take and of $\frac{b-a}{b}$ as the part I leave is thinking additively, because $\frac{a}{b} + \frac{b-a}{b} = \frac{b}{b}$. For example, if I think of $\frac{4}{7}$ as the *four one-sevenths* I take and of $\frac{3}{7}$ as *three one-sevenths* I leave, I'm thinking additively, because $\frac{4}{7} + \frac{3}{7} = \frac{7}{7}$ (Figure 10.4). On the other hand, interpreting $\frac{4}{7}$ as "4 parts of size $\frac{1}{7}$" is thinking *multiplicatively*. The

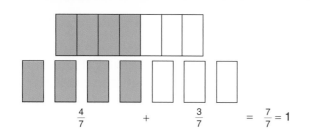

FIGURE 10.4 Separating the whole into 4 one-sevenths and 3 other one-sevenths is additive thinking.

unit is $\frac{1}{7}$ and I count "4 *copies* of $\frac{1}{7}$" to get $\frac{4}{7}$, or better yet I *multiply* "4 *times* the unit $\frac{1}{7}$" to get $\frac{4}{7}$. From a measurement perspective (a multiplicative process par excellence), saying that $\frac{4}{7}$ is 4 times as large as $\frac{1}{7}$ is saying that the quantity $\frac{4}{7}$ is measured in "$\frac{1}{7}$" units. Improper fractions are no different: $\frac{11}{7}$ means "11 copies of" or "11 times" the unit $\frac{1}{7}$ (Figure 10.5).

Generalizing this interpretation for *any* fraction $\frac{a}{b}$, we can write $\frac{a}{b} = a \times \frac{1}{b}$. The consequences of this definition of $\frac{a}{b}$ are huge. Two points are noteworthy:

1. A quotient $\frac{a}{b}$ is a product $a \times \frac{1}{b}$ just as any difference $a - b$ is a sum $a + - b$. Students learn later that there are only two operations: *addition* and *multiplication*.

2. $\frac{a}{b} = a \times \frac{1}{b}$ explains the fraction division rule, "invert and multiply." Substitute a fraction for a and one for b; dividing is multiplying by the denominator's reciprocal!

FIGURE 10.5 Seeing $\frac{4}{7}$ as four *one-sevenths* and $\frac{11}{7}$ as eleven *one-sevenths* is multiplicative thinking.

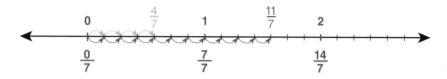

2. Other Representations of $\frac{a}{b}$

By "representations" here we mean both **inner** and **outer** representations. Inner representations are what we see with our mind's eye, or what we **think** $\frac{a}{b}$ means; outer representations are what we **see** with physical eyes. This section describes four conceptual interpretations of rational numbers (inner representations) and three models (outer representations) that students must experience in order to develop fraction sense.

Making Sense of Fractions: Inner Interpretations of $\frac{a}{b}$.

1. A Measure. A rational number $\frac{a}{b}$ can denote a *measure* or, more precisely, a fraction of a unit of measure, such as $\frac{1}{2}$ of a mile, $\frac{3}{4}$ of a kilogram, or 10½ square feet. Children first encounter rational numbers as numbers resulting from measuring experiences: sharing one cookie equally with a friend, measuring the length of a table in craft-stick units, or counting the number of square-foot tiles covering the classroom floor. As discussed in Explorations I and III, measurement situations help students transition from the world of whole numbers (answers to "how many?") to the world of rational numbers in their fractional or decimal forms (answers to "how much?" "how long?" "how heavy?" etc.). From once thinking that no numbers live between consecutive counting numbers, children gradually realize that infinitely many numbers populate each unit segment of the number line!

2. A Quotient. A rational number $\frac{a}{b}$ can also denote a *quotient* of two numbers, representing, for example, the division of 9 granola bars among 6 children. In this sense, $\frac{9}{6}$ either refers to the *process* or the *product* (result) of the division operation. The number sentence 9 ÷ 6 can be used to designate the process of sharing the 9 bars equally among 6 children, whereas the decimal 1.5 or mixed number 1½ can be used to designate the resulting share of bars per child. The quotient meaning of rational numbers is also rooted in common childhood experiences of partitioning quantities equally among two or more people.

3. A Ratio. Refer back to Question 2. If the white part of the diagram in Figure 10.1 represents the number of adults at a picnic (say 10) and the purple parts the number of children (say 30), then the *ratio* of adults to children is 10 to 30, or 1 to 3, or $\frac{1}{3}$. Conversely, the ratio of children to adults is 3 to 1, or $\frac{3}{1}$. Question 3 also pertains to ratios: $\frac{2}{5}+\frac{3}{4}$ equals $\frac{5}{9}$ when referring to ratios. For example, if there are 9 children at a party, and 2 out of the 5 playing video games are girls, and 3 out of the 4 playing board games are girls, then 5 *out of all* 9 children playing are girls (Figure 10.6). A ratio is a *multiplicative* comparison: In the picnic example, the number of children is *three times* the number of adults. In the second example, the multiplicative comparison is less obvious and requires more sophistication with rational numbers. In middle school, the *a*-to-*b* ratio notation, *a:b,* is introduced.

FIGURE 10.6   Adding ratios $\frac{2}{5}$ and $\frac{3}{4}$ gives $\frac{5}{9}$, the ratio of girls to the total number of children.

2 out of 5 children playing video games are girls

3 out of 4 children playing board games are girls

Images by © Get4net/Dreamstime

4. An Operator. Last, a rational number as *operator* means that it "changes or transforms another number or quantity by magnifying, shrinking, enlarging, reducing, expanding, or contracting it" (Barnett-Clarke et al., 2010, p. 27), depending on the nature of the quantity it's acting upon. Because the underlying operation in this "operator action" is multiplication, we must revisit multiplication in a new light. (If you thought you learned everything about multiplication, think again!). This new interpretation of multiplication, far removed from the *multiplication-as-repeated-addition* model, deserves a digression.

Seeing Multiplication in a New Light. Consider the expression, $x \times y$. A new interpretation of the multiplier x is as a *scalar operator*. Suppose y is some positive number. We represent its *unknown* value by a random line segment of length y. The number y lives y units *to the right of zero* on the number line. The scalar operator x, acting on y, can be *any* rational number, integer or fractional. How does multiplication by x affect the length y? Several cases are possible (refer to Figure 10.7 in each case):

1. **$x > 1$:** Suppose $x = 2$; then the line segment $2 \times y$, or simply $2y$, is obtained by *stretching* the segment y to twice its original length. The product by 3 stretches it to three times its original length, by 4 to four times, and so on. If x is not a whole number, say it's $\frac{9}{4}$, then $\frac{9}{4} \times y$ still *stretches* segment y but to a noninteger length.

2. **$x < 1$:** Then $1 \times y$, or y, remains unchanged.

3. **$0 < x < 1$:** Suppose $x = \frac{1}{2}$; then the line segment $\frac{1}{2} \times y$, or simply $\frac{1}{2}y$, is obtained by *shrinking* the segment y to one half its original length.

4. **$x < 0$:** In grade 6, and sometimes earlier, students learn a fourth case: multiplying by a *negative* number, such as –2 or $\frac{-3}{4}$. These numbers live *to the left of zero*, symmetric to their positive counterparts, with respect to the origin.

In short, a scalar operator (also known as *scaling factor* or *scalar factor*) "scales up" or "scales down" the other factor according to its size. The beauty of this interpretation is in its seamless transition from whole numbers to fractions, then later to negative numbers, and much later to real numbers. This stretching/shrinking way of explaining $3y$, $\frac{9}{4}y$, or $\frac{1}{2}y$ exemplifies multiplicative thinking. In contrast, additive thinking explains $3y$ as the addition $y + y + y$. But this explanation breaks down when factors are no longer whole numbers but instead are rational numbers such as $\frac{1}{2}$ or integers such as –2!

FIGURE 10.7 When x multiplies y, a positive number represented by some line segment, x either stretches or shrinks y depending on whether $x > 1$ or $0 < x < 1$ if $x = 1$ y remains unchanged.

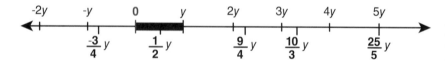

Modeling Fractions: Outer Representations of $\frac{a}{b}$

Three models, or outer representations, help foster good rational number sense:

1. Area model
2. Set or collection model
3. Number line model

1. Area Model. A popular model used in the United States for representing fractions is a part of a circular region. While this is a useful starting point—it relates to early experiences of sharing cookies, cake, or pizza fairly—we *must* graduate students beyond this sole representation in the upper elementary grades. During a recent third grade fraction lesson in a public school, I told students, "Write or draw what comes to mind when you see $\frac{1}{4}$." All but three students drew a circle divided into fourths with one part shaded (Figure 10.8a). As a first step away from circles, students represented $\frac{1}{4}$ on geoboards (Figure 10.8b).

FIGURE 10.8 (a) Common representation of $\frac{1}{4}$; (b) third-graders showing fourths on geoboards

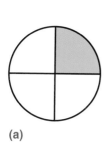

(a)

(b)

2. Set or Collection Model. Representing fractions with sets or collections is puzzling to students, partly because of their limited experience with fractions of discrete quantities. In the same third grade lesson, only Latrice drew four stars on her slate and circled one (Figure 10.9a). I called her up to teach by sharing her idea. Inspired by her work, I drew eight stars on her slate and inquired, "How many stars should I circle in this case?" (Figure 10.9b). Latrice hesitated. So did her peers. Hesitating is normal for third-graders who still see $\frac{1}{4}$ as *two* numbers—*one* out of *four*—and not yet as a relationship *between* two numbers, or better yet, a *multiplicative-comparison* relationship between the two. To guide the class down this path, I stressed the multiplicative relationship, "*times* 4," between the numbers 1 and 4, and I asked leading questions: "*What* times 4 equals eight?" "Two!" answered the class in unison. "*What* times 4 equals twelve?" "*What* times 4 equals sixteen?" and so on. To help visualize the 1-to-4 multiplicative relationships between *part* and *all* the stars, I boxed them into *four* sections and shaded *one* section (Figures 10.9c and d). Then it was clear.

FIGURE 10.9 (a) Latrice's representation of $\frac{1}{4}$; (b) My question: "What is $\frac{1}{4}$ of 8 stars ?"; (c), (d) Visuals that helped students see that 2 out of 8 and 3 out of 12 are also examples of $\frac{1}{4}$.

(a) (b) (c) (d)

3. Number Line Model. Mathematics educators, including this author, admonish the underuse of the number line—especially in the teaching of fractions and operations on

FIGURE 10.10 Fourth-grader modeling fractions on the number line

fractions. The number line is a bridge par excellence from arithmetic to algebra: Much of secondary mathematics takes place in one- and two-dimensional spaces, represented by the *x-axis* and *xy-plane,* respectively. Teachers know how difficult it is for students to conceive of a fraction as *a single number.* Developing the habit of placing a fraction on the number line to visualize its magnitude—relative to 0, 1, or another benchmark—forces students to find and mark *one point* on the line, and consequently think of a fraction as *one number* (CCSSM 3.NF and 4.NF). Figure 10.10 shows a fourth-grader answering the question, "Where does the fraction $\frac{1}{4}$ live on the number line?" He places it halfway between 0 and $\frac{1}{2}$. (*Note*: In *linear* measure, $\frac{1}{4}$ represents the length of the line segment, or the distance, from 0 to $\frac{1}{4}$.

Fractions of areas, collections, and line segments present different challenges. The differences reside in the definition of the whole and the equal parts, and in the nature of the fraction (Table 10.1). The more representations, the deeper the understanding!

TABLE 10.1 Three fraction models

	Area	Set or Collection	Number Line
The nature of the fraction	An area of a region	A number of objects	A distance from zero symbolized by a point on the line
	. . . in relation to the defined whole or unit		

3. Why Is the Unit So Important?

"Flexible reasoning about the unit is a key component of rational number sense, and it . . . develops over time and through many experiences" (Barnett-Clarke et al., 2010, p. 74). Questions about fraction representation, evaluation, equivalence, and comparison are nonquestions if the related unit is unknown. Indeed, a fraction is always understood in relation to a unit. Introductory **Questions 2**, **4**, and **5** pertain to this key idea. Mr. Mitchell's students will never forget the answer to **Question 4**, "Could $\frac{1}{2}$ be more than 1?" I have shared his story with many a teacher. At the start of his first lesson on fractions, Mr. Mitchell holds up an opaque bag, tells his students it contains chocolate bars, and asks, "Who wants a whole bar and who wants a half?" Not surprisingly, almost everyone wants a whole bar. Mr. Mitchell then draws out miniature *whole* bars, weighing 0.35 ounces each (10 g) and hands them out to the class. The conscientious few wanting to limit sugar intake end up getting 0.75 ounces (21.4 g), or *half* of a regular size, 1.5-ounce bar. Students learn from this experience that a half can be more than a whole. They learn to ask, or think, "One half *of what*?"

> ### REFLECT . . .
>
> The concept of the whole underlies the concept of a fraction.
>
> —Merlyn Behr and Thomas Post (1992, p. 213)

The Nature of the Unit

Vocabulary. The two common terms used in today's literature on fractions are *whole* and *unit*. The former is the first term students encounter in the early grades: a whole apple, a whole day, a whole number. A whole is usually represented by a circular or rectangular continuous region, symbolizing a whole pizza or birthday cake to be cut into equal parts such as halves, quarters, or thirds. By grade 3, students understand and use the word *unit* in at least three different ways: First, the number 27 is 2 tens and 7 ones or *units.* Second, in real-world problem solving, students are asked to write the *unit* beside the numerical answer, such as 5 feet, 10 minutes, or 58 pounds. The third use of *unit* is our present focus. The three instances are all related, because in all cases the unit is what we count by (whole numbers), measure with (quantities), and refer to (fractions).

One or More Than One? Discrete or Continuous? The whole or unit can be a single object or a collection of objects. It can even be a fraction (e.g., a half-pizza) or a mixed number (1½ teaspoons of baking powder for a recipe). The nature of these objects can be *discrete* or *continuous.* In the case of a collection of discrete objects, say, a can of three tennis balls, a hand of five fingers, or a busload of 30 children, students must mentally "chunk" them together and think of them as the *whole* or *unit* (Steffe, 2001). This requires the ability to *unitize*, which students have developed by the end of grade 2. **Question 2** (Figure 10.1) illustrates how even in a single, continuous region, the unit can be ambiguous: If the unit is the entire rectangle, then the purple-shaded region represents $\frac{3}{4}$, but if the unit is only *one* section, it's $\frac{3}{1}$ or 3. If the unit is not explicit, who's to say that it can't be the *half-rectangle*? In that case, the shaded region would represent $\frac{3}{2}$ or $1\frac{1}{2}$!

A Relationship

A challenge when first learning fractions is the concept of *relation* between two numbers. "First, students need to grasp the key idea that fractions name the *relationship* between the collection of parts and the whole, not the *size* of the whole or its parts" (Smith, 2002, p. 8). Consider an example where the units are collections of objects (Figure 10.11). In terms of *absolute* size or quantity, the fractional part in (a), or $\frac{1}{3}$, is greater than the fractional part in (b), or $\frac{1}{2}$. In terms of *relative* size or amount, however, the fractional part in (b) is greater. Teachers can help students focus on the relative sizes or amounts, not the absolute. When comparing fractions, we should be more explicit about the unit, even though the tacit assumption is that the fractions we are comparing refer to the *same* unit.

FIGURE 10.11   In absolute quantity, the fraction $\frac{1}{3}$ (a) is greater than the fraction $\frac{1}{2}$ (b). But the introductory concept of fraction is about the relationship between part and whole.

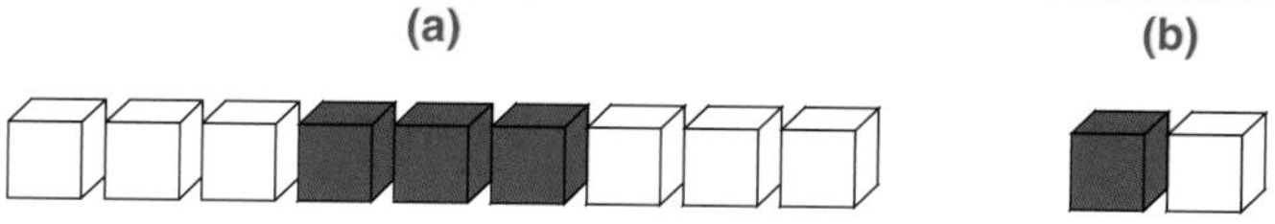

Multiple Experiences

Students need multiple experiences in order to develop a deep understanding of the concept of unit. Commonly, students are given the unit and asked to represent or find a fraction. The reverse exercise requires them to think more deeply. The following exercises help students think of fractions *in terms of the unit.*

1. Fractions With Pattern Blocks (Grade 3). When working with adults or children, after introducing pattern blocks (Figure 10.12), I routinely hold up a green triangle and ask, "What fraction is this?" Almost always, the answer is, "One sixth!" Twice I recall getting the correct answer, "It *depends*." To remedy this misconception, have students *describe the whole* if the green triangle represents $\frac{1}{1}, \frac{1}{2}, \frac{1}{3}, \frac{1}{4}, \frac{1}{5}, \frac{1}{6}, \frac{1}{8}, \frac{1}{9}, \frac{1}{12}$, or another fraction $\frac{a}{b}$. Figure 10.13 offers selected solutions.

FIGURE 10.12   Pattern blocks

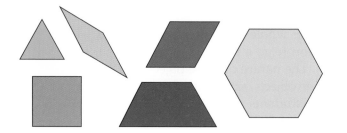

FIGURE 10.13   The same piece—a green triangle—represents different fractions depending on the choice of the whole or unit.

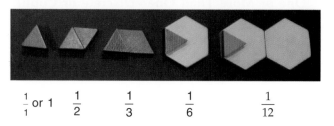

FIGURE 10.14   Given that three green triangles equal 1/16, fifth-grade teachers build the whole.

FIGURE 10.15   A fourth-grader places "$\frac{1}{12}$ of 12" on a number line. The "unit" segment is 12-long.

Photo by Karen Monroe

As students become savvy with single blocks, vary the starting piece(s). For instance, ask, "What's the whole if *three green triangles* represent $\frac{1}{16}$?" Figure 10.14 shows teachers solving this particular problem.

2. Fractions on the Number Line (Grade 4). Draw a line and mark two points, the origin O and second point P. Pose two types of questions:

FIGURE 10.16

$2\frac{1}{2}$ pizzas

a. If line segment OP is the unit, how long is $\frac{1}{3}$ of OP, $\frac{1}{6}$ of OP, or $\frac{9}{4}$ of OP? The fraction $\frac{a}{b}$ of OP can be any proper or improper fraction. In Figure 10.15, a fourth-grader is locating point A ($\frac{1}{12}$ OP), where OP has length 12. Points D ($\frac{1}{6}$), E ($\frac{1}{4}$), and C ($\frac{1}{3}$) had been placed by peers.

b. Conversely, set length OP as some fraction $\frac{a}{b}$, and ask students to draw the *unit* segment. For example, suppose OP is $\frac{1}{3}$, $\frac{1}{5}$, or $1\frac{3}{4}$ of the unit segment.

3. Fractions Can Be More Than One Piece (Grade 5). "Fractions are more than pizzas!" a colleague once exclaimed. Yet, since students routinely revert to pizzas, we need to create more challenging pizza problems. Draw a number of pizzas—whole or mixed number—such as two and a half (Figure 10.16), and ask three kinds of questions:

- Draw $\frac{1}{2}$ if Figure 10.16 represents the unit (find a fraction given the unit).

- Draw $\frac{5}{6}$ if Figure 10.16 represents $\frac{1}{3}$ (find a fraction given another fraction).

- Draw the unit if Figure 10.16 represents $1\frac{1}{4}$ (find the unit given a fraction).

A Story About Thomas

Fourth-grade teacher Kerrie approached me one day with Figure 10.2 in hand, saying, "Thomas can't see that this is $\frac{10}{5}$; he insists it's $\frac{10}{10}$!" After reviewing the importance of the unit and the ability to unitize, Kerrie realized that Thomas had been absent the day the class cut out the yellow "unit cards." For his peers, the individual card was the understood unit. But in the absence of an explicit unit, Thomas assumed both cards *combined* constituted *the unit*. The next day, Kerrie revisited the problem, explaining that either $\frac{10}{5}$ or $\frac{10}{10}$ could be correct *depending on the unit*! She thanked Thomas for the challenge and praised his *unitizing*. This story about Thomas answers **Question 5**.

REFLECT . . .

Thomas challenged me to think more deeply about my own understanding of the meaning of fraction. "What's this fraction?" I realize now has meaning only if the unit is known.

—Kerrie Jenkins, fourth-grade teacher

Delving Deeper

4. Equivalence and Comparison

Either two fractions are equal, or one is greater than the other. That is why equivalence and comparison are discussed together. In the context of fractions, equality and equivalence are synonymous, which is not the case in all contexts. Equivalent fractions are different names for the *same number*. Any given fraction has an infinite number of different names. For example, $\frac{2}{6}, \frac{15}{45}, \frac{6\frac{2}{3}}{20}$, and $\frac{\sqrt{3}}{\sqrt{27}}$ are all equivalent to $\frac{1}{3}$. They can all be simplified to $\frac{1}{3}$ by the well-known, equivalent-fraction algorithm or procedure: "Multiply or divide numerator and denominator by the same number." But while a rule can be taught and parroted by students, a concept needs time to develop for profound understanding to emerge. Hence some advice from experts in the field: "Spend whatever time is needed to ensure that students understand what it means for fractions to be equivalent at both the concrete and symbolic levels" (Cramer & Whitney, 2010, p. 21). "A serious instructional error is to rush too quickly to the rule. Be patient! Intuitive methods are always best at first" (Van de Walle & Lovin, 2006, p. 151).

How Can We Make Equivalent Fractions Come Alive?

A number (or quantity, or amount) having different names is a novel idea for students. Following are ways to make the concept of equivalence more visual and meaningful to students while planting algebra seeds, thus offering answers to **Question 6.**

Manipulatives. Using Cuisenaire rods and pattern blocks,[2] students can discover that different fractions represent the same length or area, respectively (Figure 10.17).

Number Line. Draw a line segment and call it the unit length. Students take turns marking unit fraction lengths $\frac{1}{2}, \frac{1}{3}, \frac{1}{4}, \frac{1}{6}, \frac{1}{8}$, and so on. Once unit fractions are placed, any multiple is easy to find: For instance, if I know length $\frac{1}{6}$, then $\frac{2}{6}$ is 2 times $\frac{1}{6}$, so I make 2 hops of length $\frac{1}{6}$ starting at zero. (Use different color markers for halves, thirds, fourths, and so on). Students will discover that equivalent fractions, such $\frac{2}{6}$ and $\frac{1}{3}$, share the same point on the number line and therefore are different names for a same number.

> **FIGURE 10.17** (a) $\frac{1}{2}$ and $\frac{2}{4}$ are equivalent; (b) $\frac{1}{3}$ and $\frac{2}{6}$ are equivalent; (c) 1 and $\frac{6}{6}$ are equivalent.

(a)  (b) (c)

Photo by Didier Rousselet

---

2. Both these manipulatives are 3-dimensional, but we focus on length in the first and surface in the second.

Patterns. Model a fraction of surface area with two pattern blocks—say green triangle on top of red trapezoid for the fraction $\frac{1}{3}$ — and call it the unit car (Figure 10.18a). Have students make trains with two, three, four . . . cars and name the triangle-to-trapezoid fraction in each train ($\frac{1}{3}$, $\frac{2}{6}$, $\frac{3}{9}$, $\frac{4}{12}$ . . .). While it's challenging to *see* that $\frac{1}{3}$ "equals" $\frac{3}{9}$ because the trains *look* different, the types of suggestions we make plant seeds for later understanding of the constant ratio $\frac{1}{3}$. Bring awareness to two ideas:

- First, the *inside* or *within relationship*: Within each train, the trapezoid area is *3 times* the triangle area (Figure 10.18b).
- Second, the *outside* or *between relationship*: Between any two trains, the triangle-to-triangle *and* the trapezoid-to-trapezoid relationships are the same (Figure 10.19).

Either the *within ratio* or the *between ratio* suffices to confirm equivalence.

FIGURE 10.18 (a) Unit train car; (b) the triangle-to-trapezoid relationship *within* each train is the same

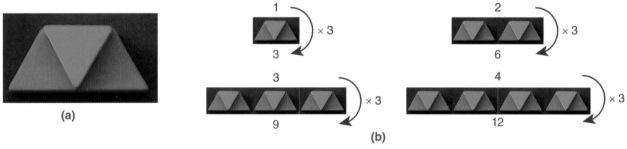

Photo by Didier Rousselet

FIGURE 10.19 The triangle-to-triangle and trapezoid-to-trapezoid relationships *between* any two trains are equal.

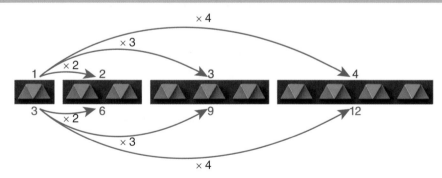

Problem Solving. Equivalent fractions often emerge as students devise different strategies for solving sharing problems: For instance, when sharing 2 chocolate bars equally among 6 friends, equivalent solutions $\frac{1}{3}$ and $\frac{2}{6}$ of one bar (or $\frac{1}{6}$ and $\frac{2}{12}$ of two bars) emerge naturally (Figure 10.20). Remind students that rational numbers came into being precisely to model situations that couldn't be described with whole numbers.

FIGURE 10.20   (a) Dividing both bars into six equal parts (sixths), each student receives $\frac{2}{6}$ of one bar (or $\frac{2}{12}$ of two); (b) dividing both bars into three equal parts (thirds), each student receives $\frac{1}{3}$ of one bar (or $\frac{1}{6}$ of two)

FIGURE 10.21   Seeing $\frac{1}{7}$ requires thinking of each column as *one* equal part.

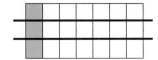

Deriving the Equivalent-Fraction Algorithm. With a looking-for-patterns algebraic mindset, students naturally discover the equivalent-fraction algorithm. If not, they should be guided to find one. The rectangular area model serves them well. A rectangle can be divided into *any* number of parallel equal slices along one direction, thus representing *any* desired fraction. Then, slicing the created fraction into one, two, three . . . congruent sections along the other, perpendicular direction produces equivalent fractions. For example, in Figure 10.21, fraction $\frac{3}{21}$ was obtained by, first, creating *sevenths* with six vertical slices and coloring in $\frac{1}{7}$. Then, with two additional horizontal slices, $\frac{1}{7}$ converted to the equivalent $\frac{3}{21}$. The horizontal slices materialize the doubling, tripling, quadrupling, . . . of numerator and denominator. And so the algorithm is this: Multiplying (or dividing) numerator *and* denominator of any fraction by the *same* factor generates equivalent fractions. Note that cutting larger regions into smaller regions is clear, as subregions can easily be counted. But the reverse is subtler. Given $\frac{3}{21}$, a student must abstract the horizontal lines and see each column as *one* in order to see $\frac{1}{7}$. This requires unitizing.

Teaching Tips

- **Thinking About the Algorithm.** Students often explain the conversion from $\frac{1}{3}$ to $\frac{2}{6}$ by saying, "I *doubled* $\frac{1}{3}$ to get $\frac{2}{6}$." Probe further to assess if they truly think $\frac{2}{6}$ *two times greater* than $\frac{1}{3}$. If so, it may be because teachers use the verb *reduce* in the reverse process of simplifying $\frac{2}{6}$ to $\frac{1}{3}$. I recommend using *simplify* in lieu of *reduce*.

- **Talking About the Algorithm.** In class visits, I typically hear students justifying that $\frac{2}{5}$ is equivalent to $\frac{8}{20}$ by saying, "I multiplied up and down by 4." To cultivate a strong algebraic mindset, I suggest inquiring further: "*Why* does that make the fractions equal?" *Possible answer*: "Because $\frac{4}{4}$ equals 1." I propose to follow with yet another *why* question: "*Why* multiply by 1?" *Ideal answer*: "Because 1 is the *identity element* of multiplication." Indeed, multiplying a number by 1 leaves it unchanged, or *identical* to itself, hence the choice of the phrase "identity element" by mathematicians. *Proof*: $\frac{8}{20} = \frac{2 \times 4}{5 \times 4} = \frac{2}{5} \times \frac{4}{4} = \frac{2}{5} \times 1 = \frac{2}{5}$.

How Can We Compare $\frac{7}{9}$ and $\frac{8}{10}$ in Meaningful Ways?

"One of the greatest errors fifth- and sixth-grade teachers typically make is introducing conversion of fractions to decimals before students have developed mastery with fractions on a conceptual level" (Collins & Dacey, 2010, p.16). While decimal conversion facilitates fraction comparison, students must also develop strong fraction sense; it is fundamental for their future work with fractions such as $\frac{1}{x+5}$ or $\frac{y}{(y-2)^2}$. Following are strategies for comparing fractions in sense-making ways, which was the focus of **Question 7.**

Three Common Comparison Strategies. In grades 3–5, students are expected to learn three strategies for comparing fractions (we assume reference to the same unit):

1. Finding common denominators and then comparing numerators;

2. Finding common numerators and then comparing the denominators; and

3. Comparing fractions to benchmarks such as 0, $\frac{1}{2}$, or 1.

The first two ways involve transforming one or both fractions using equivalent fractions *and* recalling the meaning of $\frac{a}{b}$ as "*a* times the quantity $\frac{1}{b}$." Thus, for Strategy 1, the greatest numerator implies the greatest fraction, because the numerator plays a *multiplier* role: As *a* increases the fraction's value *increases*. For Strategy 2, the greatest denominator implies the smallest fraction, because the denominator plays a *divisor* role: As *b* increases, the fraction's value *decreases*. Strategy 3 is illustrated in the following paragraphs.

- **Comparing** $\frac{7}{9}$ **and** $\frac{8}{10}$. Suppose you don't know any procedure for finding common numerators or denominators, producing equivalent fractions, or cross-multiplying (a middle school algorithm often taught prematurely). Also, withhold computation for a moment in the spirit of fostering algebraic thinking about fractions. Now refer back to **Question 7.**

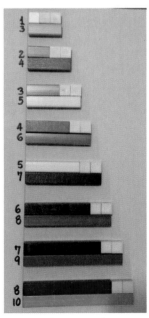

FIGURE 10.22   A pattern of "two-apart" ratios

- **A Student's Algebraic Thinking.** Both fractions are close to the benchmark 1 (Strategy 3), which makes this a challenge. I know that $\frac{7}{9}$ is $\frac{2}{9}$ away from 1, and $\frac{8}{10}$ is $\frac{2}{10}$ away from 1. I also know that $\frac{2}{10}$ is a smaller fraction than $\frac{2}{9}$, by Strategy 2. So $\frac{8}{10}$ is greater than $\frac{7}{9}$, since it is *closer* to 1. This explanation exhibits sophisticated fraction sense.

- **A Teacher's Algebraic Thinking.** The following reasoning involves pattern and generalization, two staples of algebraic thinking. It specifically addresses the common misconception—"top and bottom are both *two apart*, so they must be equal"—an example of additive thinking (7 + 2 = 9 and 8 + 2 = 10). We saw above that for two fractions to be equal, 7 and 9 on one hand, and 8 and 10 on the other, must be related by the same *multiplicative*, not *additive*, relationship (Figure 10.18). But that's hard to verify in this example. So, consider the pattern of the first eight ratios, all "two apart:" from $\frac{1}{3}$, $\frac{2}{4}$, $\frac{3}{5}$ ... $\frac{8}{10}$, represented by Cuisenaire-rod lengths (Figure 10.22). Viewed as ratios, the fractions need not refer to a common unit. In each case, two yellow unit rods represent the "two apart." We

Photo by Didier Rousselet

notice a progression from smaller to bigger: The pattern begins with $\frac{1}{3}$, which is less than one half; then, $\frac{2}{4}$ equals one half; $\frac{3}{5}$ is clearly greater than one half. Moving downward to $\frac{6}{8}$, we're at three fourths. Clearly, the values of the consecutive top-to-bottom relationships are increasing as the numbers themselves increase. The "two apart" gradually become negligible as the numbers increase. For instance, the ratio $\frac{1000}{1002}$ is so close to 1 that the "two apart" can be disregarded. We conclude that these ratios, starting at $\frac{1}{3}$, gradually approach 1. So $\frac{8}{10}$ is greater than $\frac{7}{9}$, as it's further down the pattern. Since the consecutive ratios approach 1, in mathematics we say *the limit of the sequence is 1.*

Teaching Tip. Students may say, "$\frac{8}{10}$ greater than $\frac{7}{9}$ because 8 and 10 are bigger numbers than 7 and 9"; this is faulty reasoning leading to a correct answer. Rather than saying "right" or "wrong," respond with, "Is $\frac{10}{8}$ greater than $\frac{9}{7}$ for the same reason?" Help make students' thinking more explicit to them. Help them reformulate their thinking with new words. Words are the main means by which *they* express their thinking, and *we* access it.

REFLECT . . .

Which fraction is greater, $\frac{11}{12}$ or $\frac{12}{13}$? Create a pattern starting with $\frac{1}{2}$. What is the limit of the pattern as the "one apart" fractions increase? Examine the pattern to answer the question. Can you make a generalization?

5. Can Students Make Sense of Division With Fractions?

This final section is reserved for "division with fractions." Why? Because "division of fractions is often considered the most mechanical and least understood topic in elementary school" (Tirosh, 2000, p. 6). Past president of NCTM Linda Gojak (2013) explains, "Many students learn 'flip and multiply' to divide fractions but have no idea why it works. . . . The procedure alone often leads to misconceptions." Consequently, the math standards CCSSM 5.NF.B.7a, b, and c stress the importance of using visual fraction models to explain quotients and to solve real-world problems involving fraction division to help students better grasp this "least understood topic in elementary school." In light of these challenges and charges, this section addresses

1. Ideas that enable students to build division with fractions upon their previous understandings of division with whole numbers;

2. Examples of real contexts that help make fraction division come alive; and

3. Visual models that empower students to "see what it *means* to divide by $\frac{1}{2}$ or $\frac{5}{6}$."

In the process, we'll answer **Question 8,** thus completing the answers to **Questions 1–8.**

Building on Previous Understandings of Whole-Number Division

Chapter 8, Section 1 reviewed the two main types of whole-number division problems resulting from taking the inverse of equal-groups multiplication: *partitive* division, where the number of "containers" is known, but the amount/number contained in each is unknown (Figure 8.4), and *quotative* division, where the amount/number contained in each "container" is known, but the number of "containers" is unknown (Figure 8.5).

An Example. Students must create a story context modeled by the expression 26 ÷ 4. They are given 26 objects and 8 containers (cups, or plates, or flats, etc.), purposely more than needed. They work in groups without help from Dr. Monica. Each group designates a recorder, a presenter, and actor(s). The recorder draws or writes, the presenter summarizes the group's work, and the actors model with the manipulatives. Invariably, most if not all groups devise partitive division stories such as, "Four children share 26 caramels evenly. How many caramels does each one get?" (Figure 10.23). Depending on the nature of the quantities being shared, the answer is either 6 or 6.5. Only once in a fourth grade class and once in a fifth-grade class did a quotative division problem arise: "Twenty-six fourth-graders want to ride a roller coaster together. If each car seats only 4 people, how many cars will they need?" (Figure 10.24). Since the last two students want to get on, they must ride in the *seventh* car. To better understand what follows, remember the key question in the roller coaster problem: "How many groups of 4 are in 26?" In addition to illustrating partitive versus quotative division, this problem offers rich discussions about real-world answers (6, 6.5, or 7) and the three resulting interpretations of remainders (ignore, share, or round up).

FIGURE 10.23   Modeling partitive division: 6.5 caramels is the equal share when 26 caramels are divided evenly among 4 children.

FIGURE 10.24   Modeling quotative division: 7 cars (with 4 seats each) are needed for 26 students to ride the roller coaster together.

Photo by Didier Rousselet

Photo by Didier Rousselet

From Quotative (or Measurement) Division to Fraction Division

Just as younger students must move beyond their first model of subtraction as "take away" to the more sophisticated comparison or distance model (Neagoy, 2012), so too must older students move beyond their first model of division as "fair sharing" (partitive division) to the more sophisticated quotative model if they are to succeed with arithmetic of rational numbers, whence algebra first emerged.

An Example. A challenge often used by the author with adults and students can serve us: Problem creators are asked to invent a story modeled by the expression "$2\frac{3}{4} \div \frac{1}{2}$." The story must help young students *make sense of what it means to divide by a fraction*. I plead with my audience to "withhold procedural computations and *think mathematically*." Someone typically proposes the following scenario: "I have $2\frac{3}{4}$ pizzas, and I want to divide them 'in half.'" Led astray by misuse of the English language, "divide *in half*" is the verbal interpretation of "$\div \frac{1}{2}$," which is mistaken for "$\div 2$. "Feigning ignorance, I draw $2\frac{3}{4}$ pizzas and probe further: "Without computing, *approximately* how much pizza will each person, A and B, get?" Answers include "about one and a third" or "less than one and a half" (Figure 10.25). All seem convinced. . . .

A Disobeyer. There is always someone, hiding in a corner, who can't resist the urge to apply the division algorithm (I secretly hope someone *does*.). I spot the disobeyer shaking his or her head in disagreement, because the result of "flip the fellow that follows" leads to $2\frac{3}{4} \div \frac{1}{2} = \frac{11}{4} \times \frac{2}{1} = \frac{22}{4} = 5\frac{2}{4} = 5\frac{1}{2}$. I call on the disobeyer to share the answer $5\frac{1}{2}$. "We now have a dilemma," I carry on: "A moment ago, we were convinced that person A and person B each get *fewer than two pizzas*; now we're told the *correct* answer to our division problem, produced by the algorithm, is *five and a half!* Can anyone help resolve this apparent contradiction?" Dead silence.

FIGURE 10.25 Number sentence, $2\frac{3}{4} \div \frac{1}{2}$, is misinterpreted as "dividing in half," or into two equal shares.

 OR

Quotative Division to the Rescue. Rarely, someone recalls the *other* model for division and says, "Isn't the question, 'How many halves go into two-and-three-quarters?'" "Perhaps," I reply. "But remember your task: Make up a *story* that gives *meaning to* this fraction division." More dead silence.

Three Stories and Three Ways of Modeling $2\frac{3}{4} \div \frac{1}{2}$

The frequently proposed pizza-sharing scenario demonstrates that for most children and adults, fair sharing among x people is the sole mental image for division. In order for fair sharing among x people to make sense, however, x must be a positive integer. Thus, in division by a fractional divisor, the fair sharing metaphor breaks down, and often so does sense making. Or, as in this case, we force the familiar metaphor incorrectly by interpreting, "divide by $\frac{1}{2}$" as "divide in half," or "share between 2 people." As a foundation for fractions now, and algebra later, we must ensure that *both* partitive *and* quotative division be part of children's repertoire of ideas from the start of division instruction. The CCSSM are explicit: "Interpret $56 \div 8$ as the number of objects in each share when 56 objects are partitioned equally into 8 shares, or as a number of shares when 56 objects are partitioned into equal shares of 8 objects each" (Grade 3.OA.A.2).

Following are three stories, along with three visual models, that will help teachers help students understand the most difficult topic in elementary mathematics.

1. The Beloved Pizza Fractions. Mr. Cardone is the owner of a Manhattan pizza carryout. Since 50% of Manhattan residents live alone, his *unit* portions are half-pizzas. He closes shop at 9:00 p.m. At 8:00 p.m., there are two-and-three-quarters pizzas left. Help Mr. Cardone figure out how many portions he can make from the remaining pizzas (Figure 10.26).

FIGURE 10.26   Area Model. Mr. Cardone can make $5\frac{1}{2}$ half-pizza portions from $2\frac{3}{4}$ pizzas.

2. Home Alone. Javier's parents are going out for dinner at 7:00 p.m. and will be returning at 9:45 p.m. Fascinated by space exploration, Javier just received a box set of ten 30-minute DVDs on the subject for his 10th birthday. Assuming he'll watch continuously, how many DVDs will he be able to watch while his parents are away (Figure 10.27)?

FIGURE 10.27   Number Line Model. Javier can watch $5\frac{1}{2}$ 30-min DVDs in $2\frac{3}{4}$ hours.

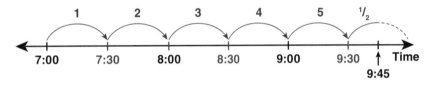

3. Aprons for the Play. Mrs. Reed is helping with costumes for the fifth grade play. She needs to make six blue aprons for the six waitresses. Each apron requires a half-yard of fabric. At the fabric store, the roll of shiny blue fabric that caught Mrs. Reed's eyes had only two-and-three-quarters yards left. Will that be enough to make all six aprons (Figure 10.28)?

We have answered **Question 8** in three ways. "Invest time in building meaning for fractions by using multiple concrete models and meaningful contexts" (Cramer & Whitney, 2010, p. 21). Indeed, students need extensive experience with, and will benefit from, a variety of manipulative models. Teachers will benefit too, as did Ms. Moore! (Figure 10.29).

FIGURE 10.28   Multilink-Cube Model. Only 5 aprons can be made out of the $2\frac{3}{4}$ yards of fabric. A half of an extra apron, in this context, is meaningless.

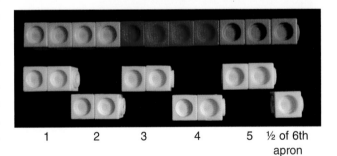

Photo by Didier Rousselet

REJOICE . . .

For the first time in my life, I truly understand how to multiply and divide fractions, not just go through the motions. This has revolutionized my teaching. Because I understand how fractions work, I am more successful at teaching fractions to my students.

—Pat Moore, fifth-grade teacher

FIGURE 10.29   Veteran fifth grade teacher Pat Moore got excited when modeling "$4 \div \frac{5}{6}$" with connecting cubes. She *saw* what division by $\frac{5}{6}$ *means*, and she didn't need the algorithm to solve the problem!

Closure

If students make sense of fractions, they will come to enjoy them and even find them fascinating. In closing this fourth and final Exploration, I come full circle and return to pi, where I began. I leave you with a fascinating way to compute pi using an infinite sum of fractions, called an *infinite series* (Figure 10.30). It requires addition, multiplication, division, and a powerful calculator. Take out your calculator and intrigue your students!

FIGURE 10.30   An infinite sum of fractions, called an *infinite series*

$$\frac{1}{1} + \frac{1}{3} + \frac{1 \times 2}{3 \times 5} + \frac{1 \times 2 \times 3}{3 \times 5 \times 7} + \frac{1 \times 2 \times 3 \times 4}{3 \times 5 \times 7 \times 9} + \ldots$$

Step 1: Compute the values of as many fractions in the series as you can; then add them together.

Step 2: Double the sum and get an approximation of pi! The more terms the better.

This infinite series is symbolic of this book:

1. It tells us something new and very different about pi—the topic of Exploration I.

2. It is appealing because it is a pattern—the topic of Exploration II.

3. It combines addition and multiplication, the two fundamental mathematical opertions, and the core of the distributive property—the topic of Exploration III.

4. It is the sum of fractions—the topic of Exploration IV.

5. It is generalizable—the heart of algebra.

6. It is beautiful in its simplicity and powerful in its complexity—the soul of mathematics.

11
Final Thoughts

The real voyage of discovery consists not in seeking new landscapes but in seeing the old ones in new ways.

—Marcel Proust, French Novelist

The opening quote by Marcel Proust summarizes the main purpose of this book: voyaging through common elementary mathematics territory, but seeing the landscapes with algebraic eyes. *Seeing* here means visual perception *and* conceptual understanding.

Algebraic Ways of Thinking, Talking, and Doing

The big idea to walk away with after reading this book is that algebra in the elementary grades is not about *x*'s and *y*'s but about ways of approaching mathematics, regardless of whether the content is numeric operations or geometric figures, linear measurement or equivalent fractions. It's about ways of thinking, reasoning, explaining, and doing that embody mathematical habits of mind, habits that teachers would do well to cultivate for themselves *and* their students. The list below recaps important algebraic approaches modeled and discussed in this book, along with one or more examples of each. These algebraic ways of thinking, talking, and doing naturally have some overlap.

Thinking About the General When Working With the Specific. "When children discern a particular object, they have to 'ascend,' to 'see through the particular to the general' in order to be able to speak about it. Doing this explicitly as part of an overt practice is part of what it means to think mathematically" (Mason, 2008). Generalizing indeed lies at the heart of mathematical thinking. *Example*:

- A student discovers that *her* square's perimeter is four times the side length. She wonders or is asked if the 1-to-4-relationship is true for *all* squares. She expresses the generalization with words, pictures, gestures, or symbols.

Interacting With Multiple Representations. Whether describing the property of an operation, expressing the solution to a problem, or studying a functional relationship, multiple representations help students deepen their understanding and communicate their knowledge. The connections between and among the various representations are key. Examine students' external representations and probe for their internal ones! *Example*:

- The functional relationship $Input \times 2 + 3 \rightarrow Output$ can be represented in many ways, including through movement or stories, with manipulatives or drawings, in function tables, as 2-D graphs, or with symbols ($I \times 2 + 3 = O$).

Looking for Patterns, Regularities, and Common Structure. Early on, children are attracted to patterns of all kinds: sounds, shapes, colors, numbers, movements, and so on. Rhythm and regularity appeal to their body-based pattern recognition. Thus, children naturally and informally notice common structure. *Example*:

- After counting the "pairs" inside a number, "Odd numbers have one left over," is a child's way of noticing the common structure of odd numbers: $7 = 3\,\text{pairs} + 1$ or $21 = 10\,\text{pairs} + 1$. The observations evolve to $7 = 2 \times 3 + 1$ or $21 = 2 \times 10 + 1$, and later generalize to $2n + 1$ for the structure of *all* odd numbers.

Distinguishing What Varies From What Remains Invariant. Understanding change is fundamental to understanding our world. In mathematics and science, students study change in patterns and functions. *Examples*:

- In the pattern 1, 4, 9, 16, 25 . . . (Figures 6.4c and 6.8), the *values* of the numbers vary, but their *structure* (perfect squares) remains invariant.
- In the function $Input \times 2 \rightarrow Output$, the *input–output values* vary, such as $2 \rightarrow 4$ or $10 \rightarrow 20$, but the *correspondence rule*, $I \times 2 = O$, remains invariant.
- In different-sized circles, the diameter and perimeter *measurements* vary, but their *ratio* remains invariant.

Making Sense of Rules, Formulas, and Algorithms. An algebraic mind tries to make sense of rules and procedures and not apply them mindlessly. Procedural fluency and conceptual understanding must go in tandem. *Examples*:

- The volume formula for a rectangular box with dimensions l, w, and h is $l \times w \times h$ *because* "$l \times w$" tells me how many cubic units are on the bottom "floor," and "$\times h$" tells me how many "$l \times w$ floors" of cubes fill the box.
- Multiplying numerator and denominator of a fraction by a same nonzero number, n, gives me an equivalent fraction, *because* I'm actually multiplying by the fraction $\frac{n}{n}$, which equals 1, and I know 1 is the identity element for multiplication.

RESEARCH . . .

If children are to become competent at mathematics, including arithmetic, those habits of mind must take precedence over rules, formulas, and procedures that do not derive from logic that the child can grasp. The fact that algebraic ideas, logic, and techniques can be organized around the development of mind makes clear that we are truly talking about habits of mind rather than features of mathematics or idiosyncrasies of mathematicians.

—E. Paul Goldenberg, June Mark, and Al Cuoco (2010, p. 549)

Pausing to Think Before Rushing to Compute. A calculator executes calculations; a student thinks before calculating. Developing the habit of mind to notice relations between expressions, recognize properties of operations, and look for structure in equations will ensure a smooth transition to algebra. *Examples*:

- I know the equation $37 + 75 - 74 = 38$ is true *without calculating* because I notice that "$75 - 74$" is 1, and I know that 38 is 1 more than 37.
- I recognize the distributive property of multiplication over addition, so I know expressions $3 \times (5 + 11)$ and $15 + 33$ are equivalent *without any calculations.*
- I know *by thinking* that $n = 10$ in the solution to $5 \times 86 = n \times 43$, because I notice that 43 is the *half* of 86, so n must be the *double* of 5 for equality to hold.

Developing the Mindset for Proof. Proof has been described as the "guts of mathematics" (Wu, 1966). "Reasoning and proof" is a process standard of the National Council of Teachers of Mathematics (NCTM, 2000) and "construct viable arguments" is a Common Core standard for mathematical practice (CCSS.Math.Practice.MP7). While we don't expect formal proofs from children, they must be given ample opportunities to reason about problems, make and test conjectures, justify and explain their thinking, and provide convincing arguments to their peers. These mathematical habits of mind are the first steps onto the path to formal proof. *Example*:

- Given the problem of finding all possible dimensions of rectangular boxes for 24 square caramels such that all 24 fit snugly in one layer, a fourth-grader produced a rainbow diagram (Figure 11.1). When asked, "How are you sure you found *all* possible boxes," she explained, "All factors of 24 are paired up, so there are none left!" Her peers found her argument convincing and aesthetically pleasing as well!

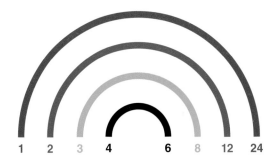

FIGURE 11.1 A fourth-grader's proof that she had found all possible dimensions of rectangular boxes for 24 square caramels.

Thinking Multiplicatively, Not Just Additively. This habit of mind, emphasized throughout the book, is particularly pertinent for` grades 3–5, when children's predominantly additive view of the world expands to include a new multiplicative perspective. Since multiplicative thinking is foundational for an entire network of interconnected concepts including multiplication, division, fractions, ratios, rational numbers, proportional relationships, and linear functions—all of which are core to beginning algebra—students must have connected experiences with a variety of multiplicative situations. Although ratios and proportions are middle school fare, research shows that preadolescent students develop intuitive and informal understandings of these notions well before encountering them in math class. *Examples*:

- Compare 5 and 15 additively (15 is *10 more than* 5) *and* multiplicatively (15 is *3 times more* than 5).
- If a family consumes 50 pounds of fruit in 2 weeks, how many pounds would they consume in 10 weeks (50 × 5), assuming their healthy eating habits don't change?

Looking at Arithmetic Through New Lenses. Fifty years ago, the purpose of teaching arithmetic in elementary school was to learn *how to compute*, and the ultimate goal was to obtain *correct numerical answers*. Today we have tools that compute more rapidly and efficiently than we do—and accurately, to boot! (See Keith Devlin's foreword on page xiii.) Thus, our technological world has raised the bar on our purpose for teaching arithmetic: Algebraic thinking is the new and higher goal. Explorations in this book, as in the previous volume titled *Planting the Seeds of Algebra, PreK–2*, offer examples of algebraic ways of teaching operations and new foci for learning them, including the following:

- Operations' inherent regularities
- Comparisons in effects of operations
- Similarities and differences in the properties of operations
- Equivalent expressions involving one or more operations
- Different ways of conceptualizing numerical relations
- Understanding computational algorithms as bridges to algebra

Very new in elementary mathematics is the functional face of operations. *Example*:

- The action of "adding 5" and "multiplying by 5" can be regarded as the functional relations, $Input + 5 \rightarrow Output$ and $Input \times 5 \rightarrow Output$, respectively, where the inputs are numbers students know. These functions can be represented verbally, concretely, pictorially, graphically, tabularly, and symbolically.

The Pivotal Role of the Teacher

"Algebraic thinking does not develop unaided in students. The role of the teacher is crucial" (Kieran, 2011, p. 592). "It requires 'an algebra sense' by which teachers can identify occasions in children's thinking to extend conversations about arithmetic to those that explore mathematical generality" (Blanton & Kaput, 2011, p. 19). We have learned from research that teachers can either contribute to or suppress the insight students manifest. The following teaching practices nurture student insight and cultivate their mathematical thinking:

- Listening to what children say about what they understand
- Questioning to help students make their own understanding more explicit
- Selecting or adapting tasks that build on what students grasp and move them forward
- Orchestrating instructional sequences that lead students to the joy of discovery
- Anticipating student questions and riding them to take the questions further
- Providing a safe setting in which children can discuss their imaginative ways of thinking
- Helping connect these ways of thinking to mathematical thinking

This book gives teachers many examples of how to support students on the road to sophisticated thinking and deep insight into mathematics.

Monica's Mottos

I closed Volume 1 of this series (Neagoy, 2012) with six mottos I regularly share with teachers. They are listed below *without* explanation.

1. Teach, Don't "Tell."

2. U-Turn Students' Questions.

3. Post: "What Did You Get?" and "The Power of Why."

4. Pose Real "Problems."

5. Don't Take Away the Manipulatives!

6. Preserve the Fun!

I close Volume 2 with six more mottos *with* explanation. If they resonate with you, incorporate them into your teaching!

> **REFLECT . . .**
>
> This shift in teaching, from telling to allowing discovery, has made a profound difference in how my students view mathematics. . . . Even if our steps in this direction are small, . . . the benefits are enormous: children smiling, even laughing, during mathematics time.
>
> —Robert B. Femiano (2003, p. 449),
> elementary school teacher, Seattle Public Schools

7. **Address the Whys, Not Just the Hows.** Dividing 5 by $\frac{1}{2}$ is equivalent to multiplying 5 by 2. Why? Because the number of *"one half's"* in 5 is *twice* the number of *ones* in 5. Said differently, there are 10 (or 5×2) halves inside of 5 wholes.

8. **Do More Than Check for Right Answers.** Despite the emphasis of late on teaching for understanding, I visit classes that begin with *checking* homework answers: They get a check or a cross. No attempt to investigate the strategies behind the answers. The subliminal message to students is: Mathematics is about *right* answers. In fact, it's so much more: It's about beautiful ideas and powerful ways of thinking. With information about students' thinking, we can help them make their own understanding more explicit, compare and contrast it with other ways of knowing, and make connections among topics they think are disconnected. It also helps us make instructional decisions. Suppose a fifth-grader gave the correct answer, $\frac{8}{9} > \frac{7}{8}$, "because 8 is bigger than 7 and 9 is bigger than 8." With that information, a teacher can follow up with the problem, "Compare $\frac{8}{9}$ and $\frac{7}{6}$." While 8 is greater than 7 and 9 is greater than 6, in this case $\frac{8}{9} < \frac{7}{6}$. The student then recognizes that her reasoning is flawed.

9. **Build on What Students Already Know.** Another thing I often see is this: A student asks a question about his strategy, because he is stuck at some point in the thinking or doing process. In response, the teacher says, "Here, let me *show* you . . . " and proceeds to explain a different method. In essence, the teacher isn't meeting the child *where he is*, nor

is the teacher *building on his knowledge,* but rather rerouting him onto the path of *her own* thinking. In such instances, students abandon their attempts at making sense of their *own* knowledge and surrender to mimicking what is shown or told to them by *others.*

10. The Teacher Is Talking! There isn't just *one* teacher in each classroom. Students learn from other students as well. But in some classrooms, students are not accustomed to listening to one another. Rather, they are trained to listen to the teacher—and even that, at times, they do with difficulty. Change the classroom culture by exclaiming, "The teacher is talking!" when a student is explaining an idea or showing a solution at the board or from her seat. You'll see the surprise in your students' eyes, taken aback at first with confusion. Then, explain that whoever is teaching in the moment is the *teacher*. Gradually students learn to respect and listen to one another with more attention. (I credit Middleburg, Virginia, teacher Jack Bowers for this idea.)

11. Instill a Sense of Wonder. The path to wonder begins with attention, continues on to curiosity, advances to intelligibility, and ends with appreciation for the new aspect of mathematics apprehended—be it a discovered pattern, an unexpected connection, or an unveiled structure. When eye, mind, and emotion converge in an unexpected aspect of mathematics, wonder occurs. Descartes called wonder the first of all passions. "The aesthetics of wonder and the poetics of thought are two sides of the same coin" (Fisher, 1998, p. 45). The teacher's direction is crucial in designing tasks that cause students to wonder (like folding paper 50 times to reach beyond the moon, two thirds of the distance from the earth to the sun) and in modeling value and appreciation not only for the usefulness of mathematics, but for its beauty and power.

12. Foster Friendliness With Numbers. The words *fluid, fluent,* and *flexible* should describe students' relationship with numbers. These are examples of friendliness with numbers:

- Knowing that 6×8 is twice 3×8, and therefore twice 24, or 48
- Understanding that $\frac{3}{5}$ is thrice $\frac{1}{5}$, and therefore thrice 0.2, or 0.6
- Seeing hidden inside of 10 the sum $1 + 2 + 3 + 4$
- Realizing that $\frac{7}{8}$ is greater than $\frac{6}{7}$ because, while both are unit fractions away from 1 ($\frac{1}{8}$ and $\frac{1}{7}$ respectively), there is a shorter distance on the number line from $\frac{7}{8}$ to 1 than there is from $\frac{6}{7}$ to 1.

I leave you with a pertinent story that marked me profoundly as a child: English mathematician G. H. Hardy paid a visit to Indian mathematician S. Ramanujan, who was in the hospital. He greeted the sick man abruptly with, "The number of the taxi-cab that brought me here was 1729. It seemed to me rather a dull number." Ramanujan's now-famous answer was, "Not at all, Hardy! It is a very interesting number. It is the smallest number expressible as the sum of two cubes in two different ways." Indeed, $1729 = 1^3 + 12^3$ and $1729 = 9^3 + 10^3$. It has been said that every positive integer was "one of Ramanujan's personal friends." Ramanujan died young, leaving behind the work of an autodidact and genius. His is a fascinating biography to research!

Teachers, math specialists, coaches, teacher educators, administrators, and parents, I hope you found in this book—through classroom vignettes (in chapters 1, 4, 7, and 10), explicit connections to algebra (in chapters 2, 5, and 8), and opportunities to extend knowledge (in chapters 3, 6, and 9)—seeds to cultivate algebraic thinking, knowing, discoursing, and doing, for yourselves and for your young ones. May these seeds blossom into a rich and colorful garden of mathematical empowerment and enjoyment!

Appendix

Answers to Nontrivial Problems in Chapter 3

Beyond *Circling Circles*: More Problems to Explore

Here you will find the answers and/or explanations to the nontrivial questions from Chapter 3.

I. Next Steps

4. Observations

The follow-up exploration sparked off more questions:

- **It looks like the points line up. Why?**

    The tips of all vertical strings line up because the ratio of vertical string (circumference) to horizontal string (radius), in each of the seven circles, is the same and equal to "a little more than 3," or π.

- **It looks like (0, 0) lines up with the rest. Why?**

    If the radius of a circle is zero then its circumference is also zero. Thus, the point (0, 0) is on the line. Note: In the upper grades students will learn that the quotient $\frac{0}{0}$ is undefined.

- **What might other points on the line represent?**

    Other points, (C, D), on the line represent the diameter and circumference values of infinitely many other possible circles, which we did not measure but can imagine.

III. For Your Students' Learning

1. Fix One and Vary the Other

Fixed Area

Figure 3.A shows the graph of the varying perimeter, P, of a rectangle whose fixed area is 48 square units, as a function of its length, L. The blue points correspond to the (L, P) integer-value data pairs in Figure 3.B. The other points on the red curve correspond to all imaginable (L, P) data pairs with *non*-integer values. We see that the perimeter is the smallest for rectangles 6-by-8 or 8-by-6. These rectangles are the most compact. (*Note*: we can get smaller perimeters if we choose a rectangle with length between 6 and 8, but that's beyond the scope of grades-3-5 mathematics, though students could grasp the idea.) The perimeter is the largest for rectangles 1-by-48 or 48-by-1. These rectangles are the most elongated ones.

Discuss with students how in some situations rectangles 6-by-8 and 8-by-6 can refer to different objects—namely when position is meaningful—and in others, such as in holding a rectangular box of chocolates, 6-by-8 and 8-by-6 can refer to the same object.

FIGURE 3.A Graph of perimeter (*P*) as a function of length (*L*)

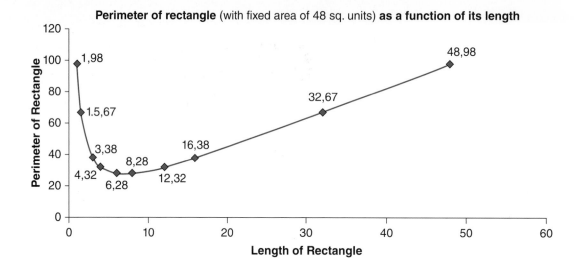

FIGURE 3.B Data values:
L **is the independent**
variable and *P* **is the**
dependent variable

W	L	A	P
48	1	48	98
32	1.5	48	67
16	3	48	38
12	4	48	32
8	6	48	28
6	8	48	28
4	12	48	32
3	16	48	38
1.5	32	48	67
1	48	48	98

Fixed Perimeter

Figure 3.C shows the graph of the varying area, *A*, of a rectangle whose fixed perimeter is 36 linear units, as a function of its length, *L*. The blue points correspond to the (*L*, *A*) integer-value data pairs in Figure 3.D. The other points on the red curve correspond to all imaginable (*L*, *A*) data pairs with *non*-integer values. We see that the area is the smallest for rectangles 1-by-17 or 17-by-1. These rectangles are the most elongated ones. (*Note*: we can get smaller areas if we choose a rectangle with length between 0 and 1 or between 17 and 18, but that's beyond the scope of grades-3-5 mathematics, though students could grasp the idea.) The area is the largest for the one and only special rectangle called a *square*. Indeed, when length equals width equals 9, the area attains the maximum value of 9 × 9, or 81 square units. This rectangle is the most compact.

Compare and contrast the two sets of findings with students. For example, as a rectangle becomes more compact, the perimeter decreases but the area increases. Discuss the units of perimeter versus area and model them with a piece of string versus a square tile. Perhaps more challenging would be to observe and comment on the symmetry or nonsymmetry of the two graphs.

Real-World Context: Family Reunion

The *number of people* in this case can be thought of as the *perimeter*: each person sitting along one side of a unit table represents a linear unit of measure for the perimeter. Students will hopefully apply their learning from the previous problems: the more compact the table, the smaller the perimeter. The maximum and minimum perimeters are 50 and 20 (Figure 3.E).

FIGURE 3.C   Graph of area (*A*) as a function of length (*L*)

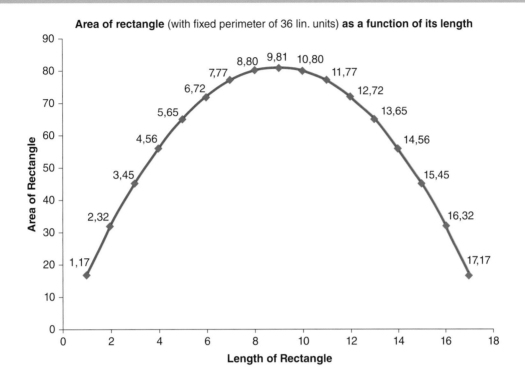

Area of rectangle (with fixed perimeter of 36 lin. units) **as a function of its length**

FIGURE 3.D   Data values: *L* is the independent variable and *A* is the dependent variable

W	L	P	A
17	1	36	17
16	2	36	32
15	3	36	45
14	4	36	56
13	5	36	65
12	6	36	72
11	7	36	77
10	8	36	80
9	9	36	81
8	10	36	80
7	11	36	77
6	12	36	72
5	13	36	65
4	14	36	56
3	15	36	45
2	16	36	32
1	17	36	17

FIGURE 3.E   Maximum and minimum number of people

Maximum number of people:
$24 + 24 + 1 + 1 = 48 + 2 = 50$
or $2 \times (24 + 1) = 2 \times 25 = 50$

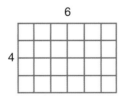

Minimum number of people:
$6 + 6 + 4 + 4 = 12 + 8 = 20$
or $(6 + 4) \times 2 = 10 \times 2 = 20$

FIGURE 3.F   Possible student suggestions

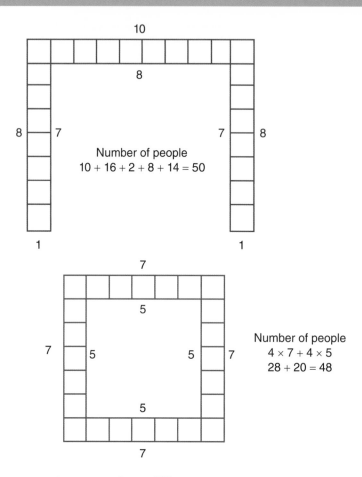

Given the opportunity to explore *different* arrangements and justify their ultimate choice, students become more creative and begin to think outside the box. Welcome creativity! Figure 3.F shows two options that students may decide on. Make sure their arguments are convincing to their peers (conviviality, number of people, aesthetics, practicality, and so on). Discuss other arrangements and propose some yourself as well.

Challenge

Depending on the nibble, the perimeter could decrease, increase, or remain equal (Figure 3.G). The area, however, would always decrease no matter how big or small the size of the nibble.

6. A Pattern of Non-Overlapping Triangles inside Polygons

The number of non-overlapping triangles (T) in a dodecagon (a polygon with 12 sides) is ten. We conclude from our observation of the pattern of polygons with consecutive numbers of sides, n (3, 4, 5, 6, 7…) that as the number of sides n increases, the number of triangles T is always 2 less than n. Algebraically, we can write this relationship as $T = n - 2$ (Figure 3.H). This relationship will come in handy in middle school when students will be asked to figure out the sum of the measures of the interior angles in an n-sided polygon. Since an n-sided polygon has $n - 2$ non-overlapping triangles inside of it, and since the sum of the measures of the interior angles in any triangle is $180°$, the answer is $(n - 2) \times 180°$.

FIGURE 3.G   Depending on the nibble, the perimeter could decrease, increase, or remain equal

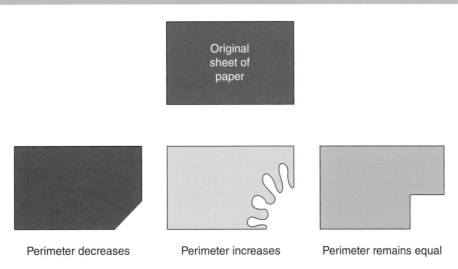

FIGURE 3.H   The number of non-overlapping triangles in an *n*-sided polygon is *n* − 2

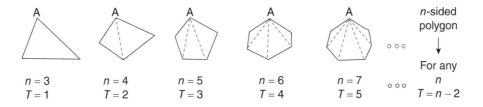

7. How Does It Change?

The relationships students will discover in this exploration will help them make sense of the notion of *dimension*. It will also help them understand how perimeter, area, and volume change no matter what the shape of the figure or solid. As a first example, have students use a piece of string to model the 1-dimensional object, a rectangle made of unit tiles to model the 2-dimensional object, and a rectangular prism made of unit cubes to model the 3-dimensional object. Help them organize their findings in a chart or table to better discern the pattern. After doubling the dimensions of all three objects, try tripling, then quadrupling the objects' dimensions. Make a larger chart and compare all findings (Figure 3.I). What do they notice? Can they put it in words? Once students learn exponential notation (which begins in grade 5), this exploration will help them better understand that if all dimensions of an object are multiplied by a factor n (be it integer or not):

- The length of a 1-dimensional object is multiplied by n^1 or n
- The area of a 2-dimensional object is multiplied by n^2
- The volume of a 3-dimensional object is multiplied by a factor of n^3

FIGURE 3.I   This chart helps students discover how length, area, and volume change as the dimensions of an object are multiplied by a factor of 2, 3, 4, and so on.

n–dimensional object	Dimensions Doubled	Dimensions Tripled	Dimensions Quadrupled	etc.
1-dimensional	Length is multiplied by 2	Length is multiplied by 3	Length is multiplied by 4	• • •
2-dimensional 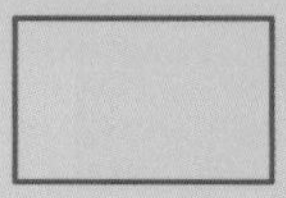	Area is multiplied by 4	Area is multiplied by 9	Area is multiplied by 16	• • •
3-dimensional 	Volume is multiplied by 8	Volume is multiplied by 27	Volume is multiplied by 64	• • •

9. Practicing With Numeric and Algebraic Expressions

1. I will multiply 5 by a factor of four, for the four equal sides of length 5. The *numeric* expression is 4×5, where four is the multiplier. If the side length is any number of centimeters s, the *algebraic* expression for the perimeter is: $P = 4 \times s$, which in later years will be simplified to $P = 4s$.

2. I can write several equivalent *numeric* expressions for the perimeter using 5, 7, and the addition symbol, including $5 + 5 + 7 + 7$ or $5 + 7 + 5 + 7$; or using 5, 7, and both the addition and multiplication symbols, which is more sophisticated: $2 \times (5 + 7)$. If the side lengths are any numbers of centimeters l and w, the *algebraic* expression for the perimeter can be written is several equivalent ways, including $P = l + l + w + w$, $P = l + w + l + w$, and $P = 2 \times (l + w)$.

10. Visualizing Unit Conversion

Linear Measure

There are 10 times more millimeters than centimeters, so 3 cm = 30 mm.

Area Measure

There are 100 times more square millimeters than square centimeters, so 12 sq. cm = 1,200 sq. mm.

Answers to Nontrivial Problems in Chapter 6

Beyond *Fancy Fences:* More Problems to Explore

Here you will find the answers and/or explanations to the nontrivial questions from Chapter 6.

I. Next Steps

3. Growing Patterns IV

See worksheet for *Growing Patterns IV* on page 198.

III. For Your Students' Learning

1. Function Table Puzzles

Function Rule: $I + 5 \rightarrow O$	
Input	Output
0	5
1	6
3	8
4	9
7	12
10	15
. . .	. . .

(a)

Function Rule: $I - 2 \rightarrow O$	
Input	Output
2	0
3	1
5	3
7	5
8	6
13	11
. . .	. . .

(b)

Function Rule: $I \times 3 \rightarrow O$	
Input	Output
1	3
3	9
4	12
6	18
11	33
20	60
. . .	. . .

(c)

Function Rule: $I \times 5 - 2 \rightarrow O$	
Input	Output
0	−2
1	3
5	23
7	33
10	48
50	248
. . .	. . .

(d)

4. Folding to the Sky

Input *# of Folds*	Output *# of Rectangles*
0	$1 = 2^0$
1	$2 = 2^1$
2	$4 = 2^2$
3	$8 = 2^3$
4	$16 = 2^4$
5	$32 = 2^5$
. . .	. . .

Young students, and even older ones, have a hard time grasping the power of exponential growth. The first few powers of 2 or 3 or 10 are clear, but as the number of factors—or the value of the exponent—increases, they lose sense of how big the numbers truly are. A wonderful film that conveys the power of the powers is the now classic film directed by Charles and Ray Eames and titled *Powers of Ten*. Click on this YouTube link to view it with your students: https://www.youtube.com/watch?v=0fKBhvDjuy0

6. Operation Patterns

Investigating

- The first pattern $10 + 10 \rightarrow 11 + 9 \rightarrow 12 + 8 \rightarrow 13 + 7 \ldots$ is constant and each sum equals 20. Depending on students' number sense, some will continue beyond the sum "20 + 0" and venture into negative addends, which is a natural outgrowth of this pattern: $20 + 0 \rightarrow 21 + -1 \rightarrow 22 + -2 \rightarrow 23 + -3 \ldots$ To look at these sums from another perspective, place the consecutive pairs of addends on the number line and ask students to observe their relative positions. They will notice that the consecutive pairs of addends are always equidistant from 10, with one on either side of 10. Even the first two addends, 10 and 10, have an equal distance of zero from 10!
- The second pattern $10 \times 10 \rightarrow 11 \times 9 \rightarrow 12 \times 8 \rightarrow 13 \times 7 \ldots$ is constructed with the same pairs of numbers but with a different operation: multiplication in lieu of addition. The sequence of products gradually decreases, as each product is smaller than the preceding one. When the second factor becomes zero, the product will too. You can delve deeper: (1) Have students notice the "jumps down" or decrements between consecutive products [1, 3, 5, 7… or –1, –3, –5, –7… depending how you phrase the question] and (2) Accompany them in their exploration if they venture beyond 20×0 into the negative zone.

9. Practicing With Equivalent Expressions

Practice

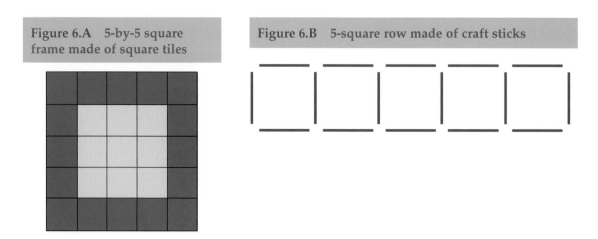

Figure 6.A   5-by-5 square frame made of square tiles

Figure 6.B   5-square row made of craft sticks

Numeric expressions for the number of tiles in the border of a 5-by-5 square (Figure 6.A) include but are not limited to: $4 \times 3 + 4$, 4×4, $5 + 5 + 3 + 3$, $2 \times 5 + 2 \times 3$, and $2 \times (5 + 3)$. Discuss the thinking behind each of these and other potential answers by asking students to model for others how they came up with their numerical expressions. Also discuss the equivalence among the different expressions. Numeric expressions for the number of toothpicks needed to make a 5-square row (Figure 6.B) include but are not limited to: $5 + 5 + 6$, $2 \times 5 + 6$, $3 + 3 + 3 + 3 + 3 + 1$, $5 \times 3 + 1$. Same comments as above.

Answering the same questions for a 10-by-10 square of tiles, and a 10-square row of toothpicks, requires replacing all "5s" with "10s," and observing if the other factors and addends need adjusting or not.

Generalizing for *any* number beyond 5 or 10 gives the following expressions, among other possible ones:

Number of tiles in the border of an n-by-n square	Number of toothpicks needed to make a 5-square row
$4 \times (n - 2) + 4$	$n + n + (n + 1)$
$4 \times (n - 1)$	$2 \times n + (n + 1)$
$n + n + (n - 2) + (n - 2)$	$n \times 3 + 1$
$2 \times n + 2 \times (n - 2)$	$3n + 1$

Exploring Growing Patterns

(Grades 3–5)

Growing Patterns IV: Log Fences (Craft Sticks Model Unit Logs)

1. Each fence below is made of unit logs, attached to each other at the ends. Make a few fences using craft sticks to model the unit logs.

Fence 1

Fence 2

Fence 3

Fence 4

2. How many unit logs are needed to make

   • Fence 1?   _____
   • Fence 2?   _____
   • Fence 3?   _____
   • Fence 4?   _____

3. What do you notice about the number of unit logs as the fence gets longer?

4. Use this table to record your data and to share your comments:

Fence Number	Log Number	Share your thinking in the box below:
1		
2		
3		
4		
Skip some…		
10		
Skip some more…		
100		
Skip some more…		
Any number N		

5. What are three ways you can represent the relationship between the fence <u>numbers</u> and the log <u>numbers</u>?

6. Call *F* any fence number and *L* the number of unit logs needed to make it. Write an equation (or mathematical model) that describes the relationship between *F* and *L*.

7. Explain your reasoning behind your answer to #6 (Use pictures or words.)

8. In what ways is this problem similar to the Fancy (Square) Fences problem?

9. In what ways is this problem different from the Fancy (Square) Fences problem?

Use the back to share at least <u>three things</u> you've learned from Growing Patterns I, II, III, or IV.

Answers to Nontrivial Problems in Chapter 9

Beyond *Multiplication Musings:* More Problems to Explore

Here you will find the answers and/or explanations to the nontrivial questions from Chapter 9.

III. For Your Students' Learning

1. The Marvels of the Multiplication Table

FIGURE 9.A "Why are they equal?" puzzles

×	1	2	3	4	5	6	7	8	9	10	11	12
1	1	2	3	4	5	6	7	8	9	10	11	12
2	2	4	6	8	10	12	14	16	18	20	22	24
3	3	6	9	12	15	18	21	24	27	30	33	36
4	4	8	12	16	20	24	28	32	36	40	44	48
5	5	10	15	20	25	30	35	40	45	50	55	60
6	6	12	18	24	30	36	42	48	54	60	66	72
7	7	14	21	28	35	42	49	56	63	70	77	84
8	8	16	24	32	40	48	56	64	72	80	88	96
9	9	18	27	36	45	54	63	72	81	90	99	108
10	10	20	30	40	50	60	70	80	90	100	110	120
11	11	22	33	44	55	66	77	88	99	110	121	132
12	12	24	36	48	60	72	84	96	108	120	132	144

Why Are They Equal?

Create puzzles requiring students to identify multiplication properties or characteristics to figure out why two cells contain equal numbers:

i. Why are the yellow cells equal ($8 \times 3 = 3 \times 8$)? Because multiplication is commutative. For any two numbers x and y, $x \times y = y \times x$. These product pairs are equidistant from the main diagonal (populated by the perfect squares). A nice way of rendering this fact concrete for children is to ask them to fold their square multiplication table along the main diagonal. They will notice that all pairs of superimposed cells contain the same products. Ask them why this is the case.

ii. Why are the green cells equal ($8 \times 5 = 4 \times 10$)? Because of the doubling/having, or *times2/divided by two* property: From left to right, 8 has been halved and 5 has been doubled. We saw that the cumulative effect of is change of $\frac{1}{2} \times 2 = 1$, and 1 is the identity element for multiplication. So the two products are equal.

iii. Why are the blue cells equal ($9 \times 4 = 3 \times 12$)? The same reason as in number ii above except that here the changes are tripling/thirding or *times three/divided by three*: from left to right, 9 has been thirded to give 3 and 4 has been tripled to get 12. The cumulative change is $\frac{1}{3} \times 3 = 1$, so the two products are equal.

iv. *Generalizing*: For any product $a \times b$, *dividing* one factor by any n (or multiplying it by $\frac{1}{n}$) and *multiplying* the other factor by n produces no change. *Note*: n cannot be 0.

Finding Equivalent Fractions

When explaining to students why fraction $\frac{3}{7}$ is equivalent to $\frac{12}{28}$, we often say that both numerator *and* denominator of $\frac{3}{7}$ have been multiplied by the same factor—in this case 4—to obtain $\frac{12}{28}$ (Figure 9.B). While this is correct, we need to delve more deeply:

i. We've multiplied numerator *and* denominator of $\frac{3}{7}$ by 4

ii. The combined effect is multiplying by $\frac{4}{4}$

iii. For any $n \neq 0$, $\frac{n}{n} = 1$ (in particular for $n = 4$)

iv. The identity element of multiplication is 1, so $\frac{3}{7} = \frac{12}{28}$. Here is the proof:
$$\frac{12}{28} = \frac{3}{7} \times \frac{4}{4} = \frac{3}{7} \times 1 = \frac{3}{7}$$

3. Multiplying by 10

One way of showing why a number n multiplied by 10 is a new number composed of the digits of n with a zero tagged on to the right is to use base-10 blocks. Begin with any number, say 23. Ask students to build the number with base-10 blocks. They will pick two 10-rods and three unit cubes. Next, line up these blocks horizontally in a row, forming a long, 23-unit rod (Figure 9.C).

Next, visualize a rolled-up window shade and imagine the length of the shade is 23 units long. In your mind's eye, "pull down" the shade until you've stretched it to 10 times as big in surface area (Figure 9.D)

We notice that the two 10-rods have been stretched to two 100-flats, and the three ones to three 10-rods. Looking at this change from the place-value perspective, multiplying the number 23 by ten results in shifting both digits to the next highest place values (Figure 9.E). As a follow-up exercise, ask students to multiply a 3-digit number, say, 123, by 10 and observe what happens. Finally, ask them to generalize.

FIGURE 9.B **Equivalence in the multiplication table**

×	1	2	3	4	5	6	7	8	9	10
1	1	2	3	4	5	6	7	8	9	10
2	2	4	6	8	10	12	14	16	18	20
3	3	6	9	12	15	18	21	24	27	30
4	4	8	12	16	20	24	28	32	36	40
5	5	10	15	20	25	30	35	40	45	50
6	6	12	18	24	30	36	42	48	54	60
7	7	14	21	28	35	42	49	56	63	70
8	8	16	24	32	40	48	56	64	72	80
9	9	18	27	36	45	54	63	72	81	90
10	10	20	30	40	50	60	70	80	90	100

FIGURE 9.C   Number 23 represented with base-10 blocks

FIGURE 9.D   Geometric visualization of 23 multiplied by 10 with base-10 blocks

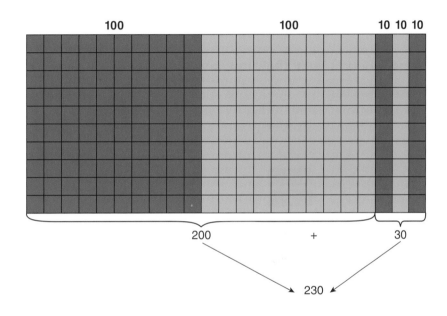

FIGURE 9.E   Multiplying 23 by 10 results in shifting both digits to the next highest place values

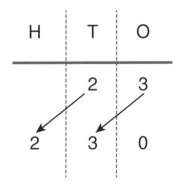

5. Differentiating Addition and Multiplication

Examining Structure

Looking at the structure of each of the four expressions below, and without evaluating them, find the ones equivalent to 9 × (8 + 7):

- (7 + 8) × 9 is equivalent to 9 × (8 + 7) because both addition and multiplication are commutative operations.
- (9 × 8) + 7 is not equivalent to 9 × (8 + 7) because applying the distributive property to the expression 9 × (8 + 7) would result in (9 × 8) + (9 × 7).
- (9 × 8) + (9 × 7) is equivalent to 9 × (8 + 7) as explained immediately above
- (9 + 8) × (9 + 7) is not equivalent to 9 × (8 + 7) as it is an erroneous application of the distributive property.

Solving by Thinking

Equivalent Sums

$5 + 100 = 10 + 95$ Explanation: "Plus 5 (5 → 10)/minus 5 (100 → 95)"

$16 + 28 = 30 + 14$ Explanation: "Plus 2 (28 → 30)/minus 2 (16 → 14)"

Equivalent Products

$5 \times 100 = 10 \times 50$ Explanation: "Times 2 (5 → 10)/divided by 2 (100 → 50)"

$15 \times 28 = 30 \times 14$ Explanation: "Times 2 (15 → 30)/divided by 2 (28 → 14)"

6. Maximizing Products Without Computing

Question: Which is greater, 94 × 72 or 92 × 74? There are several ways of answering this question *without computing* but rather by thinking algebraically.

(1) **Using the distributive property:** We can write the two products as follows, by decomposing one of the two factors into a sum:

- 94 × 72 = (92 + 2) × 72 = 92 × 72 + 2 × 72
- 92 × 74 = 92 × (72 + 2) = 92 × 72 + 92 × 2

The common partial products, 92 × 72 (highlighted in green) are equal. Since 92 × 2 is greater than 2 × 72, the second product is greater. Using Shena's rectangle method, ask students to draw a picture modeling these two expressions. The difference between the two products will become more apparent.

(2) **Using number sense:** In 92 × 74, there are two more 92s than in 92 × 72; in 94 × 72, there are two more 72s than in 92 × 72. Using these facts, and the fact that 72 and 74 are very close in size, as are 92 and 94, we conclude that 92 × 74 is greater than 94 × 72.

(3) **Using the pattern of products** (from Chapter 6, section III, problem 6): We saw that as pairs of factors move further and further apart from each other, the products become smaller and smaller: 74 ×92 > 73 × 93 > 72 × 94.

9. Magic Tricks and Multiplication

Trick 1

Multiplying a three-digit number *abc* by 7 then by 11 and lastly by 13 is the same as multiplying the number by 1001 or by 1000 + 1: $abc \times (1000 + 1) = abc \times 1000 + abc \times 1 = abc000 + abc = abcabc$.

Trick 2

Let *aaa* be the 3-digit number (N) with equal digits. The number *aaa* can be written as $100a + 10a + a$ or $111a$. The sum of the three digits (S) can be written as $3a$. So dividing N by S is equivalent to dividing $111a$ by $3a$. The answer is 111 divided by 3 or 37.

Chapter 1 Worksheet

Circling Circles (Part I)

Names: _____ _____ _____ _____

Prediction: Before measuring, discuss the number of times *you think* the diameter will fit around the lid. Agree on a number and write your group's prediction here _____.

Tasks: Decide who will do Steps 1, 2, 3, and 4.

Step 1: Cut a piece of string equal in length to the diameter of the lid.

Step 2: Cut a piece of string equal in length to the circumference of the lid.

Step 3: Use the marker to mark the number of times the short piece of string fits inside the long piece of string.

Step 4: Talk to each other and share your thoughts. Choose one idea and write about it on the back of this paper. It can be a question, an observation, a conjecture, a picture, or something else.

Circling Circles (Part II)

Names: _____ _____ _____ _____

Tasks: Decide among yourselves who will *estimate* (Steps 1 and 3), *measure* (Steps 2 and 4), and *write* (Step 5).

Step 1: *Estimate* the length of the diameter (the longest distance **across**): _____ cm

Step 2: Now use the metric tape to *measure* the length of the diameter: _____ cm

Step 3: *Estimate* the length of the circumference (the distance **around**): _____ cm

Step 4: Now use the metric tape to *measure* the length of the circumference: ____ cm

Step 5: Talk to each other and share your thoughts. Choose one observation or reaction and *write* it.

Chapter 4 Worksheets

Exploring Growing Patterns

Grades 3–5

Part I: Creating Triangles With Craft Sticks

1. Make a few equilateral triangles using craft sticks:

2. How many sticks are needed to make

   1 triangle? _____ 2 triangles? _____ 3 triangles? _____ 4 triangles? _____

3. What do you notice about the number of triangles? What about the number of craft sticks?

   _____

   _____

   _____

   _____

4. Notice the relationship *between* the number of triangles *and* the number of craft sticks needed to make them. List three different ways you could **represent** this relationship:

   _____

   _____

   _____

   _____

5. Here is a **table representation**: Continue the patterns for a few more rows.

Number of Eq. Triangles	Number of Craft Sticks	In this box, describe the patterns you see. In your own words, tell me at least three things you noticed.
1	3	1. _____
2	6	_____
3	9	_____
		2. _____
		_____
		_____
		3. _____
		_____
		_____

6. Let's call **S** *any* number of equilateral triangles (like 10, or 100, or whatever). Let's call **C** the number of craft sticks needed to make the **S** triangles. Express the relationship between **S** and **C**, first in words, and then in mathematics.

In *words*: _____

_____

In *mathematics*: _____

7. How many craft sticks would you need to build 45 triangles? Explain your thinking behind your answer: _____

_____

8. Suppose you used 102 craft sticks to build equilateral triangles. How many triangles did you build? Explain your thinking behind your answer: _____

_____

Exploring Growing Patterns

Grades 3–5

Part I: Creating Squares With Craft Sticks

1. Make a few squares using craft sticks:

2. How many sticks are needed to make

   1 square? _____ 2 squares? _____ 3 squares? _____ 4 squares? _____

3. What do you notice about the number of squares? What about the number of craft sticks?

   _____

   _____

   _____

   _____

4. Notice the relationship *between* the number of squares *and* the number of craft sticks needed to make them. List three different ways you could **represent** this relationship:

   _____

   _____

   _____

   _____

5. Here is a **table representation**: Continue the patterns for a few more rows.

Number of Eq. Squares	Number of Craft sticks	In this box, describe the patterns you see. In your own words, tell me at least three things you noticed.
1	4	1. _____ _____ _____
2	8	
3	12	
		2. _____ _____ _____
		3. _____ _____ _____

6. Let's call *S* *any* number of squares (like 10, or 100, or whatever). Let's call *C* the number of craft sticks needed to make the *S* squares. Express the relationship between *S* and *C*, first in words, and then in mathematics.

In *words*: _____

_____

In *mathematics*: _____

7. How many craft sticks would you need to build 40 squares? Explain your thinking behind your answer: _____

_____

8. Suppose you used 220 craft sticks to build squares. How many squares did you build? Explain your thinking behind your answer: _____

_____

Exploring Growing Patterns

Grades 3–5

Part I: Creating Pentagons With Craft Sticks

1. Make a few equilateral pentagons using craft sticks:

2. How many sticks are needed to make

    1 pentagon? _____ 2 pentagons? _____ 3 pentagons? _____ 4 pentagons? _____

3. What do you notice about the number of pentagons? What about the number of craft sticks?

    _____

    _____

    _____

    _____

4. Notice the relationship *between* the number of pentagons *and* the number of craft sticks needed to make them. List three different ways you could **represent** this relationship:

    _____

    _____

    _____

    _____

5. Here is a **table representation**: Continue the patterns for a few more rows.

Number of Pentagons	Number of Craft Sticks	In this box, describe the patterns you see. In your own words, tell me at least three things you noticed.
1	5	1. _____
2	10	_____
3	15	_____
		2. _____
		_____
		_____
		3. _____
		_____
		_____

6. Let's call **P** *any* number of equilateral pentagons (like 10, or 100, or whatever). Let's call **C** the number of craft sticks needed to make the **P** pentagons. Express the relationship between **P** and **C**, first in words, and then in mathematics.

In *words*: _____

_____

In *mathematics*: _____

7. How many craft sticks would you need to build 25 pentagons? Explain your thinking behind your answer: _____

_____

8. Suppose you used 200 craft sticks to build equilateral pentagons. How many pentagons did you build? Explain your thinking behind your answer: _____

_____

Exploring Growing Patterns

Grades 3–5

Part I: Creating Hexagons With Craft Sticks

1. Make a few equilateral hexagons using craft sticks:

2. How many sticks are needed to make

   1 hexagon? _____   2 hexagons? _____   3 hexagons? _____   4 hexagons? _____

3. What do you notice about the number of hexagons? What about the number of craft sticks?

   _____

   _____

   _____

   _____

4. Notice the relationship *between* the number of hexagons *and* the number of craft sticks needed to make them. List three different ways you could **represent** this relationship:

   _____

   _____

   _____

   _____

5. Here is a **table representation**: Continue the patterns for a few more rows.

Number of Hexagons	Number of Craft Sticks	In this box, describe the patterns you see. In your own words, tell me at least three things you noticed.
1	6	1. _____
2	12	_____
3	18	_____
		_____
		2. _____
		_____
		_____
		3. _____
		_____
		_____

6. Let's call **H** *any* number of equilateral hexagons (like 10, or 100, or whatever). Let's call **C** the number of craft sticks needed to make the **H** hexagons. Express the relationship between **H** and **C**, first in words, and then in mathematics.

   In *words*: _____

   _____

   In *mathematics*: _____

7. How many craft sticks would you need to build 32 hexagons? Explain your thinking behind your answer: _____

   _____

8. Suppose you used 150 craft sticks to build equilateral hexagons. How many hexagons did you build? Explain your thinking behind your answer: _____

   _____

Chapter 7 Worksheet

Visualizing the Partial Products Algorithm for Multiplication as an Area

×	Place 13 along this edge (in base-10 blocks)
Place 21 along this edge (in base-10 blocks)	

References

Abbott, E. A. (1992). *Flatland: A romance of many dimensions.* Mineola, NY: Dover.

Atiyah, M. (2001). Mathematics in the 20th century. *American Mathematical Monthly, 108*(7), 654–666.

Baek, J. M. (2008). Developing algebraic thinking through explorations in multiplication. In C. E. Greenes & R. Rubenstein, (Eds.), *Algebra and algebraic thinking in school mathematics* (pp. 141–154). Reston, VA: NCTM.

Banchoff, T. F. (1990). Dimension. In L. A. Steen, *On the shoulders of giants: New approaches to numeracy* (pp. 11–59). Washington, DC: National Academy Press.

Banchoff, T. F. (2008). Algebraic thinking and geometric thinking. In C. E. Greenes & R. Rubenstein (Eds.), *Algebra and algebraic thinking in school mathematics* (pp. 99–112). Reston VA: NCTM.

Barnett, C., Goldstein, D., & Jackson, B. (1994). *Mathematics teaching cases: Fractions, decimals, ratios, & percents: Hard to teach and hard to learn?* Portsmouth, NH: Heinemann.

Barnett-Clarke, C., Fisher, W., Marks, R., & Ross, S. (2010). *Developing essential understanding of rational numbers for teaching mathematics in grades 3–5.* Essential Understanding Series. Reston, VA: NCTM.

Baroody, A. J. (2004). The developmental bases for early childhood number and operations standards. In D. H. Clements, J. Sarama, & A.-M. DiBiase (Eds.), *Engaging young children in mathematics: Standards early childhood mathematics education* (pp. 173–219). Mahwah, NJ: Lawrence Erlbaum.

Bass, H. (2005). Mathematics, mathematicians, and mathematics education. *Bulletin of The American Mathematics Society, 42*(4), 417–430.

Behr, M. J., & Post, T. R. (1992). Teaching rational number and decimal concepts. In T. R. Post (Ed.), *Teaching mathematics in grades K–8: Research-based methods* (2nd ed., pp. 201–248). Boston, MA: Allyn & Bacon.

Bezuszka, S. J., & Kenney, M. J. (2008). The three R's: Recursive thinking, recursion, and recursive formulas. In C. E. Greenes & R. Rubenstein (Eds.), *Algebra and algebraic thinking in school mathematics* (pp. 81–87). Reston, VA: NCTM.

Blanton, M. L., & Kaput, J. J. (2011). Functional thinking as a route into algebra in the elementary grades. In J. Cai & E. Knuth (Eds.), *Early algebraization: A global dialogue from multiple perspectives* (pp. 5–23). Berlin, Germany: Springer-Verlag.

Blanton, M. L., Levi, L., Crites, T. W., & Dougherty, B. J. (2011). *Developing essential understanding of algebraic thinking for teaching mathematics in grades 3–5.* Reston, VA: NCTM.

Blatner, D. (1997). *The joy of π.* New York, NY: Walker.

Brizuela, B. M., & Earnest, D. (2008). Multiple notational systems and algebraic understandings: The case of the "best deal" problem. In J. Kaput, D. Carraher, & M. Blanton (Eds.), *Algebra in the early grades* (pp. 273–301). Mahwah, NJ: Lawrence Erlbaum.

Cai, J., & Knuth, E. (Eds.) (2011). *Early algebraization.* Berlin, Germany: Springer-Verlag.

Cameron, A., & Fosnot, A. C. (2008). *Muffles' truffles: Multiplication and division with the array.* Portsmouth, NH: Heinemann.

Carpenter, T. P., Franke, M. L., & Levi, L. (2003). *Thinking mathematically: Integrating arithmetic & algebra in elementary school.* Portsmouth, NH: Heinemann.

Carraher, D., Brizuela, B., & Schliemann, A. (2000). Bringing out the algebraic character of arithmetic: Instantiating variables in addition and subtraction. In Te Nakahara & Me Koyama (Eds.),

Proceedings of the 24th conference of the International Group of the Psychology of Mathematics Education (vol. 2, pp. 145–151). Hiroshima, Japan: Hiroshima University.

Carraher, D. W., & Schliemann, A. D. (2010). Algebraic reasoning in elementary school classrooms. In D. V. Lambdin & F. K. Lester (Eds.), *Teaching and learning mathematics: Translating research for elementary school teachers* (pp. 23–29). Reston, VA: NCTM.

Chazan, D., & Yerushalmy, M. (2003). On appreciating the cognitive complexity of school algebra: Research on algebra learning and directions of curricular change. In J. M. Kilpatrick, W. G. Martin, & D. Schifter, (Eds.), *A research companion to principles and standards for school mathematics* (pp. 123–135). Reston, VA: NCTM.

Chval, K., Lannin, J., & Jones, D. (2013). *Putting essential understanding of fractions into practice in grades 3–5.* Reston, VA: NCTM.

Clements, D. H. (2004). Major themes and recommendations. In D. H.-M. Clements (Ed.), *Engaging young children in mathematics* (pp. 7–72). Mahwah, NJ: Lawrence Erlbaum.

Collins, A. & Dacey, L. (2010). *Zeroing in on number and operations: Key ideas and common misconceptions, Grades 5–6.* Portland, ME. Stenhouse.

Columba, L. (2013). So, here's the story. *Teaching Children Mathematics, 19*(6), 374–381.

Cramer, K., & Whitney, S. (2010). Learning rational number concepts and skills in elementary school classrooms. In D. V. Lambdin & F. K. Lester (Eds.), *Teaching and learning mathematics: Translating research for elementary school teachers* (pp. 15–22). Reston, VA: NCTM.

Crowley, M. L. (1987). The Van Hiele model of the development of geometric thought. In M. L. Lindquist (Ed.), *Learning and teaching geometry, K–12* (pp. 1–16). Reston, VA: NCTM.

Darley, J. W., & Leapard, B. B. (2010). Connecting arithmetic to algebra. *Teaching Children Mathematics, 17*(3), 184–191.

Dehaene, S. (1997). *The number sense: How the mind creates mathematics.* New York, NY: Oxford University Press.

Devlin, K. (2000). *The math gene: How mathematical thinking evolved and why numbers are like gossip.* New York, NY: Basic Books.

Empson, S. B., Levi, L., & Carpenter, T. P. (2011). The algebraic nature of fractions: Developing realational thinking in elementary school. In J. Cai & E. Knuth (Eds.) *Early algebraization: A global dialogue from multiple perspectives* (pp. 409–428). Berlin, Germany. Springer.

Falkner, K. P., Levi, L., & Carpenter, T. P. (1999). Children's understanding of equality: A foundation for algebra. *Teaching Children Mathematics, 6*(4), 232–236.

Femiano, R. B. (2003). Algebraic problem solving in the primary grades. *Teaching Children Mathematics, 9*(8), 444–449.

Ferrini-Mundy, J. L., Lappan, G., & Phillips, E. (1997). Experiences with patterning. *Teaching Children Mathematics, 3*(6), 282–288.

Fey, J. T. (1990). Quantity. In L. A. Steen, *On the shoulders of giants: New approaches to numeracy* (pp. 61–94). Washington, DC: National Academy Press.

Fisher, P. (1998). *Wonder, the rainbow, and the aesthetics of rare experiences.* Cambridge, MA. Harvard University Press.

Gojak, L. (2013, October 3). *Making mathematical connections.* NCTM Summing Up. Retrieved from http://www.nctm.org/about/content.aspx?id=39616

Goldenberg, E. P., Mark, J., & Cuoco, A. (2010). An algebraic-habits-of-mind perspective on elementary school. *Teaching Children Mathematics, 16*(9): 548–556.

Greenberg, J. (2008). *No common denominator: The preparation of elementary teachers in mathematics by America's education schools.* Washington, DC: National Council on Teacher Quality.

Greer, B. (1992). Multiplication and division as models of situations. In D. A. Grouws (Ed.), *Handbook of research on mathematics teaching and learning* (pp. 276–295). New York, NY: Macmillan.

Guershon, H., & Confrey, J. (Eds.) 1994. *The development of multiplicative reasoning in the learning of mathematics.* Albany: State University of New York Press.

Harel, G., & Dubinsky, E. (Eds.). (1992). Foreword. In G. Harel & E. Dubinsky, *The concept of function: Aspects of epistemology and pedagogy* (p. vii). Washington, DC: Mathematics Association of America.

Jones, K. (2010). Linking geometry and algebra in the school mathematics curriculum. In Z. A. Usiskin, *Future curricular trends in school algebra and geometry: Proceedings of a conference.* (pp. 203–215). Charlotte, NC: Information Age.

Kamii, C. K. (2001). Representation and abstraction in young children's numerical reasoning. In A. A. Cuoco & F. R. Curcio (Eds.), *The roles of representation in school mathematics: 2001 NCTM yearbook* (pp. 24–34). Reston, VA: NCTM.

Kamii, C., & Dominick, A. (1998). The harmful effects of algorithms in grades 1–4. In L. J. Morrow & M. J. Kenney (Eds.), *The teaching and learning of algorithms in school mathematics* (pp.130–140). Reston, VA: NCTM.

Kaput, J. (2008). What is algebra? What is algebraic reasoning? In J. Kaput, D. Carraher, & M. Blanton (Eds.), *Algebra in the early grades* (pp. 1–18). New York, NY: Lawrence Erlbaum.

Kaput, J. J., Blanton, M. L., & Moreno, L. (2008). Algebra from a symbolization point of view. In J. J. Kaput, D. W. Carraher, & M. L. Blanton (Eds.), *Algebra in the early grades* (pp. 19–55). New York, NY: Lawrence Erlbaum.

Kaput, J. J., Carraher, D. W., & Blanton, M. L. (Eds.). (2008). *Algebra in the early grades.* New York, NY: Lawrence Erlbaum.

Katz, V., &. Bartob, B. (2007). Stages in the history of algebra with implications for teaching. *Educational Studies in Mathematics, 66,* 185–201.

Kieran, C. (1989). The early learning of algebra: A structural perspective. In S. Wagner & C. Kieran (Eds.), *Research issues in the learning and teaching of algebra* (vol. 4, pp. 33–56). Reston, VA: Lawrence Erlbaum and NCTM.

Kieran, C. (2011). Overall commentary on early algebraization: Perspectives for research and teaching. In J. Cai & E. Knuth (Eds.), *Early algebraization* (pp. 579–593). New York, NY: Springer.

Kilpatrick, J., Swafford, J., & Findell, B. (Eds.). (2001). *Adding it up: Helping children learn mathematics.* Washington, DC: National Academy Press.

King, J. P. (1992). *The art of mathematics.* Mineola, NY: Dover.

Lamon, S. J. (2010). *Teaching fractions and ratios for understanding: Essential content knowledge and instructional strategies for teachers* (Second Edition ed.). Mahwah, NJ: Routledge.

Linchevski, L. (1995). Algebra with numbers and arithmetic with letters: A definition of pre-algebra. *The Journal of Mathematical Behavior, 14*(1), 113–120.

Lins, R., & Kaput, J. (2004). The early development of algebraic reasoning: The current state of the field. In K. Stacey, H. Chick, & M. Kendal (Eds.), *The future of teaching and learning of algebra: The 12th ICMI study* (pp. 73–96). Boston, MA: Kluwer.

Lobato, J., Ellis, A. B., Charles, R. I., & Zbiek, R. M. (2010). *Developing essential understandings of ratios, proportions, and proportional reasoning for teaching mathematics: Grades 6–8.* Essential Understanding Series. Reston, VA: NCTM.

Lockhart, P. (2009). *A mathematician's lament: How school cheats us out of our most fascinating and imaginative art form.* New York, NY: Bellevue Literary Press.

Malara, N., & Navarra, G. (2003). *ArAl project: Arithmetic pathways towards favouring pre-algebraic thinking.* Bologna, Italy: Pitagora.

Mason, J. (2008). Making use of children's powers to produce algebraic thinking. In J. J. Kaput, D. W. Carraher, & M. L. Blanton (Eds.), *Algebra in the early grades* (pp. 57–94). New York, NY: Lawrence Erlbaum.

McCarthy, C. (1991, April 20). Who needs algebra? *The Washington Post,* A21.

Moss, J., Beatty, R., Barkin, S., & Shillolo, G. (2008). What's your theory? What's your rule? Fourth graders build an understanding of patterns. In C. E. Greenes & R. Rubenstein (Eds.), *Algebra and algebraic thinking in school mathematics* (pp. 155–168). NCTM Yearbook. Reston, VA: NCTM.

National Assessment of Educational Progress. (2007). *NAEP questions tool.* Retrieved July 27, 2013, from National Center for Education Statistics, http://nces.ed.gov/nationsreportcard/itmrlsx/detail.aspx?subject=mathematics

National Council of Teachers of Mathematics (NCTM). (1989). *Curriculum and evaluation standards for school mathematics.* Reston, VA: Author.

National Council of Teachers of Mathematics (NCTM). (2000). *Princples and standards for school mathematics.* Reston, VA: Author.

National Council of Teachers of Mathematics (NCTM). (2010). *Developing essential understanding of number and numeration: PreK–grade 2.* Washington, DC: Author.

National Council of Teachers of Mathematics (NCTM). (2011). *Developing essential understanding of algebraic thinking for teaching mathematics in grades 3–5.* Reston, VA: Author.

National Governors Association Center for Best Practices & Council of Chief State School Officers (NGA/CCSSO). (2010). *Common Core State Standards for Mathematics.* Washington, DC: Authors. Retrieved from Common Core State Standards Initiative, http://www.corestandards.org/the-standards/mathematics

National Mathematics Advisory Panel. (2008). *Foundations for success: The final report of the National Mathematics Advisory Panel.* Washington, DC: U.S. Department of Education.

National Research Council. (2009). *Mathematics learning in early childhood: Paths toward excellence and equity.* Washington, DC: The National Academies Press.

Neagoy, M. (2010, March 12). *PreK–12 algebra: Building a concrete bridge.* Presentation at the annual conference of the Virginia Council of Teachers of Mathematics, Harrisonburg, VA.

Neagoy, M. (2012). *Planting the seeds of algebra, PreK–2: Explorations for the early grades.* Thousand Oaks, CA: Corwin.

Neuschwander, C. (1997). *Sir Cumference and the first round table: A math adventure.* Watertown, MA: Charlesbridge.

Otto, A. D., Caldwell, J. H., Hancock, S. W., & Zbiek, R. M. (2011). *Developing essential understanding of multiplication and division for teaching mathematics in grades 3–5.* Reston , VA: NCTM.

Post, T. R., Behr, M. J., & Lesh, R. (1988). Proportionality and the development of prealgebra understandings. In A. F. Coxford & A. P. Shulte (Eds.), *The ideas of algebra, K–12* (pp. 78–90). NCTM Yearbook. Reston, VA: NCTM.

Radford, L. (2010). Signs, gestures, meanings: Algebraic thinking from a cultural semiotic perspective. In V. Durand-Guerrier, S. Soury-Lavergne, & F. Arzarello (Eds.), *Proceedings of the sixth Conference of European Research in Mathematics Education (CERME 6)* (pp. xxxiii–liii). Lyon, France: Université Claude Bernard.

RAND Mathematics Study Panel. (2003). *Mathematical proficiency for all students: Toward a strategic research and development program in mathematics education.* Santa Monica, CA: RAND Corporation.

Russell, S. J., Schifter, D., & Bastable, V. (2011). *Connecting arithmetic to algebra: Strategies for building algebraic thinking in the elementary grades.* Portsmouth, NH: Heinemann.

Saul, M. (1998). Algebra, technology, and a remark of I. M. Gelfand. In *The nature and role of algebra in the K–14 curriculum: Proceedings of a national symposium* (pp. 137–144). Washington, DC: National Academy Press.

Schifter, D., Bastable, V., Russell, S. J., Seyferth, L., & Riddle, M. (2008). Algebra in the grades K–5 classroom: Learning opportunities for students and teachers. In C. E. Greenes & R. Rubenstein (Eds.), *Algebra and algebraic thinking in school mathematics* (pp. 263–277). Reston, VA: NCTM.

Schliemann, A. D., Carraher, D. W., & Brizuela, B. (2007). *Bringing out the algebraic character of arithmetic: From children's ideas to classroom practice.* New York, NY: Lawrence Erlbaum.

Schoenfeld, A. H. (2008). Early algebra as mathematical sense making. In J. Kaput, D. Carraher, & M. Blanton (Eds.), *Algebra in the early grades* (pp. 479–510). New York, NY: Lawrence Erlbaum.

Sfard, A. (1991). On the dual nature of mathematical conceptions: Reflections on processes and objects as different sides of the same coin. *Educational Studies in Mathematics, 22,* 1–36.

Sinclair, N. P., Pimm, D., & Skelin, M. (2012). *Developing essential understanding of geometry for teaching mathematics in grades 6–8.* Essential Understanding Series. Reston, VA: NCTM.

Smith, D. E. (1926). A general survey of progress in the last 25 years. *The first yearbook of the National Council of Teachers of Mathematics* (pp. 1–31). New York, NY: Bureau of Publications, Teachers College, Columbia University.

Smith, E. (2003). Stasis and change: Integrating patterns, functions, and algebra throughout the K–12 curriculum. In J. M. Kilpatrick, W. G. Martin, & D. Schifter, *A research companion to principles and standards for school mathematics* (pp. 136–150). Reston, VA: NCTM.

Smith, E. (2008). Representational thinking as a framework for introducing functions in the elementary curriculum. In J. J. Kaput, D. W. Carraher, & M. L. Blanton (Eds.), *Algebra in the early grades* (pp. 133–160). New York, NY: Lawrence Erlbaum.

Smith, J. P., III. (2002). The development of students' knowledge of fractions and ratios. In B. Litwiller (Ed.), *Making sense of fractions, ratios, and proportions* (pp. 3–17). Reston, VA: NCTM.

Smith, J., & Thompson, P. (2008). Quantitative reasoning and the development of algebraic reasoning. In J. J. Kaput, D. W. Carraher, & M. L. Blanton (Eds.), *Algebra in the early grades* (pp. 95–132). New York, NY: Erlbaum.

Smith, M. S., Silver, E. A., & Stein, M. K. (2005a). *Improving instruction in algebra: Using cases to transform mathematics teaching and learning* (vol. 2). New York, NY: Teachers College Press.

Smith, M. S., Silver, E. A., & Stein, M. K. (2005b). *Improving instruction in rational numbers and proportionality: Using cases to transform mathematics teaching and learning* (vol. 1). New York, NY: Teachers College Press.

Sousa, D. A. (2008). *How the brain learns mathematics.* Thousand Oaks, CA: Corwin.

Steen, L. A. (1990). Pattern. In L. A. Steen (Ed.), *On the shoulders of giants: New approaches to numeracy* (pp. 1–10). Washington, DC: National Academy Press.

Steffe, L. P. (2001). A new hypothesis concerning children's fractional knowledge. *Journal of Mathemtical Behavior, 20,* 267–307.

Stein, S. K. (1996). *Strength in numbers: Discovering the joy and power of mathematics in everyday life.* New York, NY: John Wiley & Sons.

Stewart, I. (1990). Change. In L. A. Steen (Ed.), *On the shoulders of giants: New appraoches to numeracy* (pp. 183–217). Washington, DC: National Academy Press.

Suri, M. (2013, September 16). How to fall in love with math. *New York Times,* p. A23.

Tierney, C., & Monk, S. (2008). Children's reasoning about change over time. In J. J. Kaput (Ed.), *Algebra in the early grades* (pp. 57–94). New York, NY: Lawrence Erlbaum.

Tirosh, D. (2000, January). Enhancing prospective teachers' knowledge of children's conceptions: The case of division of fractions. *Journal for Research in Mathematics Education, 31,* 5–25.

Usiskin, Z. (1999). Doing algebra in grades K–4. In B. Moses (Ed.), *Algebraic thinking, grades K–12: Readings from NCTM's school-based journals and other publications* (pp. 7–13). Reston, VA: NCTM.

Usiskin, Z. (2004, February 6). *Should all students study a significant amount of algebra?* Keynote speech at the Dutch National Mathematics Days, Noordwijkerhout, The Netherlands.

Van de Walle, J. A., & Lovin, L. A. H. (2006). *Teaching student-centered mathematics: Grades 3–5* (2nd ed.). Boston, MA: Pearson.

Wagner, T. (2008). *The global achievement gap: Why even our best schools don't teach the new survival skills our children need—and what we can do about it.* New York, NY: Basic Books.

Warren, E. &. Cooper, T. J. (2008). Patterns that support early algebraic thinking in the elementary school. In C. E. Greenes & R. Rubenstein (Eds.), *Algebra and algebraic thinking in school mathematics* (pp. 113–126). Reston, VA: NCTM.

Whitehead, A. (1916). *The aims of education.* Leicester: Mathematical Association of England.

Whitehead, A. (1948). *An introduction to mathematics.* London, UK: Oxford University Press.

Wu, H.-H. (1966). The role of Euclidean geometry in high school. *Journal of Mathematical Behavior, 15,* 221–237.

Yerushalmy, M. & Schwartz, J. L. (1993). Seizing the opportunity to make algebra mathematically and pedagogically interesting. In T. A. Romberg, E. Fennema, & T. Carpenter (Eds.), *Integrating research on graphical representations of functions* (pp. 41–68). New York, NY: Lawrence Erlbaum.

Index